Kings, Courts and Monarchy

Harold Nicolson

KINGS, COURTS AND MONARCHY

Simon and Schuster · New York 1962

Left: *Titian's portrait of Philip II of Spain, now in the Prado Museum, Madrid*

First printing

Library of Congress Catalog Card Number: 62-14273
Printed in Italy by Istituto Italiano d'Arti Grafiche, Bergamo

Contents

CONTENTS

Acknowledgments

The author and publishers wish to acknowledge with thanks the help given by Catherine Porteous in collecting the illustrations. They are deeply grateful to H M The Queen, by whose gracious permission 61 (left) and 196 are reproduced, and to H M The Queen Mother, for her permission to reproduce 205. The author and publishers wish to thank the following people and Museums for kind permission to reproduce the illustrations of which they own the copyright:

Alinari, 71, 74 (left and right), 78, 85, 103, 169, 190, 210, 262, 268; George W. Allan, 33, 36, 245; Anderson, 64, 77 (left), 81, 97 (right); Antikvarisk Topografiska Arkives, Stockholm, 63; Ferdinand Anton, Munich, 18; Arsenal Museum, Paris, 57; Ashmolean Museum, Oxford, 47, 94, 99; Cecil Beaton, 315; Bibliothèque Nationale, Paris, 68, 124, 141, 142, 146, 186, 227, 319; Bowes Museum, Bishop Auckland, 256; Ann Bredol-Lepper, Aachen, 127, 130, 133, 138, 139; British Museum, 45, 80 (left), 118, 119, 160, 163, 166, 178, 199, 201, 203, 311, 322; Musée Carnavallet, Paris, 136; Chicago Natural History Museum, 40 (right); Musée de Compiègne, 279; Musée Condé, Chantilly, 56, 171, 261; The Dean and Chapter, Westminster Abbey, 304, 324; The Dean and Chapter, Split Cathedral, 313; Deutscher Kunstverlag, Munich, 183; Dijon Public Library, 148; Musée de Fontainebleau, 270; Fototeca Unione, Rome, 91; G. Francheschi, Paris, 68; German Archaeological Institute, Rome, 51, 97 (left); Giraudon, Paris, 49, 56, 129, 136, 142, 146, 157, 161, 172, 186, 207, 213 (left and right), 219, 223, 224, 225, 227, 249, 261, 265, 270, 272, 279; Verlag Emil Hartmann, Mannheim, 89; Heinrich Harrer, 30; Hinz SWB, Basel, 110, 111; Imperial Library, Teheran, 59, Professor Karl Kerenyi, Ascona, and the Bollinger Foundation, 21 (left); A.F. Kersting, 155; Kevorkian Collection, 249; Dorian Leigh, 307; H. Lhote, 15 (right); Dr Andreas Lommel, 15 (left); Musée du Louvre, 206, 262; Islay Lyons, 80 (right); Mansell Collection, London, 38, 40 (left), 60, 102, 174, 176, 177, 180, 184, 192, 199, 205, 215, 220, 239, 256, 257, 269, 274, 277, 281, 285, 286, 288, 290, 293, 294, 297, 299, 302, 308-9; Masters and Benchers, Inner Temple, London, 197; Metropolitan Museum of Art, New York, 27 (Gift of J. Pierpont Morgan), 153; Ministry of Works, London, 81 (Crown Copyright reserved); National Portrait Gallery, London, 282, 289; Phaidon Press, 104; Axel Poignant, London, 10; Paul Popper, 115, 235, 237, 240, 243, 254; Radio Times Hulton Picture Library, 61 (right) 232, 236, 247, 251, 253; Royal Academy, London, 164; Schulmann, Amsterdam, 214; M. Seif-Ul-Molooki, Teheran, 21 (right), 53; Edwin Smith, 259; Società Collombaria, Florence, 210; L. Stone, Wadham College, Oxford, 195; Vatican Museum, 74 (left); Musée de Versailles, 49, 213 (right), 219, 268, 272; Victoria and Albert Museum, London, 107, 117, 150, 151; Wallace Collection, London (Crown Copyright reserved), 229; Wiesbaden Museum, 87

The references above are to page numbers

The book was designed by Margaret Fraser

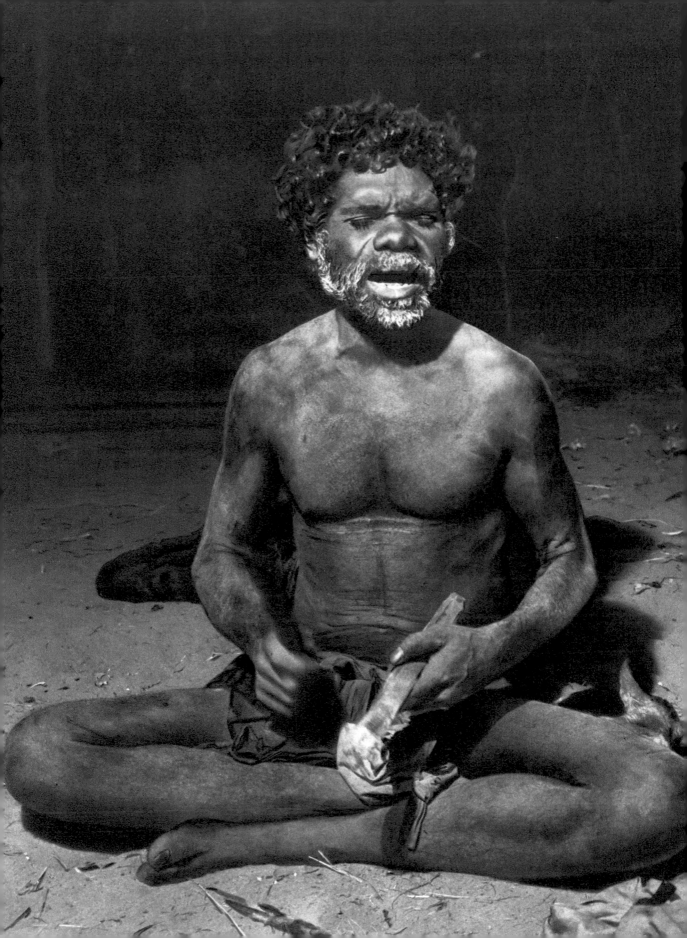

left: *An Australian aboriginal*
singing a sacred tribal song,
which can last for several hours.
Such is the basis of much
primitive monarchy

ONE

The King as Magician

PRIMITIVE SOCIETY, AS WE have now learnt from the anthropologists, was dominated by superstition. Nobody today believes in the old legends of a Golden Age, or State of Nature, when men and women would stroll naked and uncompetitive in idyllic surroundings; deriving their sustenance from the paw-paw and bananas that luxuriated around them; unimpeded by laws and regulations; drinking the pure water of their virgin springs, immune to the poisons of jealousy, greed, envy and emulation; happy in their simplicity; and free from want or fear.

Marxists do!

The vision of the Noble Savage no longer provides the dreamer with either comfort or conviction: no longer do we suppose with Columbus that the Caribs inhabited a lost Garden of Eden: no longer do we share with Montaigne the conception of primitive man as 'all naked, simply pure, in Nature's lap': nor can we echo Dryden's paean,

> I am as free as Nature first made man
> Ere the base laws of servitude began,
> When wild in woods the noble savage ran.

Even in the days when a State of Nature was associated in the minds of sentimental men and women with the concepts of gentleness, purity and peace, there were some realistic thinkers who dismissed the legend of the Noble Savage as a pathetic fallacy. Hobbes insisted that

11

the life of a savage in primitive society, so far from being idyllic, was in fact ' solitary, poor, nasty, brutish and short'. Dr Johnson stoutly denied that in primitive society men were gentle towards each other and contended that the sweet virtue of compassion was the product of experience, education and refinement and was in no sense a ' natural gift'. He was contemptuous of those who drew idyllic pictures of the State of Nature, where there existed neither pride nor envy, and when a man could satisfy his wants ' naturally', since his wants were few. ' If a bull could speak,' thundered Dr Johnson, ' he might well exclaim " Here I am with this cow and this grass: what being could enjoy greater felicity? ". '

It was not only the jeers of the realists that killed the legend of the Noble Savage. It was the patient researches, and field work, of the anthropologists. We now know for certain that primitive society was not in any way a free society; that the lives of savages, so far from being unhampered by restrictions, were and are shackled by all manner of formulas, ceremonies, taboos, and prohibitions; and that the Noble Savage is bound hand and foot by the superstitious customs handed down to him by his predecessors and maintained and rigidly enforced by the tribal medicine-men or shamans. The fears that civilised man experiences are more rational, and thus more controllable, than the superstitious terrors by which the uncivilised are assailed. Even to this day the aborigines of Australia are governed by ancestral superstitions, preserved for them, and imposed upon them, by their tribal medicine-men at the corrobborees, where dances are held in honour of the frog, kangaroo or other totem. Here still survive the ceremonies of sympathetic magic and initiation ceremonies of ghastly cruelty. These savages are naked, unwashed, famished, thirsty, strictly disciplined, and obsessed by constant terror.

Yet there will always survive some neurotic and over-civilised people who, distraught by the rush and rattle of the modern world, will long with Joseph Warton to find again

The Isles of Innocence from mortal view
Deeply retired, beneath a platan's shade
Where Happiness and Quiet sit enthroned,
Where, fed on dates and herbs would I despise
The far-fetched cates of Luxury and hoards
Of narrow-hearted Avarice, nor heed
The distant din of the tumultuous world.

Such escapes from reality are today readily provided by alcohol, opium, varied forms of delinquency, luxury cruises and sentimental day-dreams. The tribal magicians, the medicine-men, the shamans and the sorcerers have been dismissed from polite society; the totem poles have been relegated to museums; but magic survives in the mystiques of Royalty and in the ministrations of psychiatrists.

The role of the tribal magician must be given further examination since it was from the medicine-men, the sorcerers, the shamans, and the magicians that the institution of monarchy first emerged.

THE ROLE OF THE MEDICINE-MAN

The original leaders of a pre-historic tribe consisted in all probability of a caste, or oligarchy, of medicine-men, who generation by generation interpreted and transmitted the customs of the community, the traditional taboos, and the ceremonies essential to the worship of the tribal totem. By the exercise of sympathetic magic these men sought, in the palaeolithic age, to provide their fellow savages with abundant deer and bison and thus to favour successful hunting. The cave paintings at Lascaux, Alta Mira and Tortosilla are, it is now generally believed, symbols of sympathetic magic and the caves themselves are assumed to have been temples or shrines in which the medicine-men performed ceremonies and sacrifices intended to increase the local supply of game. The necessary ritual was performed by the local shaman or sorcerer who arrayed himself, as the modern medicine-men array themselves, with the bones and antlers of the animals they needed for food.

As the tribal population increased and the need for new hunting grounds became compelling, a vigorous tribe would encroach upon the preserves of its neighbours and conflicts arose. This entailed fighting. Elderly sorcerers, however magical may have been their inherited talents, however impressive their knowledge of tribal traditions, are not, owing to their state of health, well adapted to leadership in tribal warfare. The custom thus arose of choosing as leader in battle a younger man of exceptional valour and vigour, who was generally elected from the family of an ancient magician and thus assumed to have inherited something of his magic powers. This exceptional individual, who combined the hereditary magic of his family with personal prowess as a war-leader, inevitably acquired headship of the tribe.

As tribes coalesced into wider groups, he became the paramount chief. It was in this way that the magician-king succeeded the caste of elderly sorcerers, although among the Australian aborigines the stone-age system of an oligarchy of aged medicine-men is said still to survive.

In most primitive communities, however, leadership of the warrior-magician developed into the institution of monarchy, the monarch deriving his magic faculties from hereditary descent from the old sorcerer caste, and his leadership faculties from his own courage and prowess.

Sir James Frazer considers this evolution a necessary stage of development. 'The rise of Monarchy,' he writes, 'appears to be the essential condition of the emergence of mankind from savagery.' It was only the exceptional man who could snap the chain of custom, expand the hunting territories of the tribe, wage successful warfare, deprive the mumbling old sorcerers of their traditional power, and lay the road open for cultural, social and economic advance. Yet it is to be doubted whether any of these individuals could have imposed their dominance over the tribe, or founded dynasties, had it not been for the belief that magic and a popular understanding of, and relation to, the forces of nature were in some manner a hereditary aptitude possessed only by those who belonged to the hierarchy of the shamans. The connection between the hereditary principle and the transmission of magic has in vestigial shape survived until this day. It survived in the doctrine of 'The Lord's Anointed' and in the theory of the 'Divine Right of Kings'. In even more superstitious form it survived as late as the eighteenth century in the practice of the 'Royal Touching' for scrofula. Each of these phenomena of thought and feeling will subsequently be considered. For the moment it is sufficient to note that the magic element in the institution of monarchy is a survival from prehistoric times, perhaps even from the Miocene phase when man first adopted an erect stance, a million years ago.

EMPHASIS ON FERTILITY

When mankind ceased to be wholly dependent for his food on such wild animals as he could trap or spear, when, that is, he started to tame domestic animals and to grow grain, the emphasis shifted from the abundant supply of deer, bison, and fish to the productivity of live stock and the hope of rich harvests. Fertility of bulls and grain became the central preoccupation, and it was the gods of fertility - old Mother Earth, the rain, the sun and the moon, the gods of wind, the dreadful gods of thunder and lightning, the demons of blight and glanders - who had to be invoked and propitiated. Professionals were required for these ministrations and the old caste of medicine-men developed into a new kind of specialist in fertility, the priest who knew, and was known to, the supernatural powers who gave increase to man, and plant and beast. The rituals, sacrifices and incantations performed

Two sketches illustrating the influence of magic on primitive tribal societies. Left: *An Australian cave-painting brilliantly conveys the terror aroused by the medicine-man.* Right: *An archer from the Oued Djerat in the Libyan desert wearing three feathers in his head-dress. The phallus was added by a later hand*

by the priest to further productivity, became of such importance to the tribe that the priest assumed the authority of the old medicine-man, whose methods he often imitated. Gradually, out of the swirling mists of archaeology, emerges the alarming figure of the priest-king.

By identifying himself intimately with the fertility powers, by pretending on occasions that he had actually had sexual relations with some nymph or even goddess, the priest-king exposed himself to danger. Assassination has always, for monarchs, been an occupational risk. Since, if the shaman really was to be identified with the powers of fertility, then it was essential that the priest-king who personified the virility and fertility of the tribe should not be allowed to decline in vigour. The tribesmen were perfectly prepared, so long as he retained his sturdiness, to worship him as a god, to honour him with sacrifices, and to see to it that he was abundantly fed and clothed and protected from all evil influences. The fertility-priest, or priest-king, came to be regarded as a tribal fetish, was beaten with rods if he failed to produce the necessary rain or sunshine, and was not allowed out of the village unaccompanied by guards, in case he might be contaminated by evil spirits, or run away.

August and pampered were the lives of these priest-kings, but at the same time exposed to incessant scrutiny and discipline, and threatened with punishment if their magic failed to work. In many instances the priest-king was not permitted to leave the darkened chambers of his palace or to set eyes upon the sun and moon. Some priest-kings were forbidden even to make contact with the earth for fear that some of their vitality might thereby be drained from them. Being identified with the Sun-god they were not allowed to blink or wink. Their courtiers and acolytes were in fact their jailers and guards: their lives were spent in confinement and exposed to persistent menace.

It is not surprising therefore that many candidates for the post refused to sacrifice their liberty and perhaps their lives to such cere-monials, and had often to be imprisoned on low rations until they would consent to assume the priesthood and the throne. There is considerable anthropological evidence to indicate that the priest-king, once he began to manifest signs of waning vitality, was deposed by the royal family and put to death, a more fertile youngster being chosen in his place. Even in modern times, monarchs, at moments of national catastrophe, have been deposed by their people, treated as scapegoats, and obliged to take refuge abroad.

THE PRIEST OF
DIANA AT NEMI
    Sir James Frazer, in his magnificent work *The Golden Bough*, has taken as an example of this practice the story of the priest of Diana at Nemi, the lovely lapis lake cupped among the hills of the Castelli Romani. Diana, as her prototype Artemis, was not the goddess of the chase only, but also the protectress of herds and childbirth. She was in old Latium a fertility goddess, and her priest was a fertility priest and was therefore supposed, so long as he held office, to be young and brave and strong. In fact he could only obtain office if he murdered his predecessor and he knew that he in his turn would sooner or later be murdered by some tough young aspirant lurking with his dagger in the woods. Even in historic times it was believed by many Romans that an escaping slave who managed to reach the grove of Nemi, who succeeded in finding the mistletoe or golden bough of Aeneas, and who could murder the incumbent of the sanctuary, had thereafter the right to proclaim himself the king of the wood (the *rex nemorosus*) and reign over the blue waters of Nemi until he was murdered in his turn. It was in the Nemi grove moreover that Diana hid her mortal lover Hippolytus, giving to him the name of Virbius, and rejoicing in the vigour of his limbs. Sir James Frazer is so enamoured of this fairy story that he takes it to mean that before historic times in Rome the hill-tribes were ruled by ' kings, who discharged priestly duties and probably enjoyed a sacred

character as reputed descendants of deities'. The close association of monarchy with religion has persisted ever since. To this day Queen Elizabeth II has the title of 'Defender of the Faith' and those who have witnessed the coronation ceremony in Westminster Abbey will have been startled and moved by its hierophantic atmosphere, by the suggestion that the Queen, captured and surrounded, is being offered as a humble sacrifice in some service of dedication.

The hierophants who presided at the fertility feasts and ceremonies contended that to them alone had been granted understanding of the mysteries of nature, that the legend that they had been the accepted lovers of nymphs and dryads, and that in many cases they were themselves descended from some sylvan or even more august divinity, entitled them to demand that religious honours should be accorded to their persons. Not only did they aspire to divine origin, but as the centuries passed they claimed to be the personification of the great gods themselves. Temples were erected in their honour and sacrifices made. They demanded the physical obedience of their subjects in their capacity as temporal kings and spiritual obedience also in their capacity as incarnate gods. It is strange indeed that theocracy, at least in theory, should have survived so long. To this day many devout Tibetans gaze on the Potala with trembling knees, and I have seen on the faces of elderly Japanese a look of cringing reverence as they pass the wide moat that separates the imperial palace at Tokyo from a Coca Cola world.

Once the priest-king had become the personification of the vitality of the community, it was difficult for him, as I have said, to survive the decline of his faculties when middle age came to harden his arteries, stiffen his limbs and blear his eyes. The tribe could not tolerate this overt decline of their personified virility. The idea thus arose that the king-priest should, as in the case of the priest of Nemi, be put to death when his force waned and his place taken by a more vigorous incarnation of fertility. From this arose the legend of death and resurrection. The Tammuz, the Adonis, and the Osiris cults concentrate on this theme. The vigour of the old king-god was declining and a new king god must be chosen in his stead.

A curious illustration of this superstition is provided by the Aztec ceremonial centering around the murder and resurrection of a substitute king. The most handsome of the captives taken in tribal battle was chosen as king for the year. He was housed in a palace, accorded homage and rich gifts, provided with the loveliest courtesans in the

RITUAL KILLING OF AZTEC KINGS

17

A model, five inches high, of an Aztec temple, found in Mexico City. The central relief at the top of the steps represents the sun receiving offerings from the god Huitzilopochtli and King Motecuzema

realm, dressed in glittering robes, taught to play the flute, and surrounded by guards. His nights would be spent in love and his days in dalliance, when he would play the flute stretched on embroidered cushions and fanned by houris. This lasted for a year. He was then led out to execution. Surrounded by guards and priests he would be forced to ascend the high staircase of the temple pyramid, dropping one by one the flutes which had cheered his period of regal state, and casting aside the diadem and jewels with which he had been decorated. On reaching the top, he would be stripped naked; two priests would seize his feet, and two others his hands; the small of his back would be settled across the altar and his chest and stomach arched upwards; he would then be slit open by the sacrificial knife of obsidian and his heart twisted out of the body and offered to the god Tezcatlipoca. His head would then be severed from the body while his blood poured down the gutter of the pyramid to the pool below. His decapitated body would then be rolled down the ramp of the pyramid to be caught at the bottom by the waiting priests who would flay off the skin and drape it, as a sticky dressing-gown, across the shoulders of Xipe, the high priest of Chaleihuitlious, Our Lady of the Turquoise Skirt. This ceremony was supposed to celebrate the return of spring and the severed head of the ex-king was stuck on a pole in front of the Temple of Fertility. His former regalia and his flutes were recovered from the stairway on which he had dropped them on his sad climb up the pyramid to the sacrificial stone. These pyramids, with their altars, the gutters which caught the blood, the ramp down which the corpses were tumbled, still rise in the sunshine of Mexico looking across the green forests to where the smoke puffs gently above the snows of the volcanoes.

Primitive communities were curiously ignorant of the facts of life and had little understanding of the processes of insemination. Thus, whereas the maternity of the mother was an incontestable fact, doubts must always arise as to the paternity of the father. 'In contrast with physical motherhood', writes Dr Frankfort, 'physical fatherhood was a subject of theological speculation.' PRIMITIVE THEORIES OF CONCEPTION

Primitive people believed that conception could be brought about by the slightest contact and the briefest encounter. To this day the Bantu assert that a woman can be impregnated by the flower of a banana palm, and the whole of mythology is replete with stories of unnatural couplings and weird pregnancies. It was in the guise of a bull that Zeus ravished Europa; disguised as a swan he took his pleasure on poor Leda; and the gentle Danäe was impregnated by her Olympian lover in a shower of golden rain. There was thus no saying by whom, or in what circumstances, a baby might be conceived. Again and again did expectant mothers proclaim that their pregnancy had been caused, not by a mortal lover, but by the secret visitation of a god. It was thus easier than it would be today to avoid scandal or to claim divine origin.

It is curious to note the large part played by snakes in this promiscuous intercourse between mortal women and the Olympian hierarchy. The temples of Aesculapius, the god of health, were scattered far and wide across the bays and promontories of ancient Greece. These temples were staffed by sturdy young priests and a snake farm was maintained on the premises, since snakes were sacred to the healing art. Patients who visited these temples for a cure would camp out in the courtyards on hot August nights and the snakes would glide and slither over their bare limbs. Women who visited the temples in the hope of curing their sterility would often return after a month or so miraculously cured of their disability and already pregnant. It was natural for them on returning to their home town to assert that they had been visited by the god in the semblance of one of the tame snakes. Augustus himself, as we learn from Suetonius and Dio Cassius, did not seem to mind the gossip to the effect that his mother Atia, when undergoing a cure in a temple of Apollo, had been impregnated by a sacred serpent and that he thus possessed Apollonian blood in his veins. Considering, however, that it was through his mother Atia, and his grandmother Julia, that he also claimed to be the great nephew of Julius Caesar, it is curious that he should have permitted the Apollo legend to gain any currency. But people in those distant days were always vague and broad-minded on the subject of fatherhood.

This again may have been a relic of prehistoric theory. Tribes expected their chiefs to be competent rulers and effective warriors, and at the same time they expected them to have inherited the magical gifts possessed by the sorcerer families. These gifts could, to their mind, be transmitted with greater surety through the female rather than the male line; one could always be positive as to the authenticity of a baby's mother, but where the father came from must be a matter of conjecture. This theory explains, not only the matriarchal system adopted by some communities, but the belief that the magic of royalty could be transmitted with even greater assurance through the female line. Thus we have the importance attached to consanguinity, the tendency of the Pharaohs to marry their sisters, and the long tradition that, if 'royal blood' were not to become diluted, princes and princesses must always marry into some family of royal descent.

MONARCHY IN HOMERIC GREECE

In Greece the conception of monarchy assumed several distinct forms. In the heroic age, in Mycenaean and Homeric theory, the king was above all the war lord. The heroic Kings were both hereditary and elective, being chosen from the royal family by the Assembly of the armed people. They were in no sense autocrats, being controlled by the heads of the leading families in council. They presided at the assembly of the people and performed certain hierarchical functions.

A weak king or an incompetent warrior would have been immediately deposed by the assembly and some younger relation substituted in his place. But although the monarch was to this degree regarded as an elective functionary, the old sense of magic was retained in the respect paid to men of royal blood, who were regarded as superior in talent and appearance to the ordinary class of citizens and warriors. Thus in the lovely passage of the twenty-fourth book of the *Iliad*, when Hermes is despatched to earth to guide old Priam to the tent of Achilles, the god adopts the disguise of 'a young man of royal lineage, when the down first starts to spring below the chin, when youth is at her loveliest'.

What is so interesting about the Homeric conception is that the word *aisumneter* which is generally used for the paramount chief, or king, has all manner of associations. It means ' member of the royal family', and is thus endowed with hereditary distinction, beauty and magic. It is used to describe an elective monarch as distinct from a tyrant or usurper. And it is used to designate an 'umpire' at games and also a bailiff or estate manager. On his return to Ithaca after a prolonged absence, when Penelope has as yet failed to recognize him, Ulysses discourses on the qualities of the ideal monarch. He speaks of

> a king without blame, who reverences the gods, and is lord over many powerful men, practising justice. Under his wise rule the black earth bears wheat and barley, the trees are laden with fruit, the flocks bring forth their young without ceasing, the sea teams with fish, and the people prosper.

In this description we have a combination of the several elements of heredity, elective power, and fertility magic.

Another type of Greek monarchy was what they called ' tyranny ', described by Aristotle as the worst form of any human governance. The essence of tyranny, and what distinguished it from legitimate monarchy, was that it exercised rule by compulsion rather than by consent. The tyrants, in order to compel obedience, enforced their authority by means of a regiment of foreign mercenaries, who acted as the royal guard. It was seldom that any tyranny survived for more than two generations. The earlier tyrants were often demagogues or dictators, purporting to champion the proletariat against the patricians. A later type of tyranny was that established in Sicily by Dionysius and his son. The latter was a man of culture, and on two occasions Plato sought to render him a philosopher king and an ideal autocrat. Plato's endeavours proved no more successful than did Diderot's attempts to render Catherine II a philosopher despot. In 345 BC Dionysius II was deposed and retired to Corinth where he lived in luxurious ease until his death many years later.

BABYLON AND
PERSEPOLIS

A third type of monarchy known to the ancient world was that of barbarian despotism, represented by the imperial majesty of Babylon and Persepolis. These oriental traditions of theocratic despotism were to some extent adopted by Alexander who imposed them upon the more democratic traditions of the Macedonian rulers. Yet the best examples of divine kingship or the theocratic theory of monarchy is provided by the Egyptian Pharaohs. It was they who perfected the system of theocracy and represented themselves as of divine descent and as king-gods. This contention, and the doctrine of the Divine Right of Kings which arose from it, will be examined in the next chapter.

It remains to consider the survival into modern times of the pre-historic myth of the King-magician.

It all derives from Clovis the Merovingian who, having been converted to Christianity by the persuasions of his sainted wife, was solemnly baptised in the cathedral at Rheims on Christmas Day AD 406. On that occasion there was such a crowd in church that the priest who arrived with the holy oil with which the king was to be anointed was unable to push through the throng. The bishop, having no oil available, paused; a state of embarrassed tension descended on the king and the congregation. At that moment a dove fluttered into the cathedral bearing in its beak a *lekythion* or phial of scented oil brought straight from heaven. It was with this sacred oil that Clovis was anointed and the *lekythion* was thereafter preserved in a reliquary shaped like a dove. This precious relic, known as *la sainte Ampoule*, was jealously preserved by succeeding Archbishops of Rheims, who insisted that no French monarch could claim to have been properly anointed unless the ceremony were performed at Rheims and the oil of the *sainte Ampoule* (which had the magic property of renewing itself at every coronation) poured over his head and hands. Even Joan of Arc refused to recognise Charles VII as King of France and always addressed him as Dauphin until he had been anointed at Rheims. In England the first king to be anointed was Egbert, who was crowned as Bretwalda in AD 802. It is from him that England's present Queen is directly descended.

The French, not unnaturally, were proud of their *sainte Ampoule*, pointing out that, whereas their holy oil derived straight from heaven, the oil with which other monarchs were anointed was but a chemical synthesis. It was much later that scholars discovered that the whole Clovis legend had been invented by Archbishop Hincmar three centuries after the event. At the time, the myth of the sacred oil of France was believed throughout Christendom and caused much mortification to other monarchs. The English, not to be outdone by the Hincmar story, invented the tale that their oil had been given by the Virgin Mary to St Thomas Becket. It was this sacred oil that was used at the coronation of English kings until the time of James I, who, being Scottish, regarded the whole tradition as a papist myth and refused to be anointed. The ceremony of the anointment was subsequently revived. The French clung to their legend and added to it the myths that Clovis had at the time of his baptism also received the fleurs de lys and the oriflamme, or sacred standard.

The holy oil was supposed to impart to the kings an element of sanctity in that they thereby became the 'anointed of the Lord', or *Domini Christus*. It was supposed to give the kings of France and England immunity against the risk of being eaten by lions (*l'enfant de roys ne peut lyon menger*) as well as certain magic powers of healing. For some reason, which even that mighty scholar and heroic martyr Marc Bloch has been unable to identify and determine, the gift of healing by the royal touch was confined to the illness known as 'scrofula' or 'struma' and in French referred to as *les écrouelles*. The expression was employed to define what we would now call a tuberculous condition of the bones or glands. The disease was more common in the Middle Ages than it is today: the symptoms were swelling of the lymphatic glands of the neck and eyes, disfigurement and an offensive suppuration. In France this condition was called *mal le roi*, in England 'the king's evil'. The ability of the kings, once they had been anointed, to cure this malady by touching the diseased part is one of the most remarkable examples of the survival of primitive magic into historic times.

It was never perfectly clear whether the gift of healing descended to the kings by hereditary succession, or whether it was conferred only by the sacrament of the holy oil. The Church tended to adopt the latter explanation, since, as the oil was poured out by a priest, it implied that the monarchy depended on the Church for its gift of magic. The imperialists on the other hand argued that the Rheims pigeon had brought the *sainte Ampoule* to the King himself and not to the Archbishop. In any case, the king could not perform the act of healing until he had confessed, been granted absolution, and partaken of communion. Thus Louis XV for several years running was forbidden by the Church to touch for the *mal le roi*, since his private life was too disorderly for him to merit absolution.

THE ROYAL
GIFT
OF HEALING

In England the legend was that the practice of the Royal Touch dated from the time of Edward the Confessor, although the first actual mention of the ceremony concerns Henry II. It is to be noted that the legend of the royal touch became more alive in periods when a dynasty were not positive as to their hereditary sanction. In France, the Capetians and in England the Plantagenets attached much importance to this magic aptitude. Between July 1338 and May 1340 Edward III touched as many as 885 scrofulous patients. Gregory VII, as might have been expected, denied that any king could inherit this magic power, and William of Malmesbury scoffed at the whole ceremony as 'false

Left: *The coronation of Clovis, from a fifteenth-century French tapestry now at Rheims.*
Right: *Charles II of England touching victims of scrofula, ' the king's evil'. From a drawing by Robert White in* CHARISMA BASILIKON, *1684*

works '. Mary Tudor touched regular y and the liturgy she used on such occasions is to be found in her private missa'. James I touched unwillingly, and refused to make the sign of the cross on the ulcers of those who were paraded before him. Charles II, after his restoration, touched on every Friday in the Banqueting Hall in Whitehall. Pepys records that he went through the ceremony with the utmost reverence and gravity. So associated in the public mind was the royal touch with legitimacy and therefore with the mystique of royalty, that Monmouth publicly performed the ceremony, and the exiled Stuarts continued to touch for scrofula when living in France and Italy. The last recorded instance of the ceremony of the royal touch being performed by any English king or pretender was when Cardinal York conducted the ceremony in Rome before his death in 1807. William III refused to touch, but Anne did so frequently. The last occasion was on 27 April 1714, three months before her death. Samuel Johnson as a little boy was led up to Queen Anne in 1712 to be touched for scrofula. All his life he remembered a lady in black lace and diamonds leaning towards him.

In France the ceremony was conducted without remission and as late as June 1715 it is recorded that the aged Louis XIV touched 1,700 men and women suffering from *le mal le roi*. During the revolution the ceremony was abandoned and in fact the whole legend was denounced as a childish superstition. Even Saint Simon expressed doubts whether the miracle of the king's touch had ever really been proved efficacious, and Voltaire prophesied that this superstition could not possibly survive the age of reason. In spite of this Charles X attempted to revive the practice in 1825. The occasion was not a success; there were those even who made mock of the performance, and after Charles X the practice was for ever abandoned.

In England the magic powers of the monarch were to some extent compromised by the theory that similar gifts of healing were possessed by seventh sons. Supporters of the royal monopoly denounced such impostures. 'I shall presume,' wrote Dr John Browne in his *Charisma*, ' that there is no Christian so void of Religion and Devotion as to deny the gift of healing - a Truth as clear as the Sun, continued and maintained by a line of Christian Kings and Governors, fed and nourished with the same Christian milk.'

In England, moreover, in addition to the Royal Touch, there existed a belief in what were called 'cramp-rings', namely rings that had been handled and presented by the monarch on certain feast days. These rings were regarded as a cure for muscular spasms, rheumatism and even epilepsy. In the missal of Mary Tudor there is the text of an invocation of divine blessing on these cramp-rings praying that those who wear them ' may be preserved from the wiles of Satan, spasms of the nerves and the perils of epilepsy '. She would rub the rings between her fingers, praying that God would sanctify the rings ' even as he had sanctified her hands with his holy oil '. These cramp rings were believed to have been brought to England by Joseph of Aramathea and to have been used by Edward the Confessor. Henry VIII found them useful presents to give to foreign ambassadors and visitors and they soon found their way into the shops of curio dealers. Benvenuto Cellini noted in his memoirs that they were being sold most cheaply in the junk shops of the Ponte Vecchio. The magic of cramp rings having thus become inflated, the whole system was discarded. Yet the popular superstition that the king possessed some magic power of healing tuberculous glands lingered on almost to modern times. Queen Victoria made no claim to possess any magic powers; but there were those who felt that this was ungracious of her, and who longed for the old magic to be revived.

TWO

The King as God

ONCE THE MEDICINE MAN had established himself as high priest of the tribe, as the intermediary between man and the forces of nature, he inevitably came to be credited with supernatural attributes and powers. The king-priests, in order to enforce their miraculous majesty and to achieve dominance over the caste of Shamans, encouraged this theory and claimed divine origin for themselves. The early kings of Alba and Rome announced that they were descended from Jupiter himself and installed within their thrones machinery and drums that could mimic the roar of thunder, thus justifying their claim to be the representatives of *Jupiter tonans* on earth.

The identification of rulers, who were regarded as the instruments of tribal vitality, with the processes of fertility had, as I have indicated, some inconvenient consequences. It led to the theory that kings should from time to time be sacrificed or burnt alive in order to renew the vitality of the tribe through the primitive and almost universal myth of a God's death and resurrection. Powerful monarchs, being opposed to serving as scapegoats, succeeded in persuading the priests that it would be sufficient to sacrifice some substitute in their place. For example, when, after a famine of three years, the people blamed David for his failure as a fertility priest, he was clever enough to contend that it was not owing to his sins that God was visiting wrath upon the people but owing to the sin committed by Saul in massacring the Gibeonites. Thus seven sons of David's predecessor were handed over as an atonement to the Gibeonites who 'hanged them in the hill before the Lord on the first day of the barley harvest'.

Tammuz, Adonis, and Attis all represented gods of fertility who died and were born again. Their deaths were mourned by the women ululating, scratching their cheeks and beating their breasts outside the temple wall. Their resurrections were celebrated by feasts and orgies in honour of the revival of vegetation. The Christian Church was wise indeed in adopting the dates of these ancient pagan festivals as occasions for their own religious celebrations. Thus the feast of Diana became the festival of the Assumption; the feast of the dead became All Souls Day; Christmas was fixed in the fourth week of December, marking the nativity of the sun; and at the vernal equinox the great festival of Easter echoes the Phrygian worship of the resurrected Attis.

KINGS IN THE OLD TESTAMENT

As early as 3000 BC the Sumerian city kings asserted their claim to have been begotten by gods and born of goddesses. At Ur they were worshipped as the incarnations of Tammuz and the representatives on earth of Innini, or Ishtar, the virgin goddess of heaven. The Hebrew kings relied on being 'The Lord's annointed', which rendered their persons sacrosanct and enabled them to claim a special relationship to Jehovah, with whom they were constantly in secret conclave. The Hebrew kings, none the less, did not ever acquire the prestige of the ancient prophets. We know, for instance, that when Samuel became infirm he appointed his sons as judges over the people, and that the sons proved to be incompetent and corrupt. The elders therefore approached Samuel and begged him to provide them with a king. The old prophet demurred to this suggestion, pointing out to them that kings were all too liable to become tyrannical or selfish. The elders were prepared to take the risk and replied 'Nay' to Samuel, insisting that 'we will have a king over us. That we also may be like all the nations; and that our king may judge us and go out before us and fight our battles ... So all the leaders of Israel came to the king at Hebron; and King David made a league with them in Hebron before the Lord; and they anointed David king of Israel '. These passages from Samuel, I v 8 and II v 5 were frequently quoted in subsequent centuries by those who opposed the doctrine of the Divine Right of Kings and who argued that the civil authority was subordinate to the ecclesiastical. They pointed out that the Old Testament contained many instances of priests opposing kings who ' did wrong in the sight of the Lord '.

The Hebrew theory of an elective kingship was not adopted by all the other ancient monarchies; the superstition persisted that the descendants of the old magicians, or the ' royal family ', inherited some of the magic powers of their ancestors and were specially endowed with the gift of mediating between earth and heaven and thereby promoting fertility. Yet difficulty arose owing to the fact that the eldest living descendant of a medicine-man or a king-priest might not be endowed with sufficient character or intelligence to render him the consolidator of the tribes, the dispenser of justice and the leader in battle. Much of the early, and indeed the later, history of kingship is concerned with the endeavour to combine magical descent with practical efficiency. Many curious devices were adopted in the hope of reconciling myth with reality.

ELECTIVE OR
HEREDITARY
MONARCHY

In Latium the succession was not by primogeniture in the male line, since the king's daughters could marry a man from another clan, who, provided that he were competent, could legitimately succeed his father-in-law. There was certainly a tradition in Latium that after a short reign the king must be put to death, and this tradition survived in the custom by which the King of the Saturnalia was expected to cut his own throat in expiation after the carnival was over. There is some evidence also that candidates for kingship in Latium were expected to submit to ordeal by combat, in which duels were organised between likely aspirants, and the winner crowned. To this day the Queen of England possesses a hereditary champion who is supposed to fight her rivals in mortal combat, and whose functions, although in vestigial form, are performed by the eldest surviving male of the Dymock family.

It is not, however, in Greece or Rome that we must seek for theocracy. It might be said even that pure theocracy has never existed. However devoutly the king might be worshipped by his subjects as a god incarnate, there were always some checks and balances in existence that limited his autocratic power.

The Dalai Lama of Tibet photographed during a religious ceremony in the Potala Palace, Lhasa, shortly before he escaped over the Indian frontier from the Chinese in March 1959. He is surrounded by attendants

The Dalai Lama of Tibet is often cited as the sole example of absolute theocracy, in that in theory he possesses unlimited spiritual and temporal authority. He is selected as a child by the heads of the three great monasteries, who rely upon symbols and portents interpreted for them by the oracles of Lhasa and Sam-ye. He is recognised as the reincarnation of Avalokitesvara, the legendary founder of Tibet. He is brought up in the Potala Palace and subjected to monastic discipline. His powers are, however, limited, not only by the supervision of the leading monks, not only by the presence of a council and assembly, but also by his colleague the Tashi Lama, who is also supposed to possess divine descent and talents.

The Incas and the Aztecs certainly claimed to be 'the children of the sun', and as such were accorded religious honours. At the Temple of the Sun at Cuzco the Inca kings presided on great occasions, wearing golden mitres enriched with coloured plumes and bearing on their breasts a huge golden disc representing the sun and the attendant stars. Yet there always remained the conception of a supreme being to whom the Incas, or 'Lords', were subordinate, and from whom they derived such supernatural powers as they possessed. The rule of the Incas, which was far less brutal and bloodthirsty than that of the Aztecs, was in fact a patriarchal rather than a theocratic conception. In Mexico the royal family overtly claimed divine origin, and Montezuma was definitely worshipped as a god with feathers in his headdress.

In Babylon, from the time of Sargon, the kings claimed divine honours, but it does not seem that in Mesopotamia the successive dynasties were regarded as of supernatural origin. It seems rather that in primitive times the Mesopotamian provinces were ruled by assemblies of the elders who only chose a king or a dictator in times of emergency. They did not regard these kings as divine, but merely as mortals charged with a divine mission. When monarchy was established between the two rivals it became customary, in order to avoid dynastic civil war, to appoint the eldest son of a monarch as co-regent during the lifetime of his father. He was installed in what was called 'The House of Succession' where he was instructed in the arts of kingship and administration and from where, on the death of the reigning monarch, he ascended automatically to the throne. On qualifying for the monarchy, the co-regent, or heir apparent, was crowned with a diadem and anointed with sacred oil. He was permitted to be represented by a substitute at religious ceremonies, his guidance being indicated if he merely hung his state mantle on a peg. If catastrophe threatened, as at the time of a comet or an eclipse, his substitute was put to death. Yet the Kings of Mesopotamia were not regarded as incarnate gods, and in the bas-reliefs and statues celebrating their victories or hunting triumphs they were not, as were the Pharaohs, depicted as over life-size.

It was in Egypt that the deification of monarchy became a part of religion. The Pharaohs asserted that their authority extended over the whole earth and sea; they claimed even that the gods were in some manner their inferiors. Even as Horus had succeeded Osiris, so also was a Pharaoh on succeeding regarded as the incarnation of Horus, 'the Great God, the Lord of Heaven'. 'The superhuman associations,'

KINGS OF
MESOPOTAMIA
AND EGYPT

writes Henri Frankfort, 'remained valid. The uncertain services which the medicine-men had given to the community became institutionalised. Kingship in Egypt remained the channel through which the powers of nature flow into the body politic to bring human endeavour to fruition'.

Pharaoh, as god incarnate, possessed absolute power. He was supposed to be endowed with what they called *Ka*, which meant vital energy. He was expected to maintain *maat*, or justice, and the rhythm of the seasons and divine order. Even as Osiris established harmony between mankind and nature and ordered the rising and setting of the sun and regulated the ebb and flow of the Nile, so also did the Pharaohs maintain the rhythms of the seasons and protect their peoples even after their own death. Pharaoh was worshipped as 'the god by whose dealing men live'. It was Amenemhet I who proclaimed, 'I was one who produced barley and loved the corn-god. The Nile respected me at every defile. None hungered in my years or thirsted in them. Men dwelt in peace through that which I wrought'.

The caste of priests derived their powers and privileges only as delegated to them by Pharaoh. Yet they also acquired great influence over the community, and on the death of Ikhnaton were strong enough to abolish the religion of Aton and return to the old mythology. Yet always there persisted a conflict between the King and the Church, between the temporal and the spiritual authority.

So inherent in Egyptian mythology was the conviction that divinity was transmitted to Pharaoh and his sons, that when the great Queen Hatshopsitou, the daughter of Thotmes I, assumed the throne and reigned for twenty years with efficiency and success, the priests at her death erased her name from the official calendars and genealogical tables. The belief persisted that all the Pharaohs were the sons of Amon-Ra and that this sacred blood must never be defiled by alien infiltrations. It was from this belief that arose the custom of members of the royal house mating with their sisters. Only those born of this incest could be worshipped as truly divine.

DEIFICATION OF ROMAN EMPERORS

In Rome, as will be explained in a later chapter, an even more ingenious method was adopted of maintaining continuity while securing efficiency. Instead of the eldest son of the Emperor succeeding his father automatically (and in any case, in the Julian-Claudian dynasty, there was a shortage of heirs male) the practice arose for the Emperor in his declining years to nominate a successor from among his own relations and to have the young man accepted as 'Caesar' by the senate and the army.

An effigy of Horus, son of Osiris and Isis, an Egyptian solar god often represented as a falcon. The Pharaohs were regarded as incarnations of Horus, ' the Great God, the Lord of Heaven '

At the same time an endeavour was made to increase the prestige of the Emperors by investing them with supernatural or religious attributes. Julius Caesar was accorded the honour of apotheosis by the Senate and Augustus was also deified. Even before their deaths they were said to possess superhuman attributes, such as *numen* and *aeternitas*. Elaborate ceremonial marked the apotheosis of a deceased emperor. A wax image of him was laid on a high pyre and from the midst of the flames an eagle would be released to carry the soul of the emperor to the stars. The more sophisticated emperors, such as Vespasian and Caracalla, treated this superstition with a certain scepticism and even made mock of it. But the public believed in it and would file past the statue of the divine, and even the living, emperor and cast a handful of incense upon his altar. The Christians were regarded as being foolishly ' obstinate ' in refusing to save themselves from an atrocious death by performing this harmless gesture of respect, *et fungar inani munere*, 'this easy and empty function'.

With the death of Nero in 68 AD, the 'progeny of the Caesars' became extinct and the fatal practice arose of allowing the legions to choose their Emperor. Thus Galba was elected by the army in Spain, Otho by the household cavalry, Vitelius by the army of the Rhine, and Vespasian by the legions of the Danube and the Euphrates. This led to civil war and it was only under the austere rule of the Antonines that unity and order were for a space of time restored.

THE EMPERORS
OF JAPAN

A phenomenal example of the ease with which a myth can be imposed even upon a civilised community is provided by the 'restoration' in the nineteenth century of the theocracy of the Mikados of Japan. As early as the tenth century AD it became apparent that the hereditary dynasty was not strong enough to impose its authority on the several feudal princelings or *daimios*, with their trained and formidable armies of retainers, or *samurai*. A generalissimo, entitled the *Shogun*, was appointed to impose unity, order and the dominance of a central authority. As the centuries passed, the *Shogunate* in its turn became hereditary.

The Emperor in the process was deprived of all his prerogatives, prestige, and powers. He was treated almost as a state prisoner, was interned in his palace, was never seen, even by the *Shogun* himself, and was reduced to almost abject penury. So poor and hungry did the Mikado become that his wives and daughters were obliged to plait baskets which they sold in the public streets. The Mikado was treated by the *Shoguns* as a mere totem, or idol; his name was never mentioned and few of his subjects had ever set eyes upon him. So unknown and unseen had the Emperor become that when Commodore Perry visited Japan in 1853 with a view to imposing a Treaty of Commerce by force, he was totally unaware that any Mikado existed, supposing that the *Shogun* was the reigning and absolute sovereign.

Commodore Perry's visit provoked an anti-foreign agitation. The mob shouted 'Away with the barbarians' and added to this now so familiar slogan the unexpected cry 'Restore the Mikado'. Many foreigners lost their lives at the time of this nationalist hysteria and in 1863 a British naval squadron bombarded Satsuma and Shimonoseki. The Japanese were much impressed by the potency of these bombardments.

Right: *The mummy of Tutankhamun or Tutankhamen, the Pharaoh who died at the age of eighteen about 1340 BC. The boy-king is known chiefly for the splendour of his tomb, which Lord Carnarvon discovered intact in 1922*

They realised that if the ironclads of the West were to be defied, something more efficient would be needed than the swords and aprons of the *daimios* and the *samurai*. The *shogunate* was held responsible for these humiliations and a yearning developed to restore the legendary authority of the Emperors, who seemed in retrospect, and after seven centuries, to have presided over a golden age, when Japan was divine, self-sufficient, united, invulnerable, prosperous and strong.

In February 1867 the Emperor Komei, although young in age, died suddenly of smallpox. He was succeeded by his son Meiji, then a lad of fifteen. This young Emperor was not a man of exceptionally strong character or overpowering genius, but he was advised by a group of highly gifted statesmen who resolved to profit by the occasion of his accession to abolish the *shogunate* and to restore to the Mikado his ancestral mystery and power. In February 1868 the Mikado Meiji issued a rescript announcing that he had resumed sovereignty and that he was immediately leaving his internment camp at Kyoto for the new capital at Yeddo or Tokyo. There in a vast garden, sundered from the outside world by a formidable moat, heavily revetted, he would establish his theocracy. The Meiji *coup d'état* is known to the Japanese as 'The Restoration'. The reigning Shogun, Keiki, accepted the situation and resigned his powers. The *daimios* and their *samurai* also agreed to compound their feudal rights for monetary grants, official appointments and personal pensions. Apart from the easily repressed Satsuma revolt, the new Japan was accepted by all.

The architect of this revolution, the true founding father of modern Japan, was Prince Ito (1841-1909), who had spent a year in London and carefully studied the economics, constitutions, and political theories of the West. Bismarck, whom he visited in Berlin, gave him realistic advice. He advised him to replace the thousands of small deities and demons who ruled over each separate paddy-field by a centralised state religion. Rummaging among the ancient faiths and philosophies of Japan, Prince Ito decided that Shinto seemed the most suitable theology. He therefore invented State Shinto and imposed it throughout the realm. He then drafted a constitution based on the model of the Prussian constitution, and accompanied it by a curious document entitled ' The Imperial House Law ', by which in effect the Mikado reserved for himself the right of veto on all legislation. The third piece of advice that Bismarck gave to Prince Ito was to render the army and navy supreme in the new Japan. The service leaders were the only officials accorded the

PRINCE ITO'S
DEFINITION
OF THEOCRACY

37

Commodore Perry delivers a letter for the Mikado of Japan in July 1853. So sacred and remote was the Emperor, that the Commodore was unaware of his existence and his embassy was received by the Shogun, Prince of Idzu

right of direct access to the Emperor and were always in a position to ignore or counter the policies of the Prime Minister and the civil departments.

Prince Ito, in his *Commentary on the Constitution*, which he published in 1889, defines the basis of the Japanese theocracy in terms which are pragmatic rather than logically, geologically, historically, or constitutionally accurate:

The Sacred Throne was established at the time when the heavens and the earth became separated. The Emperor is heaven descended, divine and sacred. He is pre-eminent above all his subjects. He must be reverenced and is inviolable. He has indeed to pay respect to the law, but the law has no power to hold him accountable to it. Not only shall there be no irreverence to the Emperor's person, but also He shall not be made a topic of derogatory comment nor one of discussion.

Since Shinto possessed no Bible, the imperial rescripts, which dealt not so much with contemporary issues as with the ethical principles of duty and loyalty, came to be regarded as the sacred books. In the primary schools throughout the country the little boys and girls were taught to bow low in an ecstasy of subservience in front of the framed photograph of the Emperor and to weep copiously when their head-master with stylised ceremony read to them from the imperial rescripts. A whole nation was thereby conditioned by a myth, a stratagem, a legend, artificially devised by the highly gifted Prince Ito in 1889. It was in the faith of this myth that Japanese airmen flung tnemselves to death, and that Japanese soldiers, even when completely outnumbered and surrounded, preferred death to surrender. It is a rare phenomenon that a whole nation can thus be conditioned within the space of a single lifetime. The Japanese must possess a congenital instinct for subservience, and be devoid of imagination.

That the prestige and prerogatives of the Mikado were not wholly theoretical (as is the power of the purely constitutional monarch), is due to what might be called the 'pyramidical' Japanese conception of society. The whole of Japanese political theory is based on the conception that each class, or caste, of society is accorded its 'proper station' and that the Emperor is placed as a beacon of light on the summit of this pyramid.

OBEDIENCE TO THE MIKADO

To our western minds it seems illogical that an institution which had remained in abeyance for seven centuries should suddenly be revived and be able to acquire a glamour and a prestige that dated from the tenth century. The explanation of this phenomenon is to be sought in the strange Japanese doctrine of obligations. Of all the many forms of indebtedness that an individual acquires, by far the most important is the indebtedness, or *On*, that he owes to the Emperor. This is known as the 'imperial obligation' or *ko-on*, and the duty of observing and repaying this sacred obligation is known as the *Chu*. The *Chu* thus became for the average Japanese a mystic, a religious, form of patriotism. They believed that it was their duty to sacrifice themselves for their Emperor and to 'set his mind at rest'. They loved him and worshipped him as the symbol of the continuity of their country, as the divine mediator who, whatever defeats or disasters might occur, would preserve the destiny of his realm. They believed that he loved them even as they loved him, and that during the most horrible ordeals of war, famine, or earthquake, he 'turned his thoughts to them' with transcendental solicitude.

Left: *Prince Ito (1841-1909), the true father of modern Japan, who raised the person of the Emperor above all criticism.* Right: *Confucius founded a universal philosophy for China, attaching great importance to courtly etiquette*

Thus, when Japan capitulated on 14 August 1945, they obeyed the Mikado's rescript without question. 'The Emperor spoke and the war ceased.'

Ruth Benedict, in her fascinating book *The Chrysanthemum and the Sword*, has to my mind underestimated the mystique of the Japanese monarchy, rescued from oblivion only one hundred years ago. As a convinced republican she dismisses it as a sentimental emotion, comparable to the ecstasies aroused in any good American breast by the spectacle of the Stars and Stripes floating in the wind of Freedom. But the Imperial *On* is a symbol blazing at the very apex of the pyramid, in terms of which the Japanese conceive of their destiny, their country, their political and moral philosophy, their origins and traditions, and their social order. It is a mistake to regard Japan as a pure theocracy; but it is also a mistake to dismiss as sentimental what is in fact a deep and enduring religious emotion, even though it be based on a quite recent and wholly artificial fallacy.

As we might expect, the doctrines of the Son of Heaven in China, and the liturgy that encircled him, were both more elaborate and more significant than the myth established, after the Meiji restoration, by the Mikados. Although during the last four thousand years China has experienced several successive dynasties, some of them being of alien imposition, the king-god myth and the doctrine of continuity were, until 1912, reverently preserved. The Chou dynasty, which lasted for nine centuries, from 1122 BC to 249 BC, did not succeed, owing to the disobedience of local war-lords, in maintaining a united Empire; but it did certainly succeed, at a period when we in Great Britain were painfully emerging from an almost palaeolithic culture, in creating those standards of civilization and scholarship which were to render China one of the glories of mankind.

It was under the Chou dynasty that Confucius and Lao Tzu founded their philosophies. Confucius, who died nine years before the birth of Socrates, anticipated the Platonic ideal of the philosopher king. He taught that good government was righteousness and that 'the superior man' should furnish an example of temperance, compassion and self-discipline. Although he himself attained high office as Minister of Crime, he was unable to convert any of the war-lords to his own liberal ideals. Even as Plato at the court of Syracuse, he discovered that the successful are impervious to philosophy. 'No intelligent ruler,' he lamented in his old age, 'arises to take me as his master. My time has come to die.'

It was under the Han dynasty, which endured from 202 BC to 220 AD, that China was unified, that the civil service was created and recruited by examination, and that paper was invented and used. Art and literature were encouraged, the Empire was extended by the acquisition of Korea and Tongking, and in later centuries the Chinese were tempted to look back upon those four hundred years as a second golden age, calling themselves 'the Sons of Han'. Three centuries of chaos followed, known to history as 'the Three Kingdoms'. Thereafter came the T'ang emperors, the Sung dynasty, and the Mongol invasion. In the thirteenth century the audacious young Venetian, Marco Polo, visited China and managed to secure the favour of Kublai Khan, who entrusted him with high office. In 1368 the Mongol dynasty was replaced by the native Ming dynasty which maintained itself for nearly three hundred years, which crystallized the imperial technique, and in regard to the history and manners of which we have much information. In considering the theory and practice of the Dragon Throne, it is thus convenient to consider the Ming dynasty, which covers the period from the Plantagenets to the Cromwellian rebellion. It is during that stage of Chinese history that court ceremonial received its full development, and that art and literature flourished as never before.

Taoism having by then declined, it was Confucianism that became the universal philosophy. It is difficult for us, who regard etiquette as an outmoded habit, to understand the supreme importance attached by Confucius to outward patterns of behaviour. The Confucian manner of expression is as stylised as a T'ang horse, and disconcerts us by its almost infantile simplicity. Confucius himself, when having audience of the local war-lord who, at least in theory, was supposed to represent the Son of Heaven, would indulge in fantastic mimes. After addressing his master, he would not assume a 'satisfied' expression immediately, but would retain a face of 'respectful unease' until he descended the first step of the dais. If on rare occasions his master would permit him to hold the jade sceptre, 'his countenance,' we are told, 'seemed to change and become apprehensive. He dragged his feet one after the other, as if they were tied by something to the ground'.

It is owing to the seemingly exaggerated significance attached by Confucius to external gestures that we owe the classic works on etiquette known as the I-Li, the Chou-Li and the Li-Chou. These manuals prescribe the correct conduct to be observed by the superior man both on official and on private occasions. Rules are established as to the bows or genuflexions that should be exchanged and examples of dialogue are inserted indicative of abasement, humility and quite meaningless compliments. An elaborate and wholly artificial dialogue is provided to mark the correct manner of presenting gifts. If the present were a roll of silk, then the donor should not approach his host with 'great strides' but should walk trippingly and manifest 'nervous uneasiness'. If it were a piece of jade that was being presented, then the donor should 'step carefully, lifting his toes and dragging his heels'.

The protocol established for an ambassador from some distant province bringing presents or tribute to the Dragon Throne was even more stylised:

He enters the palace gate with an impressive air; he ascends the steps in a deferential manner; when he is about to hand over the symbol of authority, he looks purposeful and moves quickly. On handing over his credentials he should assume the expression of a man watching to seize an advantage; when he descends the steps of the throne he should adopt the manner of a person escorting someone else. Once he has reached the bottom of the steps, he can let his breath go and can take things more easily. He lifts his feet two or three times and thereafter steps out naturally. When he gets to the door he resumes his correct demeanour. And then he and his staff leave the palace like a flock of wild geese, one following behind the other.

It will be realised that this elaborate ballet is prescribed for visits, not to the Son of Heaven himself, but to some mandarin who represents the Dragon Throne. On the rare occasions when Chinese officials were admitted to the presence of the Emperor himself, they had to perform the ceremony of the *k'o-t'eu*, or kow-tow, grovelling on all fours and beating their foreheads upon the ground nine times in succession. The devout Confucian would willingly perform these charades, convinced that he was following the path of virtue and correctness. No monarch today would expose his courtiers to such abasement.

During the four centuries that the Ming dynasty retained its power, these ceremonies were enforced. The curious thing is that when the barbarian Manchus broke in from the north and seized the Dragon Throne they adopted the traditional ritual and proclaimed that the Mings, owing to their incompetence and corruption, had 'exhausted the mandate of heaven' which had thereafter been transferred to the Manchus.

The conception of the Emperor's status and function was cosmographical rather than constitutional. The Dragon Throne was believed to unite heaven and earth, and when the Emperor, as Son of Heaven, took his seat at sunrise on the Dragon Throne, he was believed to radiate his presence throughout the globe. The theory was that the Emperor of China really ruled over the whole earth and that such other nations as might exist were no more than his tributaries. The Son of Heaven, on one occasion, addressed a letter to the Pope offering as a supreme honour to accept a niece of His Holiness as an imperial concubine and proclaiming himself to be 'the most powerful of all monarchs on this earth, who sits on the Dragon Seat to expound the word of God'. On the imperial feast day, which was called 'The Holy Birthday of the Lord of a Myriad Years', a service was held at dawn in the Great Within. The Emperor himself, as befits a god, remained throughout the ceremony hidden behind a screen. At a signal from the drums the congregation would prostrate themselves nine times before the empty throne. 'In no religion,' wrote Lord Macartney, who in 1793 was sent on a diplomatic mission to China, 'ancient or modern, has the Divine

43

been addressed, I believe, with stronger exterior marks of worship and adoration than were this morning paid to the phantom of his Chinese Majesty. '

On the night of the winter solstice the Emperors of China would sacrifice on the Altar of Heaven, a wide marble slab, exposed to the stars in the garden of the Forbidden City. On such occasions, he would wear ecclesiastical robes embroidered with symbols of fertility. On descending from his palanquin, he would approach the altar, dragging his footsteps slowly in stylised gait. If things had been going wrong he would chant an appeal to heaven in a high-pitched voice, such as is adopted by the court poets of Iran when, at No Ruz, they intone their eulogies to the King of Kings before the marble throne. We have the text of one such memorial addressed to heaven after a period of drought by the Emperor Tao Kuang:

I, the son of Heaven, am Lord of this soil. Heaven looks to me that I preserve tranquillity. My bounden duty is to serve the people. Yet, though I cannot sleep, nor eat with appetite; though I am grief-stricken and shaken with anxiety; my grief, my fasts, my sleepless nights, have but obtained a trifling shower.' The Emperor then pauses to examine what fault he may have committed to deserve so fierce a drought. He then continues: ' Prostrate, I implore Imperial Heaven to pardon my ignorance. Truly to wait longer is not possible. I have made the three kneelings. I have made the nine knockings. Hasten and confer clement deliverance; with speed send down the blessing of rain. Wu Hu, alas! Imperial Heaven give ear to my petition. Wu Hu alas! Imperial Heaven be graciously inclined, I am inexpressibly grieved, alarmed and shaken. Reverently this memorial is presented.

This most Confucian memorial was published in the Peking Gazette for 29 July 1852. It is agreeable to record that on that very evening a thunderstorm broke out accompanied by a heavy downpour. In the following week China was granted six inches of rain.

We possess two vivid narratives, describing the ceremonial of the Great Within, and written by members of diplomatic missions despatched to the Court of China. The first is by Johan Nievhoff, who in 1566 accompanied the trade mission sent to Peking by the Dutch East India Company. The Dutch were told that they must perform the ceremony of the kow-tow, thereby recognising that the States General were trib-

Right: *A commemorative tableau produced in Holland after the Dutch embassy to the Emperor of China in 1655. On such illustrations was based the European concept of Chinese dignity and brutality*

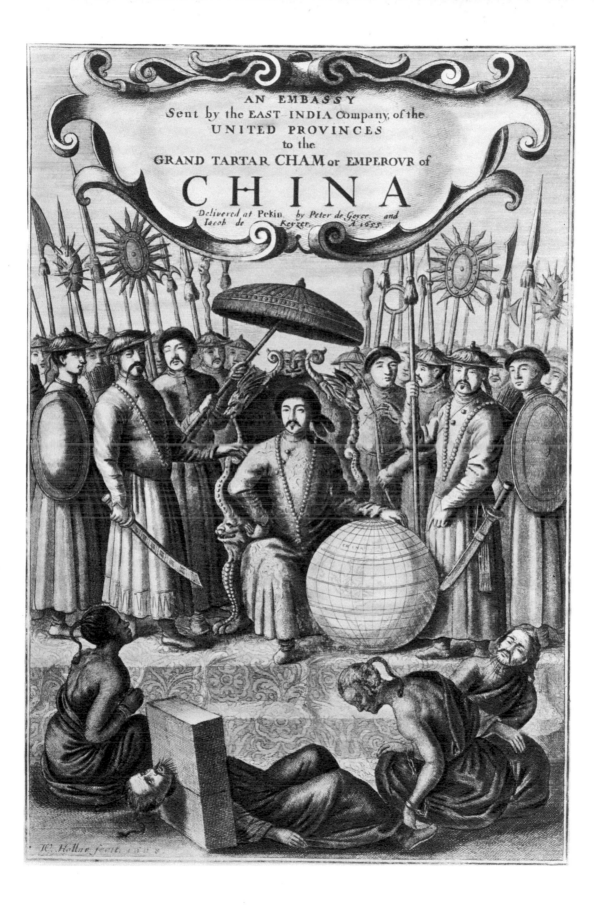

AN EMBASSY
Sent by the EAST-INDIA Company, of the
UNITED PROVINCES
to the
GRAND TARTAR CHAM or EMPEROVR of
CHINA
Delivered at Pekin, by Peter de Goyer, and
Iacob de Keyzer, A 1655

W. Hollar fecit

utaries to the Son of Heaven. Being essentially a trade mission they saw no reason why they should not perform this empty ceremony. They were obliged by the mandarins to go through a dress rehearsal of the ritual by kow-towing to the Great Seal of China laid upon a table under a cloth of yellow brocade. They grovelled on the ground before this emblem touching the floor nine times with abased foreheads. When a few days later they were admitted into the imperial presence they were accompanied by a hoard of mandarins who advanced with dragging steps to take the places allotted to them and marked with a number on their particular square of pavement. The Dragon Throne was almost hidden by the Imperial bodyguards dressed in crimson satin, by the standard-bearers wearing black hats plumed with yellow feathers, and by the senior mandarins each carrying a yellow parasol. At a given signal the whole company flung themselves to the ground on all fours and did obeisance to the empty throne by repeatedly striking their foreheads on the ground. The sound of distant music proclaimed the approach of the Son of Heaven. The congregation remained bowed to earth and all that the Dutch could see was that a figure in ' clinquant gold ' entered the throne room, and for fifteen minutes seated himself on the throne, immobile and hierophantic, facing to the south and paying no attention whatsoever to the grovelling figures below him. He then rose, and without so much as casting a glance at the congregation, walked slowly out of the throne room surrounded by his scarlet guards.

LORD MACARTNEY'S EMBASSY TO CHINA

When in 1793 Lord Macartney was despatched on a formal mission by King George III he was disconcerted to be told that the banners decorating the state barges which had been sent to meet him bore the inscription in Chinese, ' Embassy from the Red Barbarians bearing tribute '. Lord Macartney, being inhibited by Ulster obstinacy, refused to perform the ceremony of kow-tow. He was prepared to go down on one knee and bow as often as they liked; but to descend on all fours and touch the earth with his forehead was more than he could endure. His mission was a failure, and he departed without any treaty of commerce being concluded. Lord Amherst, who came on a second mission in 1817, announced in advance that he would not perform the kow-tow and was with all courtesy conducted back to his frigate.

Much powder and shot were expended before Europeans could gain admission to the Great Within and enforce their desires upon the Son of Heaven. Theocracy has always shown itself to be an exclusive and woodenheaded institution.

*A silver tetradrachma
of Alexander the Great
wearing a lion's head*

THREE

The King as Warrior

SO CONSTANT AND SO PERVASIVE is the conception of the Monarch as leader and protector of his people, that the idea of the King as Warrior has persisted throughout the ages. We have the legendary leaders from Agamemnon to Charlemagne, and:

> What resounds
> In fable or romance of Uther's son
> Begirt with British and Armoric knights;
> And all who since, baptised or infidel,
> Jousted in Aspramont and Montalban,
> Damasco, or Marocco, or Trebisond,
> Or whom Biserta sent from Afric shore
> When Charlemagne with all his peerage fell
> By Fontarrabia.

The very name Pendragon means 'chief leader in war'.

Warrior kings fall into different categories and provide divergent types, having this only in common between them, that they represent,

47

if only symbolically, the nation at war. We have the legendary warriors such as King Arthur or Fingal, who figure in epics and *chansons de geste*. We have those monarchs who were not expected actually to direct the fighting but who maintained the legend that they were the commanders-in-chief of the armed forces and that it was in their persons that the nation defied its enemies.

Thus Queen Elizabeth I, who, although a defiant woman, was by temperament a pacifist, reviewed her soldiers at Tilbury mounted on a prancing charger and carrying a truncheon in her little hand. Her speech to the troops on that occasion has a Churchillian resonance:

> I have come amongst you, being resolved in the midst and heat of the battle to live or die amongst you all, to lay down for my God, and for my Kingdom, and for my people, my honour and my blood even in the dust. I know I have the body of a weak and feeble woman, but I have the heart and stomach of a king, and of a king of England too, and think foul scorn that Parma or Spain, or any prince of Europe, should dare to invade the borders of my realm; to which, rather than any dishonour shall grow by me, I myself will take up arms, I myself will be your general, judge and rewarder of every one of your virtues in the field.

To which stimulating utterance of a warrior queen the troops responded with ' a mighty shout '.

LOUIS XIV'S SYMBOLIC VICTORIES

A less noble assertion of military leadership was enacted by Louis XIV during his Dutch Wars. An enemy city would be surrounded and beleaguered by one of his mighty marshals, such as Condé or Turenne, and when all was ready for the fall of the fortress the king and his courtiers and mistresses would hurry up to the Low Countries with their tents, their tapestries, and their chandeliers in order to arrive in time to receive the gesture and glory of the capitulation. Louis XIV managed to persuade himself that he had in person captured these fortresses, and the arms of surrendered cities were embroidered on the curtains of his great bed and on the vast Gobelin tapestries that Le Brun designed. But Louis XIV was not present in person at Blenheim, Ramillies, Oudenarde, Malplaquet, Turin, or at the victory won by Villars at Denain. It was in tapestry and oil paintings that the Great Monarch figured most frequently as the warrior king.

Since George II won the Battle of Dettingen in 1743, British monarchs have played but a symbolic role in military operations. During the two World Wars Kings George V and George VI paid frequent visits to the front, both in Flanders and at Scapa Flow or Invergordon.

The triumphal entry of Louis XIV and Maria Theresa into Arras, after his troops had captured the city. The King took no part in the fighting. A painting by Antoine-Frans van der Meulen at Versailles

'Your Majesty's presence and kindly words,' wrote Sir Douglas Haig after one such visit, 'brought home to one and all how very much our King is Head of the Army.' A more formal ceremonial appearance was staged by the German High Command in July 1918 when the Emperor William II was brought down by train to witness the final offensive in Champagne, which was accorded the title of the *Kaiserschlacht*. His Imperial Majesty was accommodated on the summit of a high wooden gazebo where, in the heat of the battle, his presence was forgotten and ignored. In the end they came to tell him that the offensive had been broken off and he returned in his train to Spa and eventual exile. It is depressing to be proved an ineffectual symbol. The spectacle of William II trundling back to Spa through the night arouses emotions of compassion.

From such symbolic soldiers we pass to those who actually led their men in war and carnage.

The Greek philosophers were interested in kingship and devoted much time to an analysis of its merits and defects. They had the advantage

49

of being able to study in the world around them many differing spec-
imens and stages of monarchy, from blatant tyranny to what purported
to be patriarchal rule. But they omitted from their analyses the phenomenon of the Warrior Kings. They came to the conclusion that, whereas
a ' good ' monarchy was the best form of governance, a ' bad ' monarchy
was worse than oligarchy, worse even than democracy.

GREEK IDEA
OF KINGSHIP

Plato's idea was that good government was based on knowledge,
an advantage which the common man could not possess. The Greeks
had but a rudimentary conception of representative institutions. Plato
felt that the world would never cease from internal and external strife
unless it were ruled by a race of philosopher kings. These supermen
would be untrammelled by law, by constitutions, or by public opinion.
The philosopher king (and Plato admitted that he was a fiction rather
than a practical proposition) would represent the organic unity of the
State; he would personify the Idea of the Good; he would possess
perfect knowledge since he would be Reason Incarnate. Unless directed
and protected by knowledge, a community might fall victim to the
' Centaurs and Satyrs ', in other words, to the politicians, who preyed
like an active virus upon its intestines. Knowledge, he felt, must be
above law or constitutions. ' Law, ' he wrote, ' is an impediment to
knowledge and knowledge is true sovereign. ' Yet when he came to
make his famous class list of the ' Law States ' and the ' Caprice States '
that existed around him, he was bound to conclude that, however flexible
and efficient might be the rule of a philosopher king, it was on the whole
preferable that the community should be protected by law against the
aberrations and fallibility of individuals who might not be philosophic.

Aristotle, while also admitting that the rule of a virtuous individual
would be preferable either to an aristocratic oligarchy or to the dictatorship of the proletariat, realised that under the hereditary principle
no dynasty could hope to produce an unbroken sequence of strong or
virtuous kings. He saw that a monarchy entailed the presence of a
body-guard, or even a standing army, to protect the monarch's person,
and that this instrument of power might well be abused for purposes
of tyranny. Moreover, an autocrat must always be swayed by personal
motives, prejudices or affections and it was purely visionary on the part
of Plato to see in an untrammelled autocrat the representative of the
organic State, incarnate reason, the creator of harmony, and the father-
image mingling authority and discipline with watchful love. A despot
must always possess personal or dynastic ambitions, and an antithesis

The so-called Sarcophagos of Alexander the Great at Constantinople, found at Sidon. It dates from the later part of the fourth century BC, *and is therefore roughly contemporary with Alexander's death at Babylon in 323* BC

is bound to arise in his conscience between private interest and public duty. The only possible guarantee that public duty will prevail is for the letter of the law to restrain the monarch from the pursuit of private gain or satisfaction. Thus law, to Aristotle, represented 'dispassionate reason' and as such must be supreme.

In advocating this admirable political principle, Aristotle may have been thinking of his ruddy, golden-haired, pupil, Alexander of Macedon, who, after subduing the Greek city-states, was conquering Asia by acts of violence of which no political theorist could approve. He tried to comfort himself with the thought that Alexander's autocracy was the form of government best suited to the Macedonian people in their barbarous phase of development. The young man's destruction of the liberties of the Greek city-states might be regrettable, but had he not been elected to his great office by the Diet of Corinth, and had he not been chosen as generalissimo, or *Hêgemôn Autokrator*, to revenge the Hellenic world for the iniquities inflicted upon them by Persia during the last hundred years? The most clear-thinking of all philosophers could find excuses for Alexander.

The Macedonians were regarded by the rest of the Greek cities as a barbaric race who could not claim to be Hellenic. The inhabitant of the smallest Greek city, as Plutarch tells us in the *Aratus*, was regarded ' as a better man than even the foremost Macedonian '. Demosthenes in his thunderous Philippics denounced the Macedonian royal family, the Argeadae, as barbarians, and contended that Philip of Macedon, the father of Alexander:

He is not only no Greek, nor related to the Greeks, but not even a barbarian from any place that can be named with honour, but a pestilent knave from Macedonia, a district from which we have never yet been able to purchase a decent slave.

These rude words were repeated to Philip, who thereafter entertained a vindictive hatred of Demosthenes.

The Macedonian kingship was of the Homeric type. The heir to the throne had, it is true, to be a member of the Argead family, but it was not invariably the eldest son who succeeded his father, and the successor had to be elected by acclamation by the assembled army. By the very circumstances of his installation the king of Macedonia was acclaimed a warrior king. The Macedonian nobility also were regarded as a military caste, being known as 'the companions' or *hetairoi*, being as feudal as the Myrmidons of the *Iliad*, and forming the pool from which the army officers were drawn. The king wore the same dress as the *hetairoi* and was not, until the time of Alexander, provided with any regalia. It was the tribal medicine-man, or seer, who wore a white robe and a circlet of gold. The king was no more than *primus inter pares* and needed vigilance and force of character to defend his authority.

On the death of Philip, the Greek city-states at first refused to accept the boy-king Alexander and threatened to recapture their liberties. By forced marches Alexander re-entered Greece. Athens trembled and submitted. Thebes was utterly destroyed with the exception of its temples and the house where Pindar had been born. The Diet of Corinth accorded to Alexander the honours that had been enjoyed by his father and, with the exception of Sparta, elected him as sole leader (*Hêgemôn Autokrator*) in the war of revenge against Persia. In the spring of 334 BC Alexander, with a mixed force of Macedonians, Illyrians and Greeks, crossed into Asia. He was not destined to see Europe again.

ALEXANDER'S CHARACTER

Plutarch had a deep admiration for Alexander's reckless courage, for his inspired daring, and for his unparalleled gift of leadership. To him the unlimited ambition of the warrior king possessed an almost mystic quality of greatness. He quotes from contemporary authorities many examples of Alexander's surpassing will-power and his trenchant gift of decision. There is the story of the Gordian knot. We are told also that Darius, having lost his army, offered an enormous ransom and the surrender of all Asia Minor west of the Euphrates if only Alexander would agree not to cross the river and not to invade Babylonia and Persia. The elder statesmen present begged the young Macedonian to accept so lucrative an offer and thereby to fulfil his mission of revenge. 'If I were Alexander,' urged his old general Parmenio, 'I should accept that offer.' 'And so would I,' replied Alexander, 'were I Parmenio.' We are told that when his counsellors, on the Eve of Gaugamela, begged him to fall upon the army of Darius at night-time when the Persians were not in orderly formation, he answered, 'I do not filch my victories.' We are told that when his men grumbled at being for ever drawn further and further into the wastes of central Asia, he refused to return to the two rivers and insisted that he must press forward towards the Ocean and complete his conquest of the world. When, after the sack of some Persian treasure house, he distributed the booty to his companions

Below: *Persepolis, about forty miles from Shiraz, was the capital of ancient Persia and was burnt by Alexander. The extensive ruins, excavated and partly restored by the University of Chicago, reflect the glories of the Persian Empire*

reserving nothing for himself, Perdiccas said to him, ' But what remains for you, my King? ' ' My hopes, ' Alexander replied. Plutarch makes much of these manly utterances.

Arrian, in his *Anabasis*, is more objective. He recognises that once Alexander, with the burning of Persepolis, had amply fulfilled his mission as the avenger of the Hellenes, he became obsessed by a ' longing ' to make himself Emperor of Asia, and dragged his soldiers ever onward in order at their expense to glut his mad personal ambition. Arrian was shocked by the deterioration of the stalwart Macedonian's character, by his repudiation of the principles of human dignity and personal austerity inculcated in him by the teachings of Aristotle. When he came into contact with Achaemenid laxity, he softened rapidly. Yet even the critical Arrian does not conceal the surpassing physical courage of Alexander, his gift for leadership, and the care and affection that he showed to his men, knowing all the petty officers by name, and sitting beside the pallets of the wounded seeking to cheer their despair and mitigate their agonies.

ALEXANDER
THE GOD

Alexander was a superstitious man, really believing he was descended from Heracles and Achilles and that his blood was divine. He would often refer to King Philip as ' my so-called father '. On one occasion, at a banquet, when Cleitus reproved him for ' disowning Philip and styling himself the son of Ammon ', he drove his spear into Cleitus' stomach in rage. He really persuaded himself that he was the son of Ammon and adopted the ram's horns of Jupiter Ammon in his official portraits. He was not a tall man; his complexion was fair and ruddy; he held his head to one side and his golden hair billowed around his scarlet face as the mane of a lion. His body exuded the delicious scent of honey. His gaze, according to his eulogists, was ' liquid and melting '. It is doubtful whether he retained this look of compassion when condemning the aged Parmenio and his son Philetas to disgraceful deaths, or when driving his spear into the stomach of his friend Cleitus. We know that his companion Cassander, who had irritated him by laughing at his Persian clothes and at his insistence on the kow-tow or *proskynesis*, had so vivid a memory of his glance of fury that when, many years after Alexander's death, he turned a corner of the sacred way at Delphi and was faced by the Lysippus statue, ' he was smitten suddenly with a shuddering and a trembling from which he could scarcely recover and which made his head swim '. Such also must have been the glance of Napoleon's icy eyes.

Aristotle had inspired his pupil with a passion for the unknown, as well as with an interest in natural, and even moral, philosophy, much to the discomfort of his generals and courtiers. Alexander regarded himself as a medical genius. Aristotle's lessons on geography were less informative. He told Alexander that the world was shaped like a plate; that India was situated at the extreme edge of this plate; and that once he had crossed the Indus he would reach the surrounding ocean, and sail home in triumph. It was this geographical misconception that determined Alexander to conquer India, and therefore the whole earth, and to round off his Empire by reaching the encircling sea. Of the Far East, it seems, he had no conception at all. He really believed when he reached the Indus that there would be no more worlds to conquer. By then he had marched some 12,000 miles across Asia, conquered the Persians, liberated the Greeks of Asia Minor, succeeded to the thrones of the Pharaohs and the Achaemenids, invaded India, crossed the Hindoo-Kush, subdued Bactria and Bokhara, penetrated almost to Tashkend, crossed the Indus, and advanced deep into the Punjab. He had seized the treasures of Damascus, Susa, Persepolis and Ecbatana, amounting to some sixty-three million pounds. He had founded numerous cities, including the great trade mart of Alexandria, destined to become the Athens of the Hellenistic world. Then, when his armies refused to follow him further, he marched back to Mesopotamia across the deserts of Baluchistan, returned at last to the Tigris, and died of fever at Babylon on 13 June 323 BC at the age of thirty-three.

Alexander in his person represented five differing types of kingship. As ruler of Macedon, as the most brilliant of all the males of the royal line of the Argeadae, as the descendant of Hercules and Achilles, as the warrior king acclaimed by the assembly of the army, he represented the Homeric type, the type of Agamemnon and Menelaus. To the Greeks he was the generalissimo, or *Hêgemôn*, chosen by the Diet of Corinth to liberate the Greek colonies in Ionia and to exact revenge upon the Persians. In Egypt he was acclaimed as Pharaoh, the incarnate Horus, the son of Ammon-Ra. As Emperor of Persia he assumed all the rights and splendour of the Achaemenids, and was as untrammelled in his autocracy as the Great King himself. In India he was the suzerain, such local rajahs as Porus or Abisares ruling as his vassals. That he was himself conscious of these different forms is shown by the fact that in his correspondence with his European viceroys he used the seal of Macedon, the seal of his earthly father Philip. In his correspondence with his Asian

MANY KINGS
IN ONE

The legend of Alexander extended deep into the middle ages. This plate is from the LIVRE DE L'APOCALYPSE *and shows a mediaeval version of Alexander at table*

satraps he employed the seal of Darius. Yet his behaviour as the elected King of Macedon, as the general representing the Corinthian League, was not unaffected by the theocratic splendour he enjoyed as Pharaoh, or the untrammelled despotism he exercised as Emperor of Persia. Having conquered the known world, he ignored the principles of democratic liberalism which Aristotle had taught him as the essence of Greek thought and habit. Warrior kings, as Demosthenes foresaw, are apt to degenerate into tyrants and to acquire megalomania.

In spite of the disruption of his Empire, the legacy of Alexander was never entirely dispersed. He broke down the barriers which until his day had separated Greek from 'barbarian' and introduced a high degree of civilization into what, before his time, had been a disordered world. His legend survived him. To the Persians he became the great Iskander, the son of their own Darius. The Mohammedans revered him as a prophet and the destroyer of idols. The Christian monks depicted him as an ascetic saint; in mediaeval tradition he figured as a mighty magician. Firdausi introduces the Iskander myth into the *Shahnahma*; the French romances of the eleventh and twelfth centuries are bright with his name; and the monk in the Canterbury Tales could contend that the Alexander legend was part of the equipment of any educated man:

> Every wight that had discrecioun
> Hath herd somewhat of his fortune.

His brutalities are forgotten; the wave of civilization and culture which, from Pella to Tashkend, accompanied his conquests is remembered and revered. Even to this day, the romance of this golden-haired stripling moves our hearts. He remains the most romantic of all warrior kings.

Comparable only to Alexander for daring and the extent of his conquests, was Jenghiz Khan the Mongol (1162-1227 AD), who founded an Empire stretching from the Dnieper to the China Seas. The very name of Jenghiz signifies ' perfect warrior ', and he succeeded in acquiring more subjects or satellites than had ever before him been ruled by a single man. The terror inspired by this Asiatic hurricane spread from Russia into Europe. The gentle citizens of Vienna or Lyons would wake screaming in the night, imagining that they had heard the blare of Asiatic trumpets, the thudding of half-a-million horses, and wild Mongolian cries.

By force or by intimidation his armies occupied Bokhara, Samarcand, Balkh, Merv and Nishapur, massacring the men, women and children whom they captured and returning to Mongolia with heavy bales of loot. They would burn and destroy the temples and the palaces and level with the parched earth the great walls that defended the cities. At Herat alone they were said to have murdered more than a million and a half of the inhabitants. They were a savage and ruthless horde. Only at the end of his life did Jenghiz order the massacres to cease.

The grandson of Jenghiz Khan, Kubla Khan, founded the Mongol dynasty of China which lasted for a hundred years. He was a lavish and civilized Emperor, who encouraged the arts and the sciences and employed many European advisers and administrators to assist him in his task. But he cannot rank as a warrior king, since, however beneficent may have been his administration, he was not a man of military genius, and his attempts to conquer Japan ended in utter failure. Until the eighteenth century the arts of civil administration and military prowess were seldom found in combination. Most of the Asiatic warrior kings were men of reckless courage who Inspired the hordes that followed them by the force of their will-power, the glamour of their personal audacity and the magic of their constant success.

TAMERLANE   Another oriental warrior-king was Timur, known to history as Timur-i-Leng or Tamerlane, who was born in 1336 in Transoxiana, in ' the green city ' fifty miles south of Samarcand. His father, chieftain of the tribe of Berlas, was a devout Moslem who preferred to any adventure a life of ascetic contemplation. Timur himself was neither ruminative nor ascetic; he was inspired by dynamic ambition and by a resolve to render himself supreme over all the Asian tribes. With subtle diplomatic skill and considerable daring he managed to collect adherents, gradually to gain mastery over the surrounding tribes, and eventually to succeed in becoming ruler of Samarcand. Even at the summit of his power Timur possessed such a veneration for the hereditary principle that he never assumed the crown but preserved as his nominal master the Khan, who was descended from Jenghiz. The sons of Timur, whose mothers were princesses of the blood royal, assumed the titles of Sultan. Timur himself was known as ' Lord Timur, the Splendid ', and ruled despotically as *Shogun*, or Mayor of the Palace, to a puppet King.

Having defeated his internal enemies Timur advanced into Russia and led his armies as far as the Volga. He then turned to the southwest, capturing Baghdad and Kerbela and subjugating Kurdistan. In 1395 he utterly defeated Toktamish, the Captain of the Mongol Golden Horde. When over sixty years of age, Timur invaded India and captured Delhi. His descendants founded the Moghul Empire which, with ever diminishing vigour, lasted until 1857. At the age of sixty-six Timur declared war upon the Turks and the Egyptians and gained possession of Baghdad, Aleppo and Damascus. In 1402 he utterly defeated the Turks at Ankara and took captive the Sultan Bayazid I who, having reached the very walls of Constantinople and constructed the castle of Anatoli Hissar on the Asian side of the Bosphorus, was obliged as a prisoner of the Tartars to suffer deep humiliation. He was not, as we have been told in Marlowe's mighty line, forced to trot and stumble beside Tamerlane's camel, and was not dragged through the villages of Anatolia in a cage. But it does appear that the Tartar conqueror forced him to attend his victory banquet, at which he was obliged to don his former regalia,

Right: *Jenghiz Khan (top right) prays for victory in the battle which has already begun at a river-crossing. An illumination from a manuscript entitled* HISTORY OF THE MOGULS, *1595, now in the Imperial Library at Teheran*

to place the jewelled aigrette in his turban, and to watch his wives and concubines, hitherto secluded in his harem, being paraded naked in front of Tamerlane and his generals. A few months later Bayazid I, the 'Thunderbolt' as the Turks had called him, died in harsh captivity and shame.

Timur the lame was not, however, the utterly revengeful warrior that Marlowe has depicted. He was a man of some culture; although he was never seen to laugh and exercised a grim dominance over his court and officers, he would play chess by himself in the very heat of battle and took great trouble to rebuild, on a plan of his own, the cities that he destroyed. He had an unexpected passion for fine apparel and even in the midst of some campaign would array himself for his evening meal in silks and richly embroidered brocades. His armies, moreover, were perfectly disciplined and he would hold regular reviews, in which the several divisions under their commanders, or *amirs*, would manoeuvre with all the precision of the Macedonian phalanx and to the sound of kettledrums and trumpets. His civil administration was elaborately organised, each province being confided to a civil governor or *daroga*, responsible to Tamerlane. He paid special attention to communications, creating wide straight roads with caravanserais at regular intervals. He established an intricate intelligence service and a secret police, his information officers being accorded priority at all posting stations. He insisted on accurate reports, any of his agents who reported inaccurately being immediately put to death. Tamerlane was quite merciless and possessed a morbid passion for building pyramids and columns from the skulls of his enemies. At the capture of Baghdad as many as one-hundred-and-twenty of these pyramids were constructed of severed heads.

WARRIOR-DESPOTS OF ASIA

In some respects Tamerlane was more typical of the Asiatic warrior-despot than his predecessor Jenghiz Khan. Each of them possessed compelling will-power, unusual endurance and magnificent physical courage. But whereas Jenghiz Khan was cautious and even patient, would direct his campaign from his headquarters and would share his responsibilities with his generals and advisers, Tamerlane preferred to enter the dust and blood of battle himself, and never to ask the advice of any minister or general. Whereas Jenghiz would sweep onward by different roads and with widely separated armies, Timur always moved with a single vast army under his own direct command. Jenghiz planned his campaigns in advance and in the smallest detail, working out the position of water wells and fodder all along his routes. Tamerlane was

Right: *Tamerlane or Timur (1336-1405), one of the greatest of the Tartar conquerors.*
Left: *The Timur ruby, now in the possession of HM the Queen. The jewel has an unimpeachable
pedigree, descending to Queen Victoria through the Shahs of Persia and Mogul Emperors*

reckless, dashing onwards with small regard for the possibility of defeat.
Each of them relied on the terror he inspired. The kettle-drums of
the Tartars, their wild battle cry of 'Hourra', aroused panic even as
the thud of the little Mongolian horses on the dry soil of the steppes
had spread fear to the banks of the Volga. Both the Mongols and the
Tartars imprinted on the Scythians and on the Russians not a physical
type only, but also a violent brand of mass courage. These desert warriors
left a lasting imprint on Central Asia; a problem and a mystery that
still exists in our own dangerous and angry world.

The warrior-despots of Asia, although their descendants created
something like the rule of law in their dominions, and achieved a high
level of civilization and culture, were themselves essentially brigand
chieftains on a gigantic scale. It was the magic of their personalities,
their iron will, the legend of their invincibility, even more than the
lust of blood and loot, that enabled them to compel the obedience of
their armies when surrounded by enemies, weakened by thirst and
hunger, exposed to icy blizzards or torrid heat, and sundered by two
thousand miles from their homes. This miraculous faith and discipline

did not survive the death of the nomad chiefs. Even as it seems inconceivable to us that Alexander could have compelled his Macedonians and Illyrians to follow him to the very edge of the known world and then back across the parched mountains of the Makran, so also do we remain perplexed by the force of personality of Jenghiz and Tamerlane.

It might be thought impossible that such almost supernatural dominance could have been witnessed in more sophisticated centuries or with armies recruited from anything but a traditionally nomad population. Yet Frederick the Great was able to maintain the iron discipline imposed on the Prussian armies by his father, owing to their conviction of his military genius and the justifiable belief that he was welding Prussia into a great European Power. And Napoleon was able to preserve the admiration of his troops owing to the legend of his invincibility and the glamour of his glory.

CHARLES XII
OF SWEDEN

Yet if we are to understand how potent can be the legend of a warrior king we must consider the career of Charles XII of Sweden, who, in spite of utter defeat and capture, was able to command the loyalty of his troops and countrymen, through twenty triumphant and disastrous years.

Charles XII, unlike most warrior kings, was devoid of personal magnetism. He was sullen, secretive, inarticulate and unwashed. He was ascetic and even austere. He never cared for women: he was indifferent to comfort and even cleanliness; he never noticed what he ate and he never touched wine: he was harsh and stark in all his ways; he seemed totally unaware of the sufferings to which, in his blind egoism, he exposed his armies and his country. At a time when Louis XIV was battling desperately with Marlborough, Charles XII could have exercised a determinant influence by taking one side or the other. But he was determined to conquer Poland and Saxony and to obtain mastery of the North and of the Baltic by defeating Peter the Great. As a result he lost his army at Poltava and had to escape into Turkish territory and seek refuge with the Sultan on the banks of the Maritza.

Fifteen years after embarking on his adventures in Eastern Europe, Charles XII returned to Stockholm, accompanied by a single adjutant. Yet such was his lust for battle that, in spite of his bitter experiences, he immediately launched a fresh war on Norway. It was while his army was investing the obscure fortress of Fredriksten that he looked over the parapet of a trench and was shot through the head by an unknown Norwegian sniper. ' His fall ', wrote Dr Johnson,

62

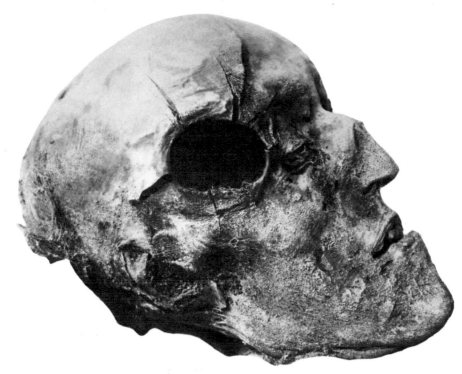

The skull of Charles XII of Sweden, who was killed during the siege of Fredriksten in Norway in 1718. This grisly relic still exhibits the huge hole made by the sniper's bullet

His fall was destined to a barren strand
A petty fortress and a dubious hand.
He left the name at which the world grew pale,
To point a moral or adorn a tale.

The moral bequeathed by Charles XII is stranger even than the vanity of human wishes. It reminds us that the spell of the warrior king is so hypnotic that a born leader, even when defeated and captured, can continue to command the obedience of his soldiers and the loyalty of his people. It reminds us that man's love of military glory and the habits of obedience are such potent human instincts that they can withstand even defeat in an unjustified war. It warns us that even the best disciplined army, led by a warrior king of genius, may experience disaster if its commissariat and supply-trains be deficient, or when faced by a scorched-earth policy on the part of a retreating enemy.

We may not always admire the daring or egoism of a warrior king, but, whether he be Tamerlane or Charles XII, he makes a powerful appeal to the vanity and ambitions of mankind. It is not only loot, advancement and rewards that can impel men to endure death and suffering: it is also the lust for glory.

63

FOUR

Principate to Tyranny

THE ROMANS HAD A MORBID HORROR of monarchy. To them it suggested the fierce Etruscans, the almost legendary Tarquins of the sixth century, and the shame and horror of foreign domination. Since their childhood they had been taught to associate the word *Rex* with myths of tyranny and enslavement, even as in my own lifetime many Americans in their little red school-houses were taught to regard dear old George III with superstitious loathing.

The Romans looked back to the virtues and institutions of the original Quirites with almost religious awe, and regretted profoundly that the egoism of war-lords should have shaken the republican fabric and exposed the Empire to a series of civil wars. They longed to become orderly again and at the same time to preserve their ancient constitution. They were prepared, in the expectation of regaining security and order, to submit to the rule of a strong man, provided that he did not trample overtly upon their traditional institutions and principles and was prepared at least to pretend that the Republic still survived.

Julius Caesar was not a tactful man: he hated shams. Having, by the force of his genius, secured supreme power, he did not possess the subtlety to disguise it, and thus, on the Ides of March 44 BC he was stabbed in the Senate House and fell dying at the foot of Pompey's statue, bleeding from twenty-two wounds.

Julius Caesar had a sister of the name of Julia whose daughter, Atia, had married a plebeian from Velletri called Octavius. Atia had a son, who came to be known as 'the young Octavian', and who was born on the Palatine hill on September 23, 63 BC. At the age of fifteen Octavian came of age and assumed the *toga virilis*. He was a youth of such surpassing beauty that his mother would not allow him to visit the temples during the day-time, since his presence distracted the devout at prayers. In 47 BC, when the consuls made their annual pilgrimage to the Alban Mount, Octavian, although aged but sixteen, was appointed by the Senate Prefect of the City. He was a precocious lad and his great-uncle, when at last he met him, decided immediately that here in truth was a worthy representative of the Julian *gens* who, as was well known, were descended through pious Aeneas from Venus herself. On Caesar's return from Asia, the young Octavian was allowed to participate in his triumph, riding behind his great-uncle's chariot followed by a herd of giraffes, stepping delicately. Gazing at him in wonder, the Roman public realised that Julius Caesar had found a successor.

Octavian was at the military academy in Epirus when the news reached him that his great-uncle had been murdered and that he had left a will appointing him heir to two-thirds of his fortune. He crossed immediately to Italy and at Pozzuoli had a meeting with Cicero, the head of the senatorial party. The great orator at first underestimated Octavian's capacity. 'He is merely a boy,' (*sed est plane puer*), he wrote; 'he is neither here nor there'; (*De Octavio Susque deque*). This was a mis-calculation. Within a few months Octavian had formed the Triumvirate with Antony and Lepidus and carried out the 'proscriptions', during which many senators, including Cicero himself, were put to death. He then successively defeated Lepidus, and Pompey's son. Antony had meanwhile escaped to Egypt, where he married Cleopatra according to Egyptian rites and proclaimed her 'Queen of Kings'. They were defeated by Octavian at the Battle of Actium on 3 September, 31 BC, and returned to Egypt where they both committed suicide. Octavian was left the master of the Roman world. He was subtle and cautious in the forms in which he concealed his power. He set himself with

THE RISE OF
OCTAVIAN

65

patient industry to create an autocracy under the guise of a republic. It is known to students of constitutional history as 'The Principate'. It was an ingenious, but not a lasting, device.

Guglielmo Ferrero, the brilliant and highly imaginative historian of the fall of the Roman Republic, disliked Octavian. He tells us that the youth's beauty was marred by his short stature, by his ugly hair, and by his bad teeth. In fact he denounces him as 'an arrant rogue', *compito briccone*. Yet even Ferrero admits that Octavian was perfectly sincere in his claim to have restored the Republic. He had no desire to impose an autocracy and it was merely the force of circumstances that rendered him unable to relax central, and therefore autocratic, control.

OCTAVIAN'S
FORM OF
DICTATORSHIP

He had learnt from the example of his great-uncle that the Romans were superstitiously afraid of kingship, that they distrusted permanent dictators, and that they still revered the senate as the symbol of ancient order. He was aware that the *comitia*, or popular assembly, were dominated by the rabble of the Roman unemployed and his aim therefore was to enhance the power of the Senate, as representing the old governing class, and to encourage the *Equites*, or middle class, through whom he hoped to create a path open to the talents and a valuable reservoir of able administrators, financiers and civil servants. The coins bearing his image bore the superscription *Libertatis populi Romani Vindex*, the 'champion of the liberty of the Roman people'. Was that hypocrisy? Ferrero does not think so. 'It is not true,' writes Arnold, 'that Augustus restored the Republic; it is equally untrue that he proclaimed the Empire.' What he did was to establish a Principate or 'Constitutional Monarchy', on solid foundations; to pacify the world; and to give the *Pax Augusta*, security, and prosperity to the Empire for forty-one years. 'He succeeded,' writes Dio Cassius, 'in creating a system, free alike from the licence of democracy and from the insolence of tyranny.'

There exists a cryptic but revealing utterance of Octavian himself. 'I excelled all,' he wrote, 'in *auctoritas*, but I had no more *potestas* than my colleagues in the several magistracies.' Even so might a President of the United States assert that he had been very much a President, but had left to his Cabinet Ministers the charge of their own departments. On what therefore was this *auctoritas* based?

Since the days of Marius it had been apparent that ultimate power rested not with the people in *comitia* assembled, nor with the Senate,

Right: *The Augustus Cameo, part of the treasure of St Chapelle, Paris. Above is Augustus deified; below, Tiberius and the imperial family*

but with the army; and that the legions would only obey and follow their own *imperator* or commander-in-chief. Thus the lynch-pin of *auctoritas* was the *imperium proconsulare*, the office of generalissimo, which gave its holder command of all the armed forces and the right of declaring war or making peace. In strict constitutional theory no proconsul could introduce his legions into the capital city: he could exercise no military authority south of the Rubicon. In practice this principle was no longer taken seriously. In any case Octavian retained command of the Fleet, and was in Rome itself protected by the *Vigiles* and the Praetorian Guard. The former were a police force and a fire brigade but could be used as security troops in times of danger. The Praetorian Guard, which in later years became such a menace to the State, were an armed and highly privileged body of household troops numbering as many as 9,000 men. The first act of Octavian on ' restoring the Republic ' was to double the pay of his household guard. At the same time he refrained from quartering more than three cohorts in Rome itself, and distributed the remainder throughout the provinces. Even Tiberius was careful not to render the Praetorians too obtrusive and decreed that when in the capital itself they must wear civilian clothes.

In addition to the *imperium proconsulare*, Octavian obtained the *tribunicia potestas*, which was regarded as a popular and honourable office, and which rendered its holder's person inviolable and enabled him to veto legislative acts. Octavian also accepted the title of *Princeps Senatus* which entitled him to summon the Senate and to be the first to speak. Even when, on 1 January 27 BC he renounced all the unconstitutional powers that he had wielded as a Triumvir, and was accorded by the Senate the title of ' Augustus ', which had ancient religious associations and prestige, he never called himself *Imperator* except when dealing with military or colonial affairs. He liked to be called *Princeps*, or ' President '. He refused the offer of the consulship for life, but he acquired the right of admitting or dismissing individual senators and no man could hope for office unless he received the *commendatio* of the Princeps. Thus, as Gibbon remarked, ' whilst he restored the dignity, he destroyed the independence, of the Senate '. He may, without ever desiring to do so, have abolished true democracy, but he certainly reimposed the rule of law, which in Rome could only be administered through republican institutions. It was when later Emperors disregarded the rule of law, and introduced arbitrary despotism, that the old constitutional formulas became entirely otiose.

OCTAVIAN
BECOMES
AUGUSTUS

69

Augustus' unwillingness to establish a dynasty is shown by his curious and dangerous hesitation to nominate an heir to the throne. He preserved the fiction that it was for the Senate to elect a successor or even to decree that the office of Imperator or Princeps should be abolished. Yet he well knew that, unless some form of automatic succession were devised, the several legions might acclaim their own Imperators, and that civil wars would then ensue. At first he decided that his successor should be the veteran Agrippa, and it was to him that, when threatened with severe illness, he handed his signet ring. But Agrippa predeceased him and one by one the successive candidates from his own family, - his nephew Marcellus, his grandsons Caius and Lucius, and his step-children Germanicus and Drusus - died while still young. He was forced to fall back upon his step-son Tiberius, a man of military and administrative ability, but disliked by his step-father owing to his timid, misanthropic and suspicious temper and his sullen ways. On 26 June 4 AD he felt obliged publicly to adopt Tiberius and to induce the Senate to recognize him as the heir apparent.

In 9 AD the army which had been despatched under Quintilius Varus to establish the Roman frontier on the Elbe was ambushed in the Teutoburgian forest by the chief of the Cherusci, Arminius, and massacred to a man. ' Arminius, ' wrote Tacitus, ' was unquestionably the liberator of Germany. ' Augustus was obliged to withdraw the Roman *limes* from the Elbe to the Rhine, thereby depriving Germany of the civilising effect of Roman rule and exposing Europe to many subsequent misfortunes. The tragedy of the Teutoburgian forest clouded the last years of Augustus' life. He surrendered to melancholy, refused to shave or wash, and would moon about the passages of his house, murmuring, *Quintilii Vare, legiones redde*, 'Varus, give me back my legions.'

At the age of seventy-five Augustus died in the arms of his devoted wife Livia in the same room in the farmhouse at Nola in which his father had died seventy years before. His body was brought to Rome amid universal lamentation.

TIBERIUS We are today less inclined to accept the conventional picture of his successor Tiberius as a ferocious tyrant and a senile voluptuary. It is at least improbable that a man who all his life had shown moderation and competence should, on succeeding at the age of fifty-eight, have suddenly changed into an almost insane despot. Nor need we credit the salacious gossip of Suetonius and believe that a man who during his youth and middle age had shown himself sexually diffident should

The Ara Pacis relief in Rome, first century AD, *showing the family of Augustus in statuesque procession. Augustus had no son, but was much aided by his stepsons Drusus (seen on the left of the group) and Tiberius who succeeded him. The boy in the centre is Germanicus, son of Drusus*

at the age of sixty-eight have developed *libido senilis*. Gregorio Marañon is probably correct in attributing the fierceness, or *saevitia*, which Tiberius undoubtedly displayed, to the fact that his youthful experiences had left him with a morbid sense of inferiority and a loathing of his fellow men. Marañon suggests that he suffered from sexual impotence, a misfortune that frequently affects left-handed people who are very tall. He was certainly an exceptionally ugly man: he was haggard, gawky, and bowed; he had a cantankerous expression and he suffered from a skin disease of a leprous nature which spread from his chin to his body and which broke out into ill-smelling ulcers. 'In his old age,' Tacitus records, 'his appearance filled even himself with shame.' During the last eleven years of his reign he refused to set foot in Rome, corresponded with the Senate in abrupt little notes, and remained perched in his villa on the precipices of Capri surrounded by his freedmen and his Chaldean astrologers.

There could no longer be any pretence that the Empire was governed in partnership between the Senate and the Princeps. Tiberius ruled by terror, not by consent; he employed a staff of secret police and paid informers, or *delatores*. Tacitus writes:

> Never before, had such apprehension taken possession of the Romans. People trembled even in their own families. Nobody dared to approach anyone else or to be seen speaking to them. The ears of everyone, whether mere acquaintances or intimate friends, were suspect. Even inanimate objects created misgiving. Uneasy glances passed over walls and partitions.

A senator could be put to death for failing to respond with sufficient alacrity to a letter from Capri, for a disapproving silence, or an ill-placed laugh or smile. Tiberius exploited the powers and offices which Augustus had assumed as Princeps, to establish what was in fact a despotism. Dio Cassius records:

> By virtue of the offices they (the later Emperors) assumed, they secured the right to raise levies, to collect taxes, to declare war or peace, to rule citizens and foreigners alike, always and everywhere, even to the extent of condemning senators and *equites* to death, even inside the city boundaries ... By virtue of holding the office of Censor they were able, apart from conducting the census, to investigate our private lives and morals, to enrol or expel senators and knights. By virtue of being chosen as High Priest, or *pontifex maximus*, the Emperor came to concentrate in his own hands all power, both sacred and profane.

THE EMPERORS
DEIFIED

Tiberius did not lay claim to the divine right of Kings. 'As for myself,' he assured the Conscript Fathers, 'I call you to witness that I am mortal, that my functions are human functions, and that I hold it sufficient if I fill the foremost place among you.' The Senators were too terrified and cautious to accept such modesty. 'The gods,' they assured the tyrant, 'have made you arbiter of all things; all that we lay claim to is the glory of obedience (*obsequii gloria*).' To such a depth of subservience had the SPQR fallen in the short space of twenty-three years. 'The show of courage,' writes Sir Ronald Syme, 'and the reality of cowardice, with dignity collapsing ludicrously at the touch of fear.'

Even Octavian, while having no pretensions to theocracy, realized that, since in so heterogeneous an Empire patriotism could not constitute a binding force, it was necessary to introduce some magical or transcendental element as well. He permitted himself to be worshipped in Asia Minor. The very title of 'Augustus', which in Greek was translated *sebastos* or 'worshipful', suggested a supernatural element. The images of the Emperor were accorded *adoration* and oaths were taken on the imperial *numen praesens*. In the later Empire this emperor-worship was no longer disguised. Imperial rescripts were called *sacrae litterae* and even the imperial mint was honoured as *sacra moneta*. By the time of Aurelian the Emperors were openly designating themselves as 'God and Master by birth', and the Emperors and Empresses were represented as sun and moon deities. Thus the *auctoritas* of Augustus became in the later Empire a mystic aura, a charismatic authority, not necessarily transmitted by hereditary succession, but associated with the semi-religious title of 'Augustus'. This title possessed a magic sanction, such as enabled the most vicious or incompetent Emperors to command, at least for a space of time, a certain reverence, a certain obedience. It is this that explains how the Quirites can have endured the tyranny of Tiberius for twenty-three years, the viciousness of Nero for fourteen years, and the lunacy of Elagabalus for almost four years. In spite of this religious aura, seven out of ten Emperors were, between 14 AD and 96 AD, either murdered or forced to commit suicide, and all of them were succeeded by their assassins.

Tiberius designated Caligula as his successor although he must have known that the boy was mad. He was so frightened of thunderstorms that when thunder threatened he would creep like a spaniel under his own bed. His jealousy was such that he could not tolerate the thought of any eminence other than his own. He openly aspired to divine honours and wished to be publicly worshipped as *Jupiter Latialis*. He erected a temple to himself and enshrined in it his own statue cast in gold. Special priests were appointed to array this statue in imperial robes and to feed it with grouse and peacocks. He treated the Senate and the old constitution with overt contempt. Senators, whatever their age or physical condition, were obliged to trot beside his chariot; if we are to believe Suetonius, he forced them to elect his favourite horse Incitatus as consul, and to provide it with a palace and a retinue of slaves. His cruelty was demented. His executioners were instructed to kill their victims slowly, while the Emperor watched their agonies. After four years of reign, at the age of twenty-nine, Caligula was murdered by a tribune of the Guard and his naked body exposed on the Gemonian steps.

Caligula was succeeded by his uncle Claudius, who, having been arrested by the Guards at the moment of his nephew's murder, succeeded, by distributing to them a bribe of £ 120 a head, in securing not only his

CALIGULA

73

Left: *A statue of Claudius dressed as Jupiter, from the Vatican Museum. This is an idealised portrait of an outwardly unimpressive man, but his achievement was remarkable, including the conquest of Britain.* Right: *The Emperor Nero, one of the most abominated of Emperors, who disgusted even the Romans by the excesses of his public and personal life. He was forced to commit suicide at the age of thirty*

release, but his acclamation as Emperor. Claudius was so ungainly, so grotesque, a figure, that Augustus had discouraged him from appearing in public lest he bring the Imperial family into ridicule and contempt. On reaching the throne at the age of fifty, he had the sense to conciliate the Senate and the Tribunes and, in semblance at least, to revive the Principate. He proved himself an able administrator, created a large civil service dependent on himself, improved the administration of justice, and sought to secure that the Senate should be composed of the most honourable and gifted men in the Empire. He chose excellent generals, such as Corbulo, Galba, Vespasian and Geta, and saw to it that the army was both disciplined and contented. He rounded off the frontiers of the Empire and gave it greater security by annexing Thrace, Mauretania, and Judaea. He pacified Britain, built a fleet to guard the Channel, and constructed a whole network of military roads in France. He enlarged the port of Ostia and dug canals and aqueducts to provide Rome with an improved water-supply; he managed the State finances with economy and skill.

For all the ability and good intentions that Claudius manifested during the thirteen years of his reign, he was a weak man who was dominated by his freedmen Narcissus and Pallas, who were determined that everything should be centralised under their own dominance. Thus although he may have been sincere in his desire to continue the Augustan system, it was under his rule that a system of highly centralised monarchy was established, and the curse of harem rule admitted. He had his own Treasury, and his own Star Chamber or *cubiculum principis*; he created his private body-guard, enrolling men from German tribes who were dependent on his personal favours: his house became a palace and his servitors and freedmen constituted a Court in the oriental sense of that term. Although in form he remained deferential to the Senate, in practice the Augustan theory of partnership between the Princeps and the SPQR was discarded and absolutism became established.

The Senators and knights resented this centralisation and the vast power and riches acquired by the foreign freedmen who became the Emperor's Cabinet Ministers. What they resented even more, and with good reason, was Claudius' utter subservience to his wives, Messalina and Agrippina. Messalina was a nymphomaniac, who caused wide scandal by her infatuation for the handsome C. Silius and for the actor Mnester. In the end, by playing on the Emperor's dread of conspiracies, Narcissus was able to secure Messalina's execution. Claudius then married his niece Agrippina, who was an intensely ambitious woman, determined that her own son by her former husband, C. Domitius Ahenobarbus, should succeed to the throne in the place of Britannicus, the legitimate heir and son of Claudius by Messalina. Such was the influence that this virago obtained over Claudius that she forced him to execute all those who might stand between the young Nero and the throne. In the year 50 AD she persuaded the Emperor to adopt Nero as his son and to marry him to his daughter Octavia. When she had perfected her plot, she murdered Claudius with a poisoned mushroom and induced the Praetorians and the Senate to accept Nero as his successor.

Nero ascended the throne on 13 October 54 AD when he was sixteen NERO years of age. For the first five years of his reign he remained under the domination of his mother, who, under the title of *Augusta Mater Augusti*, acted as Regent. He then began to resent her dominance and in March 59 he murdered her and claimed that she had been plotting against him and, that, when the plot was discovered, she had taken her own life. He abandoned himself to a life of debauchery and extravagance and fell under the influence of successive mistresses, of whom Acte and Poppaea were the most faithful and prominent. He horrified the Romans by appearing as an actor, charioteer and baritone in the public circus, and by forcing surviving members of the old nobility - the Horatii, the Fabii, the Valerii - to perform, whatever might be their ages or infirmities, in his ballets and choruses. He appointed his freedman Tigellinus, a Sicilian of the Palermo streets, as Praetorian Prefect, an appointment which caused his tutor Seneca to resign in fear and horror. How humiliating for this apostle of stoicism to witness the extremes of debauchery in which his pupil indulged! Even to the Romans of the *bas empire*, it appeared disgraceful that their Emperor should go through the ceremony of marriage with his freedman, Pythagoras, and with his catamite Scorus.

NERO SINGS WHILE ROME BURNS

In the year 64 came the burning of Rome which the public attributed to the Emperor's design. He spent fortunes on rebuilding the city and especially on his own palace, the Golden House, which embraced the site where the Colosseum now stands. In order to divert public opinion from his own detested person, he accused the Christians of having caused the fire. But the public, who already regarded him with horror as the murderer of his mother, persisted in believing that he had started the fire and that while all was burning around him, he had climbed up the high tower of Maecenas and sung his own *Sack of Troy* to the accompaniment of the lyre.

Inevitably all that remained of the old conservatives felt that he must at all costs be liquidated. A conspiracy was formed around C. Calpurnius Piso, a man of ancient nobility and of Republican views. The conspiracy was discovered and Tigellinus executed revenge on all those whom he suspected of opposition. Seneca, Petronius, the poet Lucan and the great General Corbulo, were all forced to commit suicide to avoid torture and humiliating mutilation. The rift between Nero and Tigellinus on the one hand and all that remained of Roman traditions and gravity on the other, became a gulf. Nero had always preferred Greeks to Romans and went off to Greece to receive the adulation and crowns of his Greek subjects at the Pythian and Olympic games. He appeared before them as a tragic actor and in his weak little voice sang to them his poem on the *Sack of Troy*. He forced the Greek cities to declare him victor in the Pythian and Olympic games and returned to Rome in triumph bringing with him the garlands he had won. ' A curious sort of victory, ' writes Dio Cassius, ' for a man to gain at the games a garland of wild olive, bay, parsley or pine, and thereby to lose the crown of Empire '. He then began to introduce into the Roman games

Left: *Corbulo, one of Claudius' most able generals, who restored Roman rule in Armenia and maintained the Empire's reputation for progress despite his Emperor's bad advisers. He was later executed for his part in the plot on Nero's life.* Right: *Vespasian, a man of humble origins, rose through a series of high army appointments to be proclaimed Emperor by his troops at Alexandria in* AD *69*

the same methods and principles as he had found in Greece; he created from the younger sons of the nobility a gang of *Augustiani* who were made to perform as gladiators or ballet dancers in the theatre and who constituted a personal guard of toughs. At the same time he tried to encourage the idea that loyalty to the Empire meant no more than loyalty to the Emperor's person. He did all he could to spread the oriental conception of the Emperor as God and went so far as to deify his mistress Poppaea after her death. He resolved to rename the Peloponnesus 'The Nero Island', and it was widely believed that it was his intention to change the sacred name of Rome to that of Neropolis.

The army meanwhile was showing signs of discontent. Vespasian in Judaea was keeping sixty thousand men under arms, while their Emperor was singing his songs in the theatres of Greece. The murder of Corbulo had enraged the regular soldiers. There were revolts in Gaul under Vindex and in Spain under Galba. The Praetorians refused any

A relief from the Arch of Titus in Rome, erected after his capture of Jerusalem in AD 70. *His troops are shown carrying the looted treasures of the Temple, including the seven-branched candelabrum of pure gold*

longer to obey Nero's orders. Tigellinus, scenting the coming catastrophe, made good his escape. Nero, in the hope probably of finding a refuge in Egypt, fled from Rome and hid himself in the villa of a freedman four miles outside the city. The Senate declared him a public enemy and chose Galba as Emperor in his place. Realising that he was doomed, Nero committed suicide in a back room by cutting his throat. *Qualis artifex pereo*, 'In me, a great artist dies,' are reported to have been his last words. Sadism and aestheticism mate ill together. Nero was just over thirty years old when he perished; he had reigned for thirteen years.

With the death of Nero, the Julian-Claudian line was extinguished. *Progenies Caesarum*, writes Suetonius, *in Nerone deficit*. 'From then on,' comments Tacitus, 'the will of the army was decisive'. The year 69, known as 'the year of the four Emperors', remained for the Romans an atrocious memory of cruel and destructive civil wars. Galba, Otho, Vitellius and Vespasian were each in turn proclaimed Emperor by the legions under their immediate commands. In the end, after terrible atrocities had been committed and many cities sacked, it was Vespasian who triumphed, who established the Flavian dynasty, and created an interlude of peace, regeneration and order. One of the miracles of the Roman Empire was that, after periods of collapse and degradation, as under Caligula or Nero and later under Elagabalus, it proved capable of astonishing resilience.

To us it seems inexplicable that a community which could with relief and ease settle down to Flavian reconstruction should not have possessed the vigour or unity to dispose of Caligula and Nero before great damage had been done and before the liberal principles of the Principate had been shattered for decades. Two explanations of this phenomenon are advanced. On the one hand, it is contended that the machinery of provincial and colonial administration was so massive and well established that it continued to function independently of what was happening in Rome. The Emperor himself might be insane or vicious but the provinces and colonies were governed by experienced senators who saw to it that law was properly administered and order preserved. On the other hand, as military autocracy replaced the old civilian rule, Rome gradually ceased to be the centre of the civilised world and the emperors tended to establish their headquarters in provincial capitals, such as Carnuntum, Nicomedia, Sirmium, or Treves. A flood of foreign immigrants poured into the eternal city and acquired wealth and magistracies. 'I cannot bear it, oh Quirites', lamented Juvenal. 'I cannot bear that the capital of the Roman Empire should become a Greek city.'

Vespasian was of humble origin; his grandfather had been a private soldier and his father a clerk in the Inland Revenue. He was of plebeian appearance, absurdly superstitious, given to making scatalogical jokes and comparatively austere. Such was the general dread of civil war, that Vespasian felt strong enough to force through the Senate the *Lex de Imperio Vespasiani*, by which in effect autocracy was accorded legal sanction and Ulpian's principle was accepted that the Princeps was above the law, *Princeps legibus solutus est*. Vespasian was succeeded by his able son Titus, who captured Jerusalem, erected the arch of triumph, and completed the Colosseum. Domitian, who succeeded his brother

Left: *Trajan, born in Spain and nominated by Nerva as his successor in* AD *97, was an Emperor strong enough to permit a degree of criticism unprecedented in Rome.* Right: *His successor, Hadrian, had one of the more attractive personalities among the early Emperors, and was a dominating ruler with a taste for the arts*

Titus in 81, was the least balanced of the Flavians. He would shut himself up in his study for hours and divert himself by killing bluebottles with his stylus. He persecuted the Christians, banished philosophers from Rome, and expected his subjects to address him as *divus et dominus*, as 'God and master'. In the end he became pathological, murdered all those whom he suspected of disobedience, and was himself assassinated by a freedman. His successor Nerva, during his short reign, endeavoured to return to constitutional practices and did much to reverse the caprice system which Domitian had introduced. He nominated as his successor the Spanish General Trajan, who was of liberal principles and refused to employ informers or to condemn without trial. Tacitus could write of 'the rare good fortune of an age in which we may feel as we wish and say what we feel'. As he lay dying in Cilicia, Trajan nominated as his successor his kinsman Hadrian, also a Spaniard, who, owing to his pretty little elegy to his own soul, has often been represented as a philosopher king. His admirers condone his restlessness, his architectural extravagance, his imprudent deification of Antinous, and laud his enlightenment, his passion for law and order, and his abandonment of a policy of expansion for a purely defensive policy behind firm frontiers. It was Hadrian who constructed a palisade nine feet high across the perilous gap between the Rhine and the Danube and who built the splendid wall that runs from the Tyne to the Solway Firth. Always would he repeat the patriarchal doctrine that a ' ruler exists for the State and not the State for the ruler '. He improved communications and sought to create an international civil service to administer the community of nations that the Empire was becoming. Certainly Hadrian was a man of high ability and ideals, but, whatever Mr Perowne or Madame Yourcenar may say, he lacked charm. He disbelieved in the hereditary system but chose with care as his successor the admirable Antoninus Pius, the uncle of Marcus Aurelius and the fitting founder of the Age of the Antonines.

Below: *The stone wall which Hadrian began to construct across the north of Britain from Tyne to Solway in* AD *120. It survives as one of the most remarkable monuments of the Roman Empire. It is now considered to have been more of a base for offensive action than a physical barrier for defence*

FIVE

Philosopher Kings
to Syrian Matriarchs

MARCUS AURELIUS HAD BEEN designated as the heir to Antoninus Pius
when he was eighteen years of age. He waited in all humility and patience for twenty-two years until, on the death of his uncle, he succeeded
to the throne. His youth was one of stoic austerity; he slept on bare
boards; trained himself to be indifferent to food, heat, or cold; and
spent his days in studying the teachings of the stoics. He acquired a
high sense of duty, and devoted every hour of the day and night to
the service of the Empire and its varied populations. He restored the
dignity of the Senate and would attend their meetings in person. He
had the greatest contempt for his predecessors, whom he derided as
' the Sardanapali ', and deliberately set himself to be the model king.

Renan in his study of Marcus Aurelius contends that the reigns
of his uncle and himself, which covered a period of forty-two years,
' did honour to the caste of kings '. Yet he admits that Marcus Aurelius
was ' gnawed by the disease of introspection ' and by ' the demon of
scrupulosity '; that he lacked ' what we should call keenness of intelligence '; and that, having as a young man never known pleasure, he
was somewhat devoid of imagination. A king can never possess the
freedom of the philosopher or the artist and is precluded by circumstances
from the uninhibited expression of his own originality. In their handling

of kingship, the Antonines differed utterly from the old patterns of the King as god, or the King as warrior. They were akin, rather, to great civil administators. Their private lives were austere and simple; they had no courtiers or court ceremonial and nothing to confuse their char- acters as individuals. Each of them was extremely pious; it could, indeed, be argued by the cynic that Marcus Aurelius was a moral prig. ' There is but one fruit of earthly life ', he wrote, ' that is to be inwardly holy and to do good service to mankind. '

With all his limitations Marcus Aurelius was, as Stuart Jones has written, ' a pattern of the highest virtue which the spirit of antiquity could produce '. He surrounded himself with sober men, with whom he would discuss the nature of the good, and who in fact constituted his privy council. ' Thus was realised, ' writes Renan, ' an historical miracle - what can be called the reign of the philosopher. ' It is not surprising that under such a high-minded system the defence of the Empire and the administration of finance and economics should have declined. Marcus Aurelius did his devoted best; but he was neither a great soldier nor a great financier.

PHILOSOPHY
OF MARCUS
AURELIUS
When he had passed the age of fifty, the philosopher king was assailed by pessimism. His wife Faustina, although as a blind husband he celebrated her virtues, was promiscuously unfaithful to him. ' I have been blessed, ' he wrote, ' with a wife, so docile, so affectionate, so unaffected. ' Yet Gibbon describes Faustina as a second Messalina. ' She possessed, ' he writes, ' that unbounded passion for variety which often discovered personal merit in the meanest of mankind. ' His son, Com- modus, was a brutal lout, who cared only for his grooms and racing stables. As he lay dying in his tent beside the Danube, Marcus Aurelius was assailed by the sad thought that for all his virtue and excellent intentions, his reign had not been a complete success. ' His wisdom was absolute, ' writes Renan, ' which is another way of saying that his *ennui* was without limit. ' At the same time he admits that the death of Marcus Aurelius in March 180, ' can be taken as the decisive moment when the ruin of ancient civilization was decided. '

Yet, if we read his *Meditations*, and can dismiss from our minds our irritation at his sanctimoniousness, we must admit that never has any ruler set forth in higher terms the ideals of perfect kingship. The ruler, to his mind, must be the first servant of his people. He should ' prize above all things the liberty of the subject '. No amount of wealth, no bodyguard, can ever protect a ruler, unless he ' has first of all the

Commodus, 'a cruel and lascivious boor', succeeded to the saintly Marcus Aurelius. In this second-century marble from the Museo dei Conservatori, Rome, he is shown with club and lion-skin, attributes of Hercules

goodwill of the governed'. Those kings who have enjoyed the longest and happiest reigns are those who 'capture the hearts of their subjects, not by fear of their vengeance, but by love of their virtue'. While not compromising the dignity of his office, an Emperor should see that his court is disciplined and austere and that he is not precluded by ceremonial from living the life of an ordinary individual. He should devote himself to his labours, repeating to himself the motto, 'I exist to do some work', and never skimping the most uncongenial task. He must cultivate what he called 'civic reason' (*politikos logos*) which is identical with justice. 'Injustice', he wrote, 'is impiety.'

'What then,' he asks in his *Meditations*, 'is it that calls for our devotion? This one thing: justice in thought, in act unselfishness; a tongue that cannot lie; a disposition prepared to welcome all that occurs as unavoidable'. His ideals were piety, serenity, equanimity, sweetness, patience, a sense of duty, industry, simple living, and moderation in all things. He had a vivid sense of the community of human beings. 'My nature,' he wrote, 'is civic and rational; my city, my country, is Rome; but as a man, I am a citizen of the world.' 'Such things,' he writes, 'as are of value to mankind are of value to me personally. That which is not in the interest of the hive cannot be to the interest of the bee. Social obligation (*to koinônikon*) is the dominant feature of human society. Every act that bears no relation, direct or indirect, to a common social purpose tears life asunder and destroys its unity.'

STOIC AUSTERITY

Marcus Aurelius was fully conscious (perhaps a little too conscious) that he was striving to achieve the rule of a philosopher king. He was always repeating Plato's remark, 'Well were it for States if either philosophers were rulers or rulers philosophers.' In order to realize this ideal the ruler must abide by Stoic teaching and must live his life 'according to Nature'. To the Stoics virtue meant, not merely the abstention from evil or the sins of the flesh, but a positive and active goodness. A man should govern his life according to his own controlling reason, his *daimon* or pragmatic conscience. This alone could render him superior to the ills of this world, to pain and suffering, to the temptations of the flesh, and to the final prospect of extinction in death. As a condition of active practical goodness he must hate injustice and regard all men as his fellows. He must aim at 'the simple life far removed from the habits of the rich'. He should not indulge in hot or scented baths at all hours of the day; he should not wish to have particularly handsome slaves about him; he should not be too particular about clothes or cooking. Marcus Aurelius despised those who believed too readily in portents, omens, oracles and marvels, or those who kept tame quails. A man must of course be of tidy appearance and wash his face and hands. He must cultivate 'dignity without affectation', and must 'keep pleasantry within bounds'. He must practice tolerance; 'Revenge for his own wrongs,' writes Marcus Aurelius, 'never sits well on an Emperor'. He must be 'impervious to all the passions'; he must avoid fretting and fussing; he must face misfortune with equanimity and realize that an evil borne with courage becomes a good. His motto must be, 'Revere the gods: save mankind'.

86

An altar from Wiesbaden dedicated to the Persian sun-god Mithras, a favourite deity among Roman soldiers. Here, as most commonly, he is represented killing a bull, the symbol of new life

'Let any say or do what they will,' wrote Marcus Aurelius with a touch of sanctimoniousness, 'I must for my part be good. So must the emerald, or gold, or purple, never tire of repeating "Whatever anyone else shall do or say, I must be an emerald and keep my colour"'. He was not an intellectual and distrusted imagination, or what he called 'phantasia'. It is not surprising that a man of such perfect innocence should have failed to notice that his wife was an adulteress, or that his heir, Commodus, was a cruel and lascivious boor.

Gibbon, who possessed no instinctive veneration for holiness, agreed that the reigns of Antoninus Pius and Marcus Aurelius marked the period of history 'when the human race was most happy and prosperous'. Renan, with his passionate devotion to classical antiquity, regretted that the age of the Antonines should mark 'the end of the ancient world'. It was a tragedy to him that the freedom and lucidity of Greek thought should be dimmed by Asiatic superstitions and practices. Renan had small liking for corybantic types of religion.

SEPTIMIUS
SEVERUS

With the murder of Commodus, the rule of the Antonines came to an end. Although, under Aurelian and Diocletian, there occurred two startling renewals of vitality, the massive muscles of Rome had in fact degenerated and it is with sadness that we thereafter watch the decline of 'the slowly fading mistress of the world'. Commodus had appointed no heir and the throne was seized by the elderly general Pertinax who, having really sought to discipline the Praetorians, was put to death after a reign of eighty-seven days. The post of Emperor was then overtly put up to auction by the Praetorians, the highest bidder being the rich senator Didius Julianus. The provincial legions refused to accept this nomination. The army in Syria chose Pescennius Niger, whereas Septimius Severus was acclaimed Emperor by the Legions of Carnuntum on the Danube. Didius Julianus was liquidated after a reign of sixty-six days and Septimius Severus marched triumphantly on Rome. In order to placate the Senate he changed out of uniform before entering the gates. He announced that he would follow the high example of Marcus Aurelius and promised that he would not put any senator to death. At the same time he increased the Praetorian Guard to 15,000 men and decided that henceforward barbarians could be enrolled. The Praetorians thereafter ceased to be exclusively Italian. He then proceeded to crush his rival Niger on the plains of Issus.

In Britain the election of Septimius was contested by D. Clodius Albinus, the commander of the local legions. Septimius at first sought to buy him off by appointing him Caesar, or heir to the throne. On discovering that he was engaged in treasonable correspondence with the Senate he induced the legions in Asia Minor to proclaim Albinus a public enemy. In response to this the legions in Britain promoted Albinus to the post of Augustus, or Emperor. Septimius Severus countered this by nominating as Caesar his own son Caracalla, then a lad of eight years old. Albinus crossed the Channel and established himself at Lyons where in February 197 he was surrounded by the legions of Septimius Severus and forced to commit suicide. On his return to Rome Septimius, in defiance of the pledges he had given, put to death twenty-nine senators who had supported Albinus. A rigid military dictatorship was imposed.

A reconstruction of a Roman camp of the period of Septimius Severus on its original site at Saalburg in the Taunus mountains. Only the walls, gates and more important communal buildings, but not the barracks, were reconstructed

Severus was of African origin, having been born at Leptis Magna in Tripoli. He spoke Latin with a Punic accent; he had little respect for the majesty, or traditions, of Rome; he was suspicious, vindictive, cruel and avaricious; but he was a good general and a man of strength. The Romans called him 'the Punic Sulla'. As a military dictator he considered sovereign power should be transferred from the SPQR to the army. He encouraged promising young officers to enter the equestrian order and to train themselves to become civil servants, and as such to qualify for high administrative rank. He appointed his own commissars or *procuratores* to assist and invigilate the governors of the senatorial provinces, and to provide money for the civil list (the *res privata principis*) which with his lust for money he rapidly increased until it exceeded the State exchequer. He regarded the colonies as of more importance than the mother country and packed the Senate with Africans and provincials until the native Italians found themselves in a minority. He insisted on being addressed by the title of *Dominus* and thenceforward the imperial family was referred to as *domus divina*. He forced the Senate to register and confirm his unilateral and wholly baseless claim to have been adopted into the Antonine family. He proclaimed his elder son Caracalla as heir to the throne or *Imperator*

Destinatus, and his second son Geta as joint successor. He was a short, thick-set man, who suffered much from gout. In spite of this, however, he conducted in person an audacious and successful campaign against the Parthians, occupied Ctesiphon, and assumed the title of *Parthicus Maximus*.

Septimius Severus died at York on 4 February 211 at the age of sixty-four and was succeeded by his two sons, Caracalla and Geta. Gibbon denounces him as the founder of military dictatorship and therefore as 'the principal author of the decline of the Roman Empire'. 'With Septimius Severus,' writes Professor Besnier, 'Rome renounced all constitutional fictions and definitely took the path of monarchical absolutism, imitated from Asia and Egypt and based on force'. These are harsh judgements. Septimius Severus maintained discipline in the army, fortified and enlarged the boundaries of the Empire, and, with the advice of Ulpian, reformed the penal code. On the other hand, he destroyed the old constitution, deprived the Senate of the last vestiges of power, and introduced African and Asian theories of governance and conduct, thereby destroying the ancient *gravitas* that had rendered the city of the seven hills the mistress of the world.

Septimius Severus married a Syrian lady of intelligence and strength of character. He first met the girl when he was in command of the fourth legion in Syria. He is said to have chosen her since an oracle had predicted that she would marry a soldier who would one day be Emperor. She was called Julia Domna and was the managerial type of wife. She was accorded the titles of Augusta *mater patriae*, *mater senatus* and *mater castrorum*. She insisted on being admitted into the Senate and on occupying a throne, or curule chair, set only one step below that of the Emperor. It was with sullen rage that the senators surrendered to this monstrous regiment of women.

THE CRIMES
OF CARACALLA

Caracalla, who succeeded his father in 211, was demonstrably insane. He left the administration of the Empire to his mother, Julia Domna, and concentrated upon his pleasures and sadistic passions. One of his first acts was to murder his brother and colleague, Geta, in their mother's boudoir. He thereafter executed some 20,000 of Geta's suspected sympathisers. He ordered a general massacre of the citizens of Alexandria, having heard a voice in the crowd utter an exclamation in Geta's favour. He suffered from the illusion that he was a reincarnation of Alexander the Great, would hold his head sideways, and trained a phalanx of 16,000 men on the Macedonian model. He was an ugly, dark little man,

Caracalla, although one of the least impressive of the Roman Emperors, left behind in Rome a palatial bath-house of which these are the towering ruins. The picture shows the palaestra

and from the golden locks of a German prisoner he had a wig contrived which assisted him in his personification of the mighty Macedonian. He discarded the Roman toga and would wear a tunic, or bush shirt, of Gallic style, called a *caracallus*. He was a poor economist, ran the exchequer into debt, and in order to increase the number of those subject to death-duties, accorded Roman citizenship to all free-born subjects of the Empire. On 8 April 217 Caracalla was murdered at Carrhae by the prefect of his Praetorian Guard, Opilius Macrinus, who at once claimed the succession.

Macrinus was a Moor by origin and from the lobes of his ears depended two earrings, a most un-Roman form of adornment. Dio Cassius writes that 'being a Moor, he was excessively timorous' - a remark that would not be supported by those who have known the Riffs or the Goums. In any case, in spite of having his election confirmed by the Senate, he was not able to retain his throne for more than a few months and was defeated and killed in 218.

Julius Bassianus, a citizen of Emesa or Homs in Syria had two gifted daughters, the elder being Julia Domna whom I have already mentioned, and the younger being Julia Maesa. Julia Domna, as we have seen, married the Emperor Septimius Severus, and by him had two sons, Caracalla and Geta. Julia Maesa, Bassanius' younger daugher, had two daughters. The elder, Julia Soemias, married Sextus Varius Marcellus and became the mother of Varius Avitus Bassianus, known to history as the Emperor Elagabalus. The second daughter, Julia Mammaea, married Gessius Marcianus and became the mother of Alexianus Bassianus who succeeded his cousin as the Emperor Alexander Severus.

THE FIRST MATRIARCH

On the accession of Septimius Severus Julia Domna insisted upon being accorded all the titles and privileges of an imperial consort. She was an intellectual woman, a mathematician and an astronomer. She gathered round her poets such as Oppian and scholars such as Diogenes Laertius. It was she who persuaded Philostratus to write his *Life of Apollonius of Tyana*. She accompanied the Emperor on his tours of the provinces and took a direct interest in imperial administration. Thus, when Septimius was succeeded by his brutal son Caracalla, it was Julia Domna who ruled as Matriarch. To her, rather than to her son, is to be attributed the introduction of the Constitution of 212, under which the rights of citizenship were extended to all subjects of the Empire. The scope and importance of this enactment have been somewhat exaggerated, since it had already become comparatively easy for provincials to acquire citizenship. The main purpose of the edict was fiscal rather than democratic, and even after the constitution of 212 there remained many subjects of the Empire who were excluded from the franchise. Julia Domna was an authoritative and ruthless woman by whom Caracalla was entirely dominated. It was rumoured that the Alexandria massacre was occasioned by the fact that the mob had made jokes regarding Julia Domna as well as raised cries in memory of Geta. On the murder of Caracalla and the accession of Macrinus, the dowager Empress refused either to be captured by the usurper or to live on in powerless exile. She committed suicide by starving herself to death.

Her sister Julia Maesa, wife of Julius Avitus, was made of more durable stuff. She had been able, during the reign of her brother-in-law Septimius Severus, to accumulate a large personal fortune and she managed to transfer the money to Emesa, her home town. The descendants of Julius Bassianus stood in high repute in Homs, since they held the hereditary office of High Priests of the local sun-god, El Gabal, the Syrian Baal, the ' lord of the high place '. The grandson of Julia Maesa, the son of her elder daughter Soemias, although but a lad of fourteen, had become hereditary high-priest. He was a beautiful youth and performed the rites of fertility, or phallic worship, with grace and ecstasy. Julia Maesa conceived the ambition of using the boy-priest as a means of recapturing matriarchal power. She spread the rumour that her daughter Soemias had been living adulterously with her cousin Caracalla and that the boy was not the son of the obscure Varius Marcellus, but in fact the grandson of Septimius Severus. She instructed the boy to assume the name of Marcus Aurelius Antoninus, although he possessed no legitimate right to so august a name. With the help of the boy's tutor, Gannys, and the prefect Comazon Eutychianus, and by lavishly expending her personal fortune on bribing the legionaries, she succeeded in having her grandson, the boy-priest of a Syrian cult, acclaimed as the Emperor Marcus Aurelius Antoninus, or, as the troops called him, Elagabalus, the priest of Baal.

Macrinus and his son Diadumenius, who had been proclaimed ELAGABALUS Caesar, were defeated in a battle outside Antioch. At one moment it seemed that Macrinus would win the victory, but Julia Maesa and her daughter Soemias, who had accompanied the legions into battle, leapt from their chariots and ran shrieking into the melée, thereby rallying the troops. Macrinus escaped from Antioch disguised as a common soldier and hoping to reach Rome before the news of his defeat. He was recognised at Chalcidone and decapitated. His son who escaped in the direction of Parthia was intercepted by a troop of cavalry and pierced with lances. Julia Maesa as a victorious grandmother had no further rivals to fear. The boy priest was chosen Emperor and his election accepted by the Senate. He assumed all the titles enjoyed by his predecessors, adding thereto the name of *Pius Felix Augustus*, and the alien appellation of *Sacerdos Dei Solis Elagabali*. The ancient Syrian name of El-Gabal, meaning the ' Lord of the high place, ' was transliterated into Greek as ' Heliogabalus ' meaning the ' Sun-god '.

Elagabalus the boy-emperor did not leave immediately for Rome. He spent some months at Nicomedia, where he executed his old tutor, Gannys, to whom, more than to anybody apart from his grandmother, he owed his throne. He spent his time chanting wild hymns to Baal, dancing in front of his altar, indulging in phallic worship, and practising in front of an awe-struck congregation, the lascivious ceremonies which formed an important element in the fertility rites of El-Gabal. Eventually,

Three Syrian matriarchs. Left to right: *Julia Maesa, grandmother of Elagabalus, whose empire she controlled; Julia Soemias, his mother, a woman of little political consequence; and the formidable Julia Mammaea, regent for Alexander Severus who succeeded at the age of fourteen and was murdered in* AD *235*

accompanied by his grandmother, his mother, and his aunt, he entered Rome on 29 September 219. He was dressed in a silken purple shift embroidered with gold; his arms tinkled with bracelets; he was draped in jewels; his eyes were darkened and his cheeks rouged. The Romans were startled by the arrival of this Asian ingle as their Emperor. His gestures were not those of an *imperator* but those of a male prostitute: he minced.

THE
DECADENCE
OF ELAGABALUS

It is a sad comment on the decadence of what the French call *le bas-empire* that Elagabalus could have been tolerated for so long as three years and nine months. His mother Soemias was a frivolous woman who indulged in love-affairs, was indifferent to the lechery and extravagance of her son, and had no political tastes or ambitions. It was to his formidable grand-mother, Julia Maesa, that the administration of the Empire was transferred. She ruled with the assistance of Comazon Eutychianus. It was a perfectly competent and not entirely ruthless administration.

Those warm-hearted writers who enjoy white-washing the reputation of history's bad characters, have sought to refurbish the sullied repute of Elagabalus. They contend that the sources from which his biography has been derived are all tainted. The *Scriptores Historiae Augustae* are admittedly unreliable: Aelius Lampridius, who composed the section on Elagabalus, was an even worse scandal-monger than Suetonius himself. The accounts written by Herodian and Maximus were composed by men anxious to emphasise the contrast between Elagabalus' eccentricities and the simpler, sweeter reign of his cousin Alexander Severus. Dio Cassius, a more conscientious historian, was so blinded by his conservative prejudices, by his esteem for the old republican virtues, that he could not find a good word to say for the Syrian matriarchs or the decadent boy emperor.

His apologists like to represent him as a young man of profound religious belief, whose aim in life was to establish monotheism in the place of the discredited mythology of Greece and Rome. He certainly made every effort, at the risk of arousing deep and lasting animosity, to establish his own god El-Gabal, as master of the Roman Pantheon. He proclaimed Baal as the supreme god of the Empire; he had the black stone of Emesus (a conical meteorite held sacred to Baal), brought from Homs to Rome and constructed for it the Elagabalium on the Palatine. Within this shrine he assembled the most sacred fetishes of republican Rome, - the vestal fire, the *palladium*, the shield of Mars, and the black stone of Cybele. He transported from Carthage the statue of the heavenly mother, or *dea caelestis*, and celebrated with great pomp the marriage of this goddess with the black meteorite of Homs. Once a year the sacred stone of Emesa was carried in a chariot drawn by four white horses from the Elagabalium to a suburban temple. The Emperor, dressed in his hieratic robes, would walk backwards in front of this sacred car, chanting what Dio calls the 'barbaric chants' of his rite, and from time to time performing a little dance. He seems to have been sincere in his ambition to render sun-worship, the worship of the El Gabal of Homs, a monotheistic cult that would embrace all other religions - the old paganism, Mithraism, the Egyptian rites, the mysticism of Apollonius of Tyana, even perhaps the revelation of Christ. He proclaimed that his sun-god was superior to Jupiter Capitolinus and to Vesta. So objective a historian as Professor Bury contends that in endeavouring to establish a monotheistic religion combining all existing beliefs, Elagabalus was seeking in all sincerity to benefit mankind.

His religious purposes and ceremonies left him little time for the affairs of state. He entrusted all legislation and administration to his grandmother, Julia Maesa, and it was this formidable matriarch who sought to preserve peace in the Empire and discipline in the army. She paid lip service to the Senate and to the ancient traditions, and refrained from introducing any internal reforms such as might disturb the established classes or authorities. There is no record of any important legislation having been introduced during the period of her rule. She was a shrewd woman and soon realised that her grandson Elagabalus and his frivolous mother were becoming unpopular and that the atrocious conduct of the boy-emperor was losing him the respect, not of the senators only, but of the legions also. She decided therefore that, if all power were not to desert the Syrian family, she must abandon Soemias and

JULIA MAESA

95

the foolish Emperor, and concentrate on her younger and more serious daughter, Julia Mammaea, and the latter's sober son, Alexander Severus. This boy, who was even younger than his cousin the Emperor, had been kept by his mother aloof from the orgies and hysteria of the court and carefully educated in the principles and philosophy of Marcus Aurelius. If Julia Maesa were to retain her authority it might become necessary to dispose of Elagabalus and to put Alexander in his place.

The boy-emperor was wholly oriental in his tastes and habits and had no respect whatsoever for the Roman aristocracy or their traditions. He gave high office to his palace favourites. He appointed his barber as director of the food-supply of Rome and handed over the Treasury to a young man from Homs of the most degraded origins and character. He divorced his wife and married a Vestal Virgin, Aquilia Severa, claiming to justify this outrage on the ground that a child born from such a union must surely be divine. He would sacrifice boys to his beloved Baal and in the inner sanctuary he installed a lion, a serpent and a monkey which he would feed on the genitals of slaves.

Dio Cassius disapproved of these Asian ways. He refers to Elagabalus as ' the false Antoninus ', as ' the Assyrian ', or as ' Sardanapalus '. The boy-emperor indulged without restraint in a practice to which even to this day royalties are specially addicted — the vice of practical joking. He would serve his guests with sweets or fruit made of wax, and would seat elderly senators or generals on air cushions which his slaves would suddenly deflate. He enjoyed forcing old gentlemen to drink too much; they would be carried insensible to bedrooms prepared for them, and when they woke in the morning they would find a tame bear or lion or leopard beside their couches. He would excite their appetites by describing the houris whom he had provided for their pleasure, and then shut them up in a bedroom with a toothless Abyssinian crone. The Romans, who set great store by dignity, did not at all relish practical jokes when applied to senators.

His extravagance also caused displeasure. His carts and chariots were of gold and ivory; his slaves and guards were drenched in the most expensive scents; his bath-water was heated by Arabian herbs; his saucepans were of silver and he fed his lions on Parakeets. He disliked wool and linen as much as he disliked the toga; he dressed entirely in oriental robes of silk and wore necklaces and bracelets of emeralds and pearls. At a single dinner party he provided his guests with the fried brains of six hundred ostriches. The tongues of nightingales were heaped

Left: *Elagabalus, the boy-priest of a Syrian cult, who became Emperor of Rome through the influence and deception of his grandmother Julia Maesa. His reign lasted for under four years, but they were years which witnessed a degradation of the Imperial court which even by Roman standards was shocking.* Right: *Alexander Severus, successor of Elagabalus, the persecutions of whose reign he did much to remedy with the aid of his mother, Julia Mammaea*

in huge golden bowls, powdered with pearl dust and smothered in the precious hydrogarum sauce of the Sybarites. He never had written menus at his banquets, but each new service was announced by a change of tablecloth on which the nature and the composition of the expected dish were embroidered in gold.

The dowager, Julia Maesa, realised that if the scandal of the Emperor's degraded habits were allowed to continue, the whole dynasty might be discredited. She therefore insisted that Elagabalus should publicly adopt as his colleague and successor his cousin Alexander Severus, then a pious and popular boy of thirteen. The Emperor, obedient as always to the old matriarch, ordered the Senate to register the appointment of Alexander as heir and Caesar. On realising however how popular this appointment proved to the Senate and the soldiers, he immediately sought to cancel it. This enraged the praetorians who burst into the palace clamouring that Alexander should immediately become Augustus. Elagabalus hid in a chest but was discovered. He and his mother Soemias were immediately decapitated and their naked trunks dragged through the town and flung, first into *Cloaca maxima*, or main drain, and thereafter into the Tiber.

ALEXANDER
SEVERUS

He was succeeded by his cousin Alexander Severus, then only just fourteen years of age. The regency fell to Alexander's mother Julia Mammaea, the third of the great Syrian matriarchs. She was an austere woman who fully realised that the new reign must be conducted on more traditional lines. The black stone was sent back to Homs and the fetish restored to Carthage. The ancient gods were accorded all their former prestige. The great jurist Ulpian was recalled from exile and assumed the office of Prime Minister. The council of sixteen was created, composed of the leading senators, lawyers and generals. All Elagabalus' favourites were either exiled or executed. Religious tolerance became the policy of the new regime. It was rumoured even that the ' virtuous and pathetic ' Alexander, as Renan calls him, had admitted a statue of Christ into his family shrine, and the regent Julia Mammaea was reported to have been converted to Christianity at Antioch, by Origen. The progressive policy of Julia Mammaea is said to have included the organisation of trades unions among the artisans. There was but one error of policy that she commited. Wishing to restore the finances of the Empire she insisted upon strict economy and put an end to the recurrent system of doles by which Elagabalus had managed for more than three years to retain the support of the soldiers and the urban proletariat. Her reputed stinginess infuriated the praetorians. Ulpian, the chief minister, was murdered in her presence. And finally, in March 235, when absent in Germany campaigning against the barbarians, Julia Mammaea and her most unwarlike son were murdered in the camp near Mainz. They were succeeded by a Thracian soldier of the name of Maximinus, a professional wrestler of gigantic stature, who was notorious for his violence and cruelty. The Empire thereafter became the prey of war-lords and it was not until the advent of the Emperor Aurelian in 270 that the central authority was re-established, the *limes* regained, and the barbarians driven back from the frontier.

The dominance of the Syrian matriarchs, of Julia Domna, of her sister Julia Maesa, and of her niece Julia Mammaea, lasted for almost twenty-five years. It constitutes a strange interlude in the long history of Rome; in the even longer story of kingship.

Constantine the Great, adorned by a halo indicating his hieratic status

SIX

Sacerdotal Kingship

THE RULE OF THE FOUR SYRIAN MATRIARCHS marked a final severance between the Empire and the traditions of republican Rome. Under the Augustan theory an aspirant to the throne must be of a patrician family and must be able to claim, if only by a fiction, descent from some formerly deified Emperor; he must be a Roman citizen, or at least a native of Italy; he must be elected by the Senate and must have held the main offices of State, according to the traditional *cursus honorum*; he must be an adult male and capable of leading the legions in battle. With the election of the Syrian boy-priest Elagabalus and the rule of his female relations, these conventions and principles were discarded. I must repeat that it is a matter of perplexity that the grave Romans should not have been more horrified than they were by a system which enabled Elagabalus to be elected and his Syrian family to rule. Even Julian the Apostate, who was a stubborn Puritan, writes almost affectionately of Elagabalus, calling him ' the pretty boy (*paidarion*) from Homs '.

The office of Emperor thereafter became purchasable by anyone possessing sufficient cash and audacity to subborn the legions or the

99

praetorian guard. A rapid succession of claimants followed each other, being often of foreign and plebeian origins, and in the ensuing struggles for power the legions were withdrawn from their posts on the frontier and the barbarians seeped in. From time to time, however, the armies would choose as their Emperor a competent general and under him the frontier would at least temporarily be re-established and the barbarian invaders driven back.

In 260 the Emperor Valerian, an old man of sixty, virtuous and gentle in character, was defeated by the Persians near Edessa and taken captive by Shapur I, ruler of the unified Sassanian Empire. Grovelling in homage before the King of Kings, the Roman Emperor was led in triumph through the avenues of Hamadan.

DISINTEGRATION
OF THE EMPIRE

Already the Empire was disintegrating; the Gauls established a kingdom of their own and in the Middle East Oedanathus and his wife Zenobia created the Empire of Palmyra, including Mesopotamia, Armenia, and Cilicia. Then came the election of the veteran general Aurelian, the son of a Pannonian peasant, who defeated the invading Alemanni and Hungarians, built the Aurelian wall round Rome, smashed the Gallic Kingdom, destroyed Palmyra, and led Zenobia in golden chains behind his triumphal chariot. It was Aurelian who proclaimed himself 'the unconquered Sun-God' and established sun-worship throughout the Empire. Yet internal disintegration was checked rather than cured by the victories of Aurelian. Under his immediate successors (Tacitus, Probus, Carus, Carinus and Numerian) the old rivalries and corruption reappeared. The *pax romana* ceased to be observed. The federation of the Germanic tribes - the Chauci, the Cherusci and the Gatti - calling themselves the Franks, or freemen, crossed the Rhine and the Pyrenees and raided as far as the Straits of Gibraltar. The Suevi, calling themselves the Alemanni or Germans, invaded Italy itself and pushed on as far as Ravenna. The Goths seized the Balkans and obtained command of the Black Sea. During the reign of Gallienus there were as many as nineteen pretenders to the throne, all of whom were eventually assassinated. And then in 284 came the great reformer Diocletian.

Diocletian, the son of a Dalmatian slave, was a statesman rather than a soldier. He styled himself the 'father of a golden age' (*parens aurei saeculi*) and was in fact the first to realise that the Empire had become unmanageable under a single Emperor and that some division

Right: *The four Tetrarchs, seen in a fourth-century porphyry group outside St Mark's, Venice. They were the successors to Diocletian (284-304) and governed the Roman Empire according to his rule*

of responsibility had become essential. He decided to break entirely with the past; to restore discipline in the army; to split up the provinces into smaller units; to introduce economic and fiscal reforms; and to give to the personal position of the Emperor an aura of aloof splendour. He thus created what is known as 'the Tetrarchy of Diocletian' under which there were to be two Emperors assisted by two younger deputies, or Caesars, who would eventually succeed, without conflict, to the throne. He thus raised his old crony Maximian to the rank of Augustus in the West with Constantius as his Caesar, taking for himself the superior *auctoritas* as 'Jovian' Augustus of the East with Galerius as his deputy. Diocletian ruled over Egypt, Libya, Arabia, Bithynia and Illyricum. Maximian, under the protection of Hercules, ruled over Rome, Italy, Sicily, Africa and Spain, while Gaul and Britain were entrusted to the care of his deputy Constantius. At the same time Diocletian did all he could to enhance the glamour and majesty of the imperial position. He surrounded himself with a regular court, insisted on the kow-tow, or *adoratio*, wore golden robes studded with jewels, and openly claimed to be accorded divine honours during his life-time. 'Ostentation,' writes Gibbon, 'was the first principle instituted by Diocletian'. He adopted the *nimbus* or sun-burst as an imperial symbol. He elaborated court etiquette or *basiliké pompé* and created castes or classes of nobles, called *cubicularii*, to form his own imperial household. He called even his bedroom 'sacred' and the heads of his government departments, or *skrinia*, were called the 'sacred council'. In the provinces he separated the military from the civil governorships, entrusting the command of the troops to senior officers under the title of *duces*, and attaching civil commissars to them with the titles of *correctores*. By such a separation of powers he hoped to prevent a provincial governor from inducing the local garrisons to proclaim him Imperator.

DECLINE OF DIOCLETIAN

Diocletian was a superstitious man and was convinced that the city of Rome was unlucky. He preferred Ravenna or Nicomedia and only visited the capital on very rare occasions. He thus reduced the Senate to impotence. 'The Senate of Rome,' writes Gibbon, 'losing all connexion with the Imperial Court and the actual constitution, was left a venerable but useless monument of antiquity on the Capitoline hill'. In May 305, worn out by the strain of maintaining the Tetrarchy, Diocletian had a nervous breakdown at Nicomedia and solemnly abdicated his functions. He persuaded his unwilling colleague Maximian to do the same. Diocletian retired to his native Dalmatia, and at Aspalathos

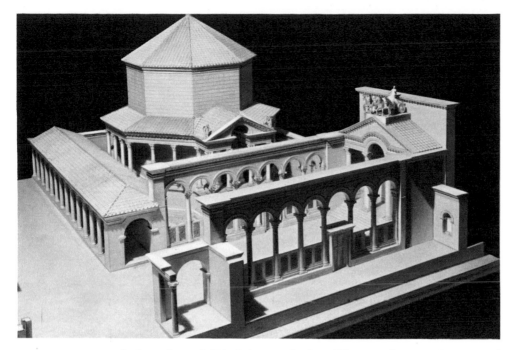

A reconstruction of the palace of Diocletian at Spalato. His mausoleum is the octagonal building in the background

constructed the superb palace, the remnants of which so impressed Robert Adam in 1757. Maximian, regretting the loss of imperial power, went sulkily to his estates in Lucania, where he sought to mitigate the dullness of retirement by the pleasures of senile debauchery. In the gardens of his mighty palace Diocletian collected and cherished all the rarest vegetables that Europe, Africa and Asia could produce. He was, as Gibbon wrote, more of a statesman than a warrior. The 'wily Diocletian' was wise to retire in time. He died a natural death in 313 and thirteen years later Constantine the Great decided to transfer to Constantinople the seat of the Empire of the East. The West dwindled under the onslaughts of the barbarians, until eventually in 475 the boy Romulus Augustulus, the last Roman Emperor, surrendered to Odoacer, the Rugian king of Italy. The Empire of the East, the Byzantine Empire, survived until the capture of Constantinople in 1453 by Mahomet.

Much as I admire the Byzantines for having defended Christianity against the barbarians for a thousand years, I find the history of that magic city monotonous, incomprehensible and dull. I agree with Gibbon:

The subjects of the Byzantine Empire, who assume and dishonour the names both of Greeks and Romans, present a deadly uniformity of abject vices, which are neither softened by the weakness of humanity, nor animated by the vigour of memorable crimes.

The marble base of an obelisk showing Theodosius I (379-395), Valentinian II, Arcadius and Honorius in the imperial box at the Hippodrome, Byzantium. Theodosius was the last of the Emperors of all Rome, and father of Honorius and Arcadius. The latter is usually regarded as the first purely Byzantine Emperor

Although they never excelled in literature or science, the Byzantines created a deeply significant type of art or iconography and their buildings have inspired great architecture down to our own day. Santa Sophia, designed by Anthemius of Tralles and by Isidore of Miletus, was consecrated by Justinian in 537 and remains one of the wonders of the world. Against the golden, and often blood-stained, monochrome of Byzantine history a few vivid and extraordinary individuals emerge. They perfected a new type of kingship, what might be called the sacerdotal type. The Basileus became the high priest; his court ceremonial a religious ritual.

Constantine and his immediate successors certainly regarded themselves as the inheritors of Rome and as the legitimate representatives of the great Caesars. Even Justinian, the boy from Skoplye, would style himself a Roman Emperor, would use Latin as the official language and would address his Byzantine subjects as *populus Romanus*. Yet in fact, once Rome itself had been abandoned for Constantinople, the Empire of the East became increasingly Levantine and the venerable Latin language ceased, as the centuries slid by, to be the imperial tongue.

As dynasty succeeded dynasty and Greeks and Bulgars reigned in the Sacred Palace by the Golden Horn, the traditions of Rome became obliterated and even its legends dimmed. The Emperor and his court bore no relation at all to the old republican Principate, but were moulded on the apparatus of Persian monarchy. High on its column the golden statue of Constantine, bearing the radiant diadem of Helios, soared above the churches, the baths and the palaces; he was worshipped as sun-god by Christian and pagan alike.

The Byzantine conception of kingship combined the oriental idea of the divine right of kings, with the old Roman idea of the monarch as the chief magistrate of the State. Once he had been crowned and the holy oil had been poured upon his head, breast and hands by the Patriarch at his coronation, he became 'the Lord's anointed' and head of the Christian Church. It did not signify from what origins he had come, or whether his virtue was such as to command reverence; the moment he had been anointed he was hailed as semi-divine.

What rendered the Byzantine kingship different from other forms of autocracy, was that the Basileus was not merely the Commander-in-Chief or Imperator, was not merely the head of the administration and above the law, but was essentially the Pope of the Eastern Church. It was he who nominated and could depose the Patriarch; it was he who decided theological questions and could impose his own doctrines upon the priests and monks; alone of laymen the Basileus was allowed to pass behind the iconostase and even to touch the consecrated wafers. The autocracy became a sacred priesthood and the Basileus was regarded by all as a member of the clergy. It was he who, arrayed in sacred vestments, conducted the great ceremonies, the slow stylised processions, of the Church. 'Nothing,' wrote a patriarch of the sixth century, 'should be done in the holy Church contrary to the opinion and the will of the Emperor'. When it happened, as with Justinian, that the Emperor was a trained and pedantic theologian, who prided himself on his gift of dialectic, and who much enjoyed presiding at theological synods, the ecclesiastical discipline enforced was rigid and often cruel. Of his many titles, those most frequently used were 'Autocrat of the Romans', 'Elect of God', 'Vicar of Christ on Earth', and 'Apostolos', or the equal of the holy apostles. Justinian proclaimed, and perhaps believed, that he 'proceeded from God and not from Man', that he ruled by Christ's desire, and that he was therefore the 'supreme master of the universe' and could claim 'absolute obedience from all'.

The Basileus, moreover, was the symbol of unity. 'The Empire,' wrote A. Rambaud, 'was an entirely artificial creation, comprising twenty nationalities united by the single formula, "one master, one faith"'. Thus orthodoxy took the place of patriotism, and heresy came to be identified with the rebellious nationalism of the subject races.

Throughout those thousand turbulent and dangerous years all power was centralised in the hands of the Basileus. The doctrine of State supremacy was almost universally accepted, and since there existed no feudal nobility and no self-assertive middle class or proletariat, the despotism of the Emperor remained unchallenged. In place of the hereditary territorial classes which arose in Europe during the Middle Ages, Byzantium, like Tsarist Russia, was organised on a caste system or *tchin*. There were eighteen carefully graded classes, bearing distinguished names, such as Anthypatos, Protospatharios, Dishypatos, Spatharocandidatos, Spatharios and so on. There were as many as eight distinct classes reserved for the eunuchs. The Prime Minister received the title of 'Grand Logothetos', and the prefect of the guard became the 'Eparch'. The First Lord of the Admiralty had the sturdy title of 'Grand Drungarius'. From these castes the civil service was recruited and, as in all highly centralised systems, it was the bureaucrats, or *sekrétikoi*, who preserved tradition and precedent. The provinces were divided into *themes*, and by the tenth century there were as many as thirty-one themes. The military control of the provinces was entrusted to a strategos, who was assisted by a civil commissar called a protonotary. All this elaborate machine was entirely in the hands of the Basileus.

THE POLITICS OF BYZANTIUM

The Emperor, in that he was the anointed of God and his Vice-regent on earth, could not be deposed; he could only be murdered. 'It can fairly be said,' writes Charles Diehl, 'that imperial power in Byzantium was autocracy tempered by revolution and assassination'. Mommsen went so far as to say that palace revolts were almost part of the constitution. The Senate, which had been reduced to a mere Council of State, were entitled to tender their advice to the Emperor although there was no obligation for him to take it. In a community as superstitious and gullible as were the Byzantines, the Church was bound to exert great influence: the monks, who were popular figures and who, amid the filth of their cells, would mumble criticisms and protests, formed the element of opposition. The Army was ultimately the decisive voice. The Basileus, in his coronation oath, swore to rule in the interest of the people. Yet the fact remained that his powers were

*Ariadne, daughter of the
Byzantine Emperor Leo I,
and wife of the Emperor Zeno.
A sixth-century ivory of the Empress*

universal and his actions constitutionally limited by dagger and poison only. Of the 107 Emperors who reigned at Byzantium between 396 and 1453, only thirty-four died natural deaths. During those thousand years as many as thirty-five revolutions were contrived either in the camps of the legionaries or in the harem and colonnades of the sacred palace. There was no generally accepted rule of succession, although an emperor was often allowed to designate and even to crown his successor. Thus the Macedonian dynasty and that of the Commeni each managed to survive for a century. A palace made of dark purple bricks was specially constructed as a lying-in hospital for the birth of princes and princesses, and the expression *porphyrogenitus* or ' born in the purple ' was used to designate those of royal blood.

THE GREENS
AND THE BLUES

Yet in Byzantium there did exist one democratic check on the kingship which was unique and strange. The citizens of Constantinople were divided into two sections, or parties, known as ' the Greens ' and ' the Blues '. Symbolically, the Greens were supposed to represent the fertility of the earth and the Blues the adventure and riches of the sea. In the Hippodrome the Greens and the Blues occupied opposite blocks and would hurl across at each other invectives, melons and rotten eggs. Although they were supposed only to represent opposed factions, backing one team of athletes or jockeys against the other, they were in fact organised and fiercely antagonistic democratic gangs. The young sparks of the Green faction let their beards grow, shaved the front of their heads allowing long locks to flap behind, and wore coloured blouses, the sleeves being taut at the wrists and bulging loose above the biceps. The Blues were equally fierce, attacking their rivals in the streets of the capital, and beating up peaceful citizens at night. In the Hippodrome these factions would demonstrate against unpopular ministers, would clamour for their impeachment, and, if their request were granted, would howl with delight when the disgraced minister was led slowly round the arena, mounted on a donkey with his face to the tail. On occasions even they would demonstrate against the Emperor himself. They provided a safety-valve for the expression of public opinion, and occasions arose, as we shall see, when the valve had little to do with safety.

One of the most remarkable personalities in the long history of Byzantine kingship was Theodora, wife of the Emperor Justinian. She was born, probably in Syria, in the year 500, the daughter of the man who kept the bears in the Hippodrome. When he died and his widow was left penniless, the three children, dressed in rags, were made by their mother to circle the arena making piteous pantomime appeals to the audience for some mitigation of their distress. The Greens laughed long and loud at this spectacle. The Blues showed some compassion for the tattered suppliants. Theodora from that moment became a fervent Blue. In any case their mother shortly afterwards married her late husband's successor as keeper of the bear pit, and the three children were brought up and educated, so to speak, on the stage.

Theodora herself was a pretty child and soon made her mark as a mime in the lascivious scenes acted in the interludes between the athletic events. She was specially adept at the stomach dance. While little more than a child she became a star of the circus. Her performances on the last day of the New Year celebrations, known as 'The Harlots Day', were particularly commended. She became the most noted of all the Byzantine prostitutes. At the age of seventeen she had an illegitimate son of whom, when she became Empress, she was so ashamed that when the boy had the audacity to visit her in the sacred palace, she had him strangled in the basement. Justinian, the prim, proper, religious and austere heir to the throne became wildly enamoured of this highly gifted strumpet. He married her in 527 and when, a few months later, he succeeded his uncle as Emperor, he had her solemnly crowned as Empress, and allowed her for twenty-one years to share the kingship with him and to exercise imperial power. Other remarkable women, such as Irene, Teophano, and Eudocia, played a leading part in Byzantine history; but none of them exercised such unquestioned dominance as Theodora. Justinian, for all his purity, for all the excellence of his intentions, was a fundamentally weak man, and surrendered gladly to the dominance of his gifted and resolute wife. She even induced him to share her prejudice against the Greens and to adopt towards the Monophysite heresy a more lenient attitude than that of which strict orthodoxy would have approved.

It must be noted that most of our evidence for the early lechery of Theodora comes from her vindictive assailant, Procopius, the Jew from Caesarea. He calls her 'the common abomination of the universe'. Considering that Procopius also represents Belisarius as corrupt and cowardly and contended that the austere Justinian was the prince of demons and the destroyer of the Empire, complete credence cannot be given to his account of Theodora's debauchery. His references to her are so detailed and so obscene that they well merited Gibbon's famous remark that they are best 'veiled in the obscurity of a learned language'.

RISE OF
THEODORA

The Emperor Justinian (527-565) with priests and attendants, from the mosaic of the Church of S. Vitale, Ravenna. His reign marked the most brilliant period in the history of the Byzantine Empire

Once Theodora became Empress she certainly changed her mode of life, and posed as the perfect example of a devout and constant wife. Yet the memory of her brothel period never faded from her mind; at great cost she built and endowed a palace on the sea of Marmora as a hospice for fallen women. Theodora never displayed any lack of moral courage. Nor of physical courage either. When the hostility between the Greens and the Blues reached a sudden climax in 532 and culminated in what is known as the Nika riot, she alone retained her equanimity of mind and her determined dignity. Justinian weakly surrendered his unpopular ministers to the fury of the populace. Clasping the gospel in his hand, the Emperor appeared in the imperial box at the Hippodrome and swore to grant the people all their desires. He was greeted with hoots of 'idiot' and 'liar' and was so terrified by this demonstration that he decided to escape to Asia. He loaded his treasures, his jewels and his most sacred icons into caiques moored at the Seraglio Point and urged his Empress to escape with him from the clamour of the

The Empress Theodora, wife of Justinian, from the same group of mosaics in Ravenna, attended by her ladies-in-waiting. From obscure and even disreputable origins, she became one of the most powerful women in history.

mob battering at the gates. She refused to budge. 'The imperial purple,' she said, 'will make the finest of all shrouds.' The situation was then taken over by the unconquerable soldier Belisarius. He burst into the Hippodrome from both ends of the arena and slaughtered all within. The rebellion was repressed; the Hippodrome closed until further notice; and about 30,000 of the mutineers were put to death. Theodora, having by her courage saved the throne, became more dominant than ever.

She was a superstitious woman, believing in portents, oracles, prophecies and the utterances of holy men. During the most degraded period of her life, when she was earning her living in the brothels of Alexandria and Antioch, she had been befriended by Severus, patriarch of Antioch, and by Anthimos, Bishop of Trebizond, who was subsequently elected oecumenical patriarch. The Pope, Adapit, determined to have nothing to do with the Monophysite heresy, and insisted that Anthimos should not only be deposed but should be exiled from

Constantinople. Although they searched diligently, they were unable to find the deposed patriarch and in fact he was only discovered twelve years after Theodora's death. He had been concealed by the heretical Empress in her private apartments. The widower Justinian preserved his life in tribute to the memory of his dead wife.

The Emperor, who had a tidy mind, much disliked all forms of heresy and decided that orthodoxy must be throughout the Empire imposed by force. Theodora allotted the Palace of Hormisdas to heretical refugees and as many as five hundred monks were housed there and impressed even the Emperor by their austerity, piety and good works. In 536 Pope Adapit died suddenly and Theodora decided that the next Pope should be chosen by herself. Her candidate was Vigilius, the papal nuncio at Constantinople and, as she imagined, a subservient priest. The city of Rome was at that date occupied by the Ostrogoths, and the barbarian King, Theodatus, refused to recognize Vigilius and chose in his place the deacon Silverus. Theodora thereupon ordered Belisarius to enter Rome, to depose Silverus and to instal Vigilius on the papal throne. Belisarius entered the city, deprived Silverus of his papal regalia, had him forcibly tonsured, arrayed in the garb of a monk and interned in the island of Palmaria, where he died. Vigilius having been by Theodora's insistence installed as Holy Father, then changed his mind and became more orthodox than the orthodox. The Empress had him arrested while he was celebrating mass in the Church of St Cecilia, transported down the Tiber and shipped across to Syracuse. From there he was brought to Constantinople, repented of his audacity in opposing the will of Theodora, and at Easter 548 issued the rescript exculpating the Monophysists of the charge of heresy. A few weeks later, on 29 June 548, Theodora died of cancer; she was buried in a golden coffin in the Church of the Holy Apostles.

THEODORA
AS EMPRESS

She was in truth a remarkable woman. She was loyal to her friends, but pursued her enemies with ferocious vindictiveness. She was not a tall woman but her body, owing to her long training as an acrobat, was seductively supple. She had a sallow complexion, a long solemn nose and enormous black eyes; her eyebrows met above her nose, a defect that was regarded by the Byzantines as a delicious adornment. She was witty and formidable. In her own quarters she maintained a host of guards, eunuchs, serving maids and pages; her guards were dressed in long white tunics with golden helmets surmounted with eagle plumes. She would receive ambassadors and barbarian kings surrounded by her personal court. She insisted upon being accorded the *proskynesis* or kow-tow, an honour never until her time paid to the Empress. Procopius, writes:

> In the case of Justinian and Theodora, all the members of the Senate and those who held the rank of Patricians, whenever they entered into their presence, would prostrate themselves to the floor, flat on their faces, and holding their hands and feet stretched far out would touch with their lips one foot of each before rising.

She was particular also about minor forms of protocol and etiquette, and if any foreigner from ignorance violated one of the regulations which she had herself laid down, he was conducted from her presence while her ladies shrieked with derisive laughter. Unlike the austere Justinian, who only allowed himself water and vegetables, she had an excellent cook and took great interest in the preparation of exotic or luxurious dishes. Like most royalties (and it is, as I have said, one of their most unpleasant habits), she derived pleasure from practical jokes. She took great care of her appearance, taking two baths a day and being constantly smeared with grease and unguents. She employed a spy system of her own and attached her private agents to all officials and ambassadors. She was not modest about her attainments and boasted openly of her hold over her husband. She had the effrontery to write to the King of Persia saying ' the Emperor decides nothing without consulting me '.

Her dominant vice was rancour. She was jealous of the great general Belisarius but was confident that she could control him through his adored wife, Antonina (also a retired prostitute), whom she appointed Mistress of the Robes. Priscus, a favourite of Justinian, was smuggled off to Cyzicus, forcibly tonsured, and interned in a monastery. The patrician Germanos, a nephew of the Emperor and a man of high integrity, was regarded by the Empress with suspicion; he was forbidden the Court and only returned to Constantinople after Theodora's death. A more dangerous antagonist was John of Cappadocia, Justinian's Minister of Finance and in fact his Grand Vizier. The Emperor realised that Byzantium owed her survival and supremacy as much to the stability of the byzant as to any other cause. He could not manage without the ingenious if unscrupulous John of Cappadocia and remained deaf to Theodora's hints that he was not a friend to be trusted. John was in fact an unreliable person; he speculated in grain and army contracts and amassed a huge private fortune; he was debauched and drunken

INTRIGUES
AT COURT

and had low tastes. He became so self-confident that he displayed lack of reverence to Theodora and was even suspected of trying to put the Emperor against her. She determined that he must be crushed and in order to gain her purpose and to destroy the confidence that Justinian continued to place in his Grand Vizier, she devised a most byzantine stratagem.

JOHN OF
CAPPADOCIA

She induced Antonina, the wife of Belisarius, who, according to Procopius, had the character of a scorpion, to complain to John of Cappadocia of the ingratitude with which her distinguished husband was treated, and to hint that if only she had a friend at Court, she might arrange to depose Justinian, and see that Belisarius was suitably rewarded for his splendid services to the State. The implication was that, on the murder of Justinian, John of Cappadocia would himself become Emperor. A secret interview was arranged in the garden of a villa belonging to Belisarius in the suburb of Rufinianae. Theodora instructed the chief eunuch Narses and Marcellus, the captain of the guard, to hide behind the garden wall and to arrest John of Cappadocia once any treasonable words were exchanged. Antonina was clever enough to trap John of Cappadocia into the most damaging statements as they paced the garden paths together. Marcellus rushed out of the bushes and started to arrest the Prime Minister but was checked by the arrival of the personal guard which John of Cappadocia had had the prudence to bring with him. The Minister escaped to the shore where a boat took him to the Seraglio Point. He took refuge in the sanctuary of Santa Sophia. Narses and Marcellus reported to the Emperor what they had overheard in the garden; the Cappadocian was deprived of his offices, scourged, thrown into prison, stripped of his huge fortune, and exiled to Egypt. On the death of Theodora he returned to Constantinople but never recovered his former power.

It was a dangerous thing not to bow to every whim that the Empress might manifest. While she lived in grandeur, surrounded by her eunuchs and women, the Emperor toiled away at his codifications and his laws for the improvement of public morals. He was a good dull man and it is consoling to believe that during their long marriage Theodora gave him more pleasure than pain. But although he was much respected, he was not loved. In fact he was worthy but unattractive, nor can we forgive his treatment of Belisarius, which in the long history of human ingratitude, can be compared only to Queen Anne's abominable repudiation of Marlborough, who by his transcendent genius

The ruined interior of the palace of Justinian on the shores of the Sea of Marmora, Istanbul. The palace was one of great grandeur, based on the architectural tradition of Imperial Rome, and was the scene of regal pomp, terror and intrigue in which the Empress Theodora was the central figure

added such lustre to her reign. Gibbon, while appreciating his sobre virtues, is waspish about his passionless egoism. 'The character,' he writes, 'of Philip II and of Justinian are distinguished by the cold ambition which delights in war and declines the dangers of the field.'

It would be possible to contend that it was during the reign of Justinian and Theodora that the Byzantine Empire reached its apogee. Internally, there was great economic prosperity, and after the collapse of the Nika riot, the excesses of the Greens and the Blues were curbed.

Orthodoxy was combined with tolerance and the Emperor glittered as the supreme pontiff. Externally, the genius of Belisarius had triumphed over the Persians, the Ostrogoths and the Vandals; he restored Africa and Italy to the Empire, brought two captive kings in triumph to the Hippodrome and laid at the feet of Justinian the treasures of Genseric and Theodoric. In his old age he saved Constantinople from the Bulgars. The Empire, for a space of time, was triumphant and at peace. Justinian survived Theodora for seventeen years, dying a natural death in 565 at the age of eighty-three and after a reign of thirty-eight years.

COURT
CEREMONY

The best description of the elaborate sacerdotal ceremony which became the apparatus of Byzantine kingship, is provided by the Emperor Constantine VII, who reigned from 912 to 959 under the name of Constantine Porphyrogenitus, and who left behind him a *Book of Ceremonies* for the guidance of his successors. In the introduction to this strange manual the Emperor answers those who contend that court ceremonial was mere outward show devoid of any true significance. ' Those, ' he writes, ' who do not care very much for what is unnecessary might regard this my work as superfluous. To me, however, the book is very dear, and appears deserving of all care. Since, thanks to a praiseworthy order of things, the imperial power appears more majestic, acquires prestige, and by that very fact attracts the admiration of foreign visitors and the subjects of the Empire. ' Confucius himself was not more insistent on the civilising effects of ordered ceremonial.

Constantine Porphyrogenitus demonstrates clearly how liturgical was the protocol that the Byzantine Emperors observed. On the great feasts of the Church the Emperor would, as High Priest, conduct the services. Surrounded by the royal family, escorted by the clergy and the palace guards, he would proceed in slow motion and with stylised gait towards Santa Sophia, while the choirs chanted litanies and the acolytes, swinging their golden censers, would dim the mosaic corridors with clouds of incense. The procession would on most occasions form up in the *Chrystotriclinius*, or throne room, from which it would proceed slowly and to the sound of hymns and litanies along the blue and gold colonnades and galleries that connected the imperial palace with the church of Santa Sophia. Constantine lays down exactly what route they should follow on each occasion, in what order the several dignitaries should process and at what point he would be greeted by the Patriarch or by the prefects of the Greens and Blues. In the course of this ritual progress the Emperor would change his vestments and his regalia. He

ΙΣ ΧΣ

The coronation by Christ
of a Byzantine Emperor,
possibly Constantine Porphyrogenitus.
An ivory now in Moscow

would start wearing the green crown, and then change into the blue crown, and finally, at the climax of the service, adopt the great royal tiara, blazing with jewels. He would wear the *scaramangion*, a tunic descending to the feet and caught at the waist by a jewelled belt. Above the *scaramangion* would be worn the *saigion*, a waistcoat stiff with pearls. At a certain stage of the service he would put on the *colobion*, a very sacred jacket. In his hand he would carry, not a sceptre, but the *akakia*, a form of satchel filled with the dust of tombs, and carried as a reminder of mortality. They walked in step and in slow motion. Their vestments were in fact so stiff with gold embroidery and jewels that it was impossible for them to bend. They made no reply to the paeans which the choirs intoned. They slowly lowered themselves on to the throne beside the altar and remained rigid throughout the service, never wavering from their hierophantic poise. Stiff as images they hardly glanced at the congregation prostrating themselves under the huge dome. All that was visible behind the billowing clouds of incense was an immobile effigy and at moments the flash of large jewels in the light of candles. Such was the attitude and etiquette demanded of the priest-basileus.

The solemn sacerdotal grandeur of the court of Constantine VII did not survive. It happens that we have a description of Byzantine etiquette from the pen of Luidprand, Bishop of Cremona, who was sent on a mission by the Emperor Otto to Nicephorus Phocas in 968. It was not an auspicious embassy, since Nicephorus much resented Otto calling himself 'Holy Roman Emperor' and thereafter attacking the Byzantine possessions in Apulia. Luidprand was ill-received, housed in a tumble-down house, kept under domiciliary arrest, allowed no water,

The two sides of a coin of Nicephoros Phocas, seen on the right with the Virgin Mary

and given only resinated wine to drink. On being admitted to an audience with the Emperor, he was obliged to kneel on the floor and keep his forehead to the ground. When allowed to rise he was startled to find that the imperial throne had in the interval risen to the ceiling and that the Emperor during these minutes of levitation had changed his clothes. The throne, moreover, was flanked by two golden lions who 'beat the ground with their tails and gave a dreadful roar with open mouth and quivering tongues' (*linguis mobilibus*). The Bishop of Cremona did not take to Nicephoros Phocas, the Byzantine Emperor, and wrote to the Emperor Otto:

> He is a monstrosity of a man, a dwarf, fat-headed, and with the tiny eyes of a mole; his face is disfigured by a short, broad beard growing grey; his neck is hardly an inch long; he resembles a pig, because of the thick bristles on his head. In colour he is like an Ethiopian and, as the poet says, 'one would not wish to meet him in the dark ..' He has a huge belly, a thin posterior; is very long in the thighs considering his short stature; small legs, and ordinary-sized ankles and feet. He was dressed in a tunic of fine linen, but old, stained and smelling foul. He is a fox by nature, a Ulysses in perjury and falsehood. My Lord and Emperor, you always seemed handsome to me, but you seem even more handsome now that I have seen Nicephoros Phocas.

NICEPHOROS
PHOCAS

Luidprand describes a ceremony which he witnessed at Santa Sophia. 'As Nicephoros, like some crawling monster, waddled along, the choirs burst into a litany of adoration. "Behold," they sang, "the morning star approaches; the day-star rises; in his eyes the rays of the sun are reflected. Long life to our Prince Nicephoros, the dealer of death to the Saracens. Adore him, ye nations of the earth, bow the neck to his greatness". How much more truly might they have sung, "Come, come you wretched burnt-out coal; with the walk of an old woman and the eyes of a wood-devil; you clodhopper, you goat-footed, horned, bristly, rough barbarian; you Cappadocian usurper".'

When Luidprand at last had the opportunity to deliver his messages from Otto, Nicephoros 'sweated like a toad with rage'. In the end Luidprand was dismissed by the Emperor with a present of two goats, and returned to his master with his mission unaccomplished. The next year Nicephoros was murdered by his wife's lover John Zimiskes, and his severed head displayed, like a pig's head in the shop front of a Berlin butcher, upon the gate of the palace, where it was gaped at by the crowds in the Forum of Constantine.

Comment nře seigr par son ange enuoya les trois fleurs de lis dor en vn escu dasur au roy clouis

SEVEN

Charlemagne

WITH THE DECLINE OF THE ROMAN EMPIRE and the withdrawal of the legions from the frontiers, ancient Gaul was split into several separate kingdoms. The Burgundians occupied the Saône valley; the Alemanni were settled in what is now Alsace; an island of Gallo-Romans under the rule of a Roman general, or *magister militum*, survived between the Somme and the Loire; the large section of western Europe that stretched from the Loire to the Straits of Gibraltar was held by the Visigoths; and northern Gaul had been occupied by the Salian Franks as far as the Somme. This German tribe, the ancestors of the French nation, still spoke a barbarous teutonic dialect, still sacrificed to Thor and Odin, still retained some of the old Germanic traditions, and were still convinced that their gods derived satisfaction from human sacrifice.

The King of the Franks, when first the nation emerges from the mists of legend into the daylight of history, was Merouechus, or Merovech, or Mérovée, the reputed son of a sea god and the founder of the Merovingian dynasty. His grandson Chlodovech or Clovis ruled from 466 to 511 and was the true founder of the *regnum Francorum* or the kingdom of France. In 486 he attacked and defeated his neighbours the Gallo-Romans under their general Syagrius who called himself ' Rex Romanorum '. In 496 he defeated the Alemanni and was baptised an orthodox Christian by Saint Remigius at Rheims. Three hundred years later, as I have already recounted, the legend was invented that on the occasion of this baptism, Remigius, whose duty it was not only to baptise Clovis, but to consecrate him as the Lord's anointed, mislaid the bottle of sacred oil, and that while Clovis and the congregation sat there waiting in embarrassed inaction, a pigeon was seen to fly into the cathedral bearing in its beak the *sainte ampoule* or sacred phial, which played a prominent part in the coronation of the Kings of France until 1824. Clovis thus acquired the prestige and responsibilities of secular head of the Orthodox Church and was regarded by the Vatican as the heaven sent champion of the true faith against the Arian heresy, which to the papal mind represented a more dreadful enemy than Odin even, or Thor. In 496 Clovis made war against the Visigoths, killed their king Alaric with his own hand, and annexed the northern realm of the Visigoths, thus extending the Regnum Francorum from the Channel to the Pyrenees. He accepted the old Roman title of ' Augustus '. He established his capital at Paris which, as Julian the Apostate had observed, was a gay and easily defensible little city upon an island in the River Seine. Clovis died in 511.

SUCCESSORS OF CLOVIS

One of the fatal illusions of the Merovingian dynasty was to regard their kingdom, not as an organic unity, but as a private property or estate. On the death of the reigning sovereign the estate was divided up more or less equally among his sons. The great realm that Clovis had won and unified was therefore partitioned among his four sons and chaos ensued. The Merovingian monarchs, who became known as the ' Donothing Kings ' or *Les Rois Fainéants*, lost all executive authority, whereas, as the descendants of sea-gods, they still retained a powerful mystic prestige.

In the long and varied history of kingship, which culminated in the excellent device of constitutional monarchy, the *Rois Fainéants* filled a strange interlude between 511 and 751, during which the executive power of the Merovingian dynasty was practically abolished, whereas the mystique of hereditary monarchy never lost its appeal to the nation. We witness a rapid succession of Contrans, Gondovalds, Childeberts, Dagoberts, Theodeberts, Clotaires, Thierrys and Childerics, whose names have survived in the decrees and official documents which they were made to attest. Legend has represented them as besotted old gentlemen, with long hair and beards, who for most of the year were interned in outlying farms near Soissons or Sens, but who from time to time were bundled into ox-wagons and trundled along to preside at some national festival. As a matter of fact, few of them reigned for more than eight years, most of them died before reaching the age of twenty-five, and a large number of them were from childhood onwards deliberately debilitated by wine, drugs, and women, in order to destroy their reputations, wills and energies. Dagobert, who reigned from 628 to 638, was the only one of the descendants of Clovis who made a fleeting attempt to revive the fallen monarchy. At his death the Merovingian kings returned to inanity.

Their powers and responsibilities as rulers were usurped by the controllers of the Household, the major-domos, the *proceres palatii* or 'Mayors of the Palace'. This office was of ancient origin; Sidonius Apollinaris refers to it as the summit of political ambition, and the eunuch Narses had held the title of *praepositus palatii* to Justinian. Under the *Rois Fainéants* all central authority collapsed and, since the palace had become the only seat of government, the mayor of the palace became Grand Vizier. When, as so frequently happened, the legitimate king was a minor, the mayor became his guardian or *nutricius* and saw to it that he remained in his farm or villa and drank much. In 656 the mayor, Grimoald, decided to abolish the fiction of a Merovogian dynasty and on the death of the legitimate monarch, Sigebert, proclaimed his own son as King of the Franks. Yet such was the prestige of the legitimate dynasty that the lords and bishops denounced this usurpation and Grimoald was put to death. Even when the legitimate descendants of the sea god had petered out, even when the mighty Martel was Mayor, the fiction was preserved that a King was still living in one of the farms; and under the rule of the Pépins a feeble-minded and forgotten member of the Merovingian family was dug out of a monastery and proclaimed King Childeric III.

The partitioned Empire of Clovis had by then consolidated into two main blocks, the Austrasians to the east, and the Neustrians to the west. It is not correct to describe the former as 'German' and the latter as 'French': they were of mixed nationality. Each of these two kingdoms had its hereditary king and its, by then, practically hereditary Mayor. The most important family, or dynasty, of the Mayor was that founded by Pépin I, called Pépin of Landen, who ruled Austrasia until his death in 639. His grandson Pépin II, called Pépin of Heristal, defeated Ebrion, the rival mayor of Neustria, at the battle of Tertry in 687, and united all Gaul with the exception of Aquitaine.

THE DYNASTY OF PEPIN

123

King Pépin III, on whose head a divine hand places a diadem, and two priestly attendants. From the 'Sacrammentaire de Metz'

It was the illegitimate son of Pépin II, by his concubine Alpaidis, who is known to history as 'Charles the Hammer' or 'Charles Martel'. It was he who checked the Arab invasion of western Europe by utterly defeating Abd-ur-Rahman, who had advanced to within two hundred miles of Paris, at the battle of Poitiers in 732. He rendered himself master of Burgundy and forced the Duke of Aquitaine to acknowledge his suzerainty. He is rightly regarded as the saviour of western Europe from the Moors and as the true founder of modern France. He died in 741 and was succeeded by his two sons Pépin III, known as *Pépin le Bref* or 'Pépin the Short', and Carloman. The latter abdicated in 747 and retired to a cave on Mount Soracte and eventually to the monastery of Monte Cassino. Pépin III ruled alone under the aegis of the last of the Merovingians Childeric III.

The main menace at that date to the Frankish kingdom was Alboin, the savage ruler of the Lombards, a barbarous tribe settled between the Elbe and the Oder. Alboin was a ferocious tribal leader. He had with his own hands murdered Cunimund, king of the Gepidas, as well as his son and heir. He had forced Cunimund's daughter Rosamund to marry him. He then invaded Italy and made Pavia the capital of the Lombard Kingdom, a kingdom that lasted for two hundred years. At a banquet at Verona he became very drunk and called for the drinking cup which he had scooped from the skull of his victim and father-in-law Cunimund, King of the Gepidas. He was so intoxicated that he forced his wife Rosamund to drink from her father's skull. This outrage was too much even for the Lombards; Rosamund was able to have her revenge: Alboin was murdered and succeeded by Aistulf. The new Lombard leader started by invading the strips of territory in southern Italy which had been retained by the Emperors of the East. The Byzantine exarch at Ravenna appealed to Pope Stephen II for assistance, and the Pope appealed to Pépin, King of the Franks. Pépin entered Italy by the Mont Cenis pass, defeated Aistulf, and took him prisoner. The Pope, in gratitude for this rescue, decided to pay a visit to Pépin. He was warmly received and the King of the Franks sent to meet and to escort him his eldest son Charles, then a lad of eleven. It thus happened that successive Popes fell into the habit of regarding the Franks as their natural allies and defenders; that Charles, in his mystic manner, regarded himself as 'Patrician of the Romans', as chosen by God to be the champion of God's Vicar on Earth. France thereafter claimed to be 'the eldest daughter of the Church'. It is not known where exactly the young Prince Charles first met Pope Stephen II on his journey to the Frankish Court of Soissons. European history is indebted to that almost chance encounter.

In 751 Pépin III decided that his power was now sufficient to enable him to abolish the farce of the *rois fainéants*, yet he hesitated to

KINGDOM OF
THE LOMBARDS

commit this act of usurpation without papal approval. The Pope Zacharias decreed that 'he who exercises the king's power should enjoy the king's title'. Childeric III was thus bundled into an ox-cart and brought to Soissons where he was shaved and tonsured in the presence of the nobles and thereafter interned in the monastery of St Bertin. Pépin was acclaimed and crowned by St Boniface as *Gratia Dei Rex Francorum*, King of the Franks by the grace of God. He died at St Denis in September 768 and was succeeded by his sons Carloman and Charles who divided the kingdom between them. Carloman died in 771 and Charles ruled alone over the Empire left by his father.

Pépin III, conscious that he was in fact an usurper, set great store by being anointed as the chosen of God. The coronation ceremony was not in the teutonic tradition. The German kings were elected and acclaimed by the leading warriors and raised aloft by them on their shields. Had not David, although of upstart origin, been rendered sacred on Jehovah's own instructions by being anointed with holy oil? Had not Saul and even Aaron been similarly consecrated? Thus Pépin, having received the oil of the *sainte ampoule* from the hands of St Boniface, was again crowned and consecrated two years later by the Pope. 'The royal unction,' writes Gibbon, 'of the kings of Israel was dexterously applied; the successor of St Peter assumed the character of a divine ambassador; the German chieftain was transformed into the Lord's anointed; and this Jewish rite has been diffused and maintained by the superstition and vanity of modern Europe.' The coronation ceremony came in later centuries to be regarded by the Vatican as some sort of contract between the Holy See and the Kings of France.

THE RISE OF CHARLEMAGNE

Charles, King of the Franks, who so rightly earned the title of Charles the Great, was born, (probably at Aachen) on 2 April 742. His mother, a strong-minded and resolute woman, was the daughter of the Count of Laon; she was known to her contemporaries as 'Bertha of the Big Foot'. King Pépin, as has been said, died in 768 partitioning his dominions between his two sons, Charles, then aged twenty six, and Carloman, then aged seventeen. The line of partition did not follow the former boundary between Neustria and Austrasia, but cut across it in an eccentric manner; in general it can be said that Charles received the western, or what has incorrectly been called the 'French', portion, whereas to Carloman was allotted the eastern or 'German' sector. Charles on his accession established his court at Paris, whereas Carloman chose Soissons as his headquarters. Carloman died at the age of twenty,

The throne of Charlemagne in Aachen Cathedral, subsequently used for the coronation of the Holy Roman Emperors

and although he left two infant sons behind him, Charles then seized the whole of Pépin's dominions and Neustria and Austrasia were united once again.

Almost immediately Charles started upon the long series of campaigns that rendered him the terror of Europe and earned him immortal fame as the defender of the faith and the hero of romance and legend. Not since Alexander the Macedonian has any conqueror been the subject of so great a mass of fiction.

Before considering what constitutes the most interesting of Charlemagne's achievements, namely the establishment of the theory of responsible kingship, it is necessary to examine the series of campaigns which brought him world prestige. His first triumph was the swiftness with which he crushed a revolt in Aquitaine and captured the rebel king Hunold. According to the custom of the age Hunold should have been convicted of disloyalty and either hanged on the gallows, or blinded, or mutilated; the best that could have happened to him was to have his locks sheared in public, to be tonsured, and thereafter confined for life in some remote monastery. Charles, who was temperamentally magnanimous, merely imprisoned Hunold for a few months and then granted him his liberty. This eccentric action might have been regarded by his contemporaries as a sign of weakness; they had not long to wait before they were forced to recognize that there was no fault or fissure in Charles' iron will.

Desiderius, King of the Lombards, invaded papal territory; his mercenaries even captured the Lateran Palace and held Pope Stephen III under house arrest. The Pope appealed to Charles for help, but Big Foot Bertha intervened and managed to patch up an agreement between Charles and the King of the Lombards, under which Desiderius was to refrain from disturbing the Pope and as a pledge of amity Charles was to marry the Lombard Princess, Desideria, daughter of Desiderius. She was a dull girl who bored the young King of the Franks so atrociously that, in spite of the protests and warnings of Big Foot Bertha, he packed her back to Pavia, and in her place married the bright and beautiful Swabian, Hildegarde. Desiderius and his Lombards were hurt by this affront.

In 772 Pope Stephen died; he was succeeded by a man of greater ability, Adrian I. Desiderius, profiting by the confusion caused by a papal election, again invaded papal territory and Adrian appealed to Charles for help. Although a mighty warrior, Charles did not really like war. He offered Desiderius what in those days was a fantastic bribe of half a million pounds, if he would withdraw from papal territory and restore the cities he had seized. Desiderius refused and there was

INVASION OF LOMBARDY

nothing further that Charles could accomplish by subsidies, diplomacy and bribes. Charles collected a large army at Geneva and embarked on the invasion of Lombardy. Desiderius manned the defiles of the Mont Cenis and for a while blocked any advance on the part of the Franks. Charles then discovered a mountain path, which is still called ' The Way of the Franks ', by which he could turn the Lombard barriers. On finding that the Franks had managed to outflank their positions and to get behind them, the Lombards broke in disorder and fled as far as Pavia, where within a few weeks they were closely invested by the Franks. While Desiderius and his Lombards were shut up in Pavia and pending the time when starvation would compel their surrender, Charles decided to see Rome. His restless curiosity had for long impelled him to visit that eternal city; he wished to meet Pope Adrian, in whom

Charlemagne in his tent with his knights, servants and suppliant prisoners. A mediaeval representation of the great king by the French illuminator Renaud de Montambant. Now in the Arsenal Museum, Paris

he had detected a fellow spirit; and above all he desired to discover Roman scholars, musicians and artists who he hoped would be able to instruct the then untutored Franks in at least the elements of culture. The visit was a great success; he formed a lasting friendship with Pope Adrian; and he returned to Pavia with a team of scholars in time to receive the surrender of Desiderius and the Lombards in June of 774.

Once again he startled contemporary opinion by behaving with the utmost magnanimity. Instead of executing Desiderius, or gouging out his eyes and tongue (which was at that date the favourite method of mutilation), he merely interned him in the Abbey of Corbie. He then annexed the Lombard lands to his own dominions and was crowned King of the Lombards. He thereafter assumed the titled of ' Rex Francorum, Rex Langobardum, and Patricius Romanorum '. He could claim

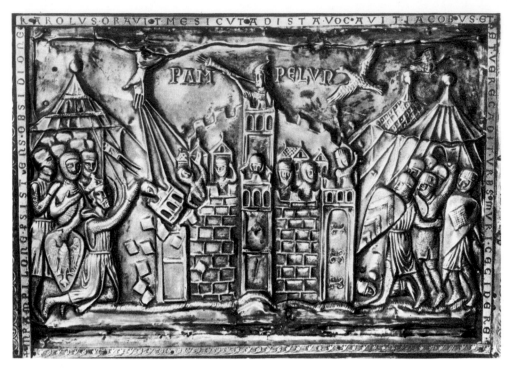

Charlemagne at the siege of Pampeluna. On his return-march occurred the incident described in the Chanson de Roland.

with justice that he had acted as champion of the Papacy and the eldest son of the Church:

> Quando il dente longobardo morse
> la Santa Chiesa, sotto alle sue ali
> Carlo Magno vincendo la soccorse.

Charlemagne was not merely a splendid fighter, who, wielding his great sword *la joyeuse*, would kill all those who confronted him; he was also a fine strategist and tactician. He had the Napoleonic gift of the unexpected and would appear suddenly, when least awaited, on the flank or in the rear of his enemies. His mobility caused great fear. At the very rumour of his approach whole armies would disperse.

His most persistent enemies were the Saxons, who in those days occupied the area between the Elbe and the Weser, who still made human sacrifice to Thor and Odin, and who were said to indulge in the sin of cannibalism. Great missionaries, such as Boniface of Crediton in Devonshire, had failed to convert them; Boniface himself was murdered by the Frisians, and their cousins the Saxons would again and again sacrifice Christian missionaries to their pagan gods and burn the chapels they had built. Charles was determined that they should be punished for their raids into Frankish territory and that they should by force be baptised into the Holy Church. Alcuin, his saintly teacher, disapproved of these forcible conversions.

Charles' first invasion of Saxony occurred in 772. He occupied their sacred grove and destroyed their tribal fetish, a high totem-pole which they worshipped as Irminsul. Two years later the Saxons again revolted and made repeated raids on the Franks. Charles, who was then in Italy, dashed back to his northern frontier and at his approach the Saxons fled. He pursued them and managed in 775 to impose a new treaty upon them; their tribal leaders were baptised, presumably under compulsion, in the river Lippe. In 778, when Charles was in Spain fighting the Moors, another revolt broke out in Germany. The Saxons on this occasion had discovered a talented national leader, Widukind. Under his leadership they penetrated far into Frankish territory and even captured Cologne. Charles dashed back from Spain and again defeated them and forced them to surrender. He sought to pacify the country by appointing as governors men of Saxon nationality, but this expedient was not successful, and in a fit of impatience Charles published his ' Saxon Capitularies ' or regulations, which were oppressive in intent and practice. The fury aroused by this cruel legislation furnished a further chance to Widukind, who assembled his savage hordes and inflicted a defeat on a Frankish army under Count Theodoric near Minden. Charles was so angered by this obstinate renewal of revolt that he slaughtered four thousand five hundred Saxon hostages at Verden on the Aller. The massacre of Verden has remained a dark stain upon his repute.

On Charles' return to the scene of action his prestige led the Saxon hordes to disperse in panic and in the end Widukind himself was obliged to surrender. Charles received him generously at Attigny, stood godfather to him at his inevitable baptism, and created him Duke of Saxony. But the rebellious Saxons were not really pacified until 808. It had taken Charles thirty years and eighteen campaigns to subdue this stub- born race.

Less important, although far more renowned in fable and song, was his expedition against the Moors in Spain. In 777 he entered Spain at the invitation of one of the insurgent Caliphs and pushed as far as Barcelona. But the local Christian population, who were mainly Visigoths by origin, hated the Franks and even joined with the pagan Moors against them. Charles was so shocked by such infidelity that he withdrew from Spain in disgust. On recrossing the Pyrenees in August 778, his rear-guard and his baggage train were ambushed and slaughtered in the pass of Roncevalles by Basque brigands. Among those killed was

CHANSON DE
ROLAND

Charles' cousin, Hruoland, prefect of the Breton march, who commanded the rear of the army. Charles, who had already crossed the mountains and debouched into the plain, returned too late to avenge this disaster; the brigands had dispersed. Yet this comparatively trivial episode formed the theme of the *Chanson de Roland* and of endless romances of the age of Chivalry, from the *Chansons de Geste* to the *Rolandslied* and the *Willehalm*.

The *Chanson de Roland* is almost entirely apocryphal. The King at the time of the Roncevalles misfortune was only thirty-six years of age but is represented as a centenarian with a long white beard (*Li emperere od la barbe flurie ... Il est mult vielz*). His sword, Durandal, his horn, the Olifant, his banner the Oriflamme, are all fictional. The catastrophe was not as serious as was later represented. The assailants were not the Saracens or the Moors but the local robbers from the Basque province. Only a small rear-guard with the baggage was severed from the main army. The main Frankish army did not suffer lastingly from the ambush set for the baggage train. There was in fact no reason for Charles to exclaim that the flower of the French army had been taken from him (*De France dulce m'ont tolute la flur*) or to call upon future generations to pity poor sweet France (*pleindre povum France dulce, la bele*). In this case at least fiction was stranger than history and great poetry flowed from a false spring.

CAMPAIGNS IN
BAVARIA AND
PANNONIA

Further trouble then arose in Bavaria, where Luitberga, sister of the outraged Desiderata, and daughter of Desiderius, urged her husband, the Duke of Bavaria, and her brother-in-law, the Duke of Benevento, to attack the papal territories, regardless of the fact that Charles was then recognised as the Pope's devoted champion. The Duke of Benevento was rapidly disposed of and forced to restore the cities that he had seized. Tassilo, Duke of Bavaria, was encircled by three Frankish armies, descending unexpectedly. He was arrested, deposed, and interned in the Abbey of Jumièges. Luitberga was confined in a convent and Charles assumed the additional title of Duke of Bavaria.

A further menace to civilisation were the Avars, a Mongol tribe related to the Huns, who had settled in Pannonia and were a constant menace to their neighbours. They had by frequent raids amassed a huge treasure which they guarded in their central stronghold, protected by as many as nine circles of entrenchments. Charles invaded this vast perim-

Right: Charlemagne's reliquary bust made in the mid-fourteenth century to contain his bones. The crown is a hundred years earlier. The bust, which is of silver and enamel, is in the treasury at Aachen

eter but was unable to pierce beyond the first circle. It was left to his son Pépin to break through all nine circles and to capture the vast treasure of the central fortress. This treasure, the dispersal of which, according to some experts, caused a revolution in European economy, certainly brought great riches in gold and silver to the King of the Franks. Part of it he distributed among his troops, but he also gave a large sum to the Church, which the Popes devoted to the repair of the Lateran. From then on the Avars disappear from history.

Certainly Charlemagne was a fine warrior, and a strategist and tactician of genius. But what is more interesting than his many campaigns was his civilising energy. What differentiates Charlemagne from other warrior kings is that he introduced into kingship the doctrine of responsibility.

He was an enormous man, being six foot four in height and obese as well. He was muscular, loved hunting, and could kill a man with a single blow of his club. His hair and moustache were reddish in colour and his eyes, which were unusually prominent, were of searching blue. He had a short thick neck and vast wide hands. Contrary to the legend, he never grew a beard. Like so many enormous men (including Bismarck and Reza Shah), his voice was as squeaky as that of a boy of twelve. He dressed simply and tidily; he was punctilious about personal cleanliness and had two hot baths a day. He loved bathing with his courtiers in the huge swimming bath of Aix. He was temperate in eating and drinking and imposed austerity upon his bishops and counts. He was a very garrulous man, affable but alarming. Being a poor sleeper, he would in the early hours of the morning prowl about his camp or palace, startling sentinels and monks. He was very fond of women, had four wives and a succession of mistresses. Gibbon (who found Charlemagne too manly to be interesting) states waspishly that of his many qualities ' chastity was not the most conspicuous '. He had eighteen children, of whom eight were certainly legitimate; but, as Douglas Woodruff notes, even in his marriages ' there was a certain amount of overlapping '. Of his wives, the fair and gentle Hildegarde exercised a soothing influence, whereas her successor, the vixen Fastrada, was a nuisance to all. He was so fond of his daughters that, while encouraging their lascivious tastes, he would never allow them to marry and leave him. The wise old Alcuin disapproved of the Carolingian princesses, calling them ' the crowned doves ' (coronatae columbae).

The intellectual strength of Charlemagne derived from his immense powers of concentration. His critics might accuse him of obstinacy and

An equestrian statue of Charlemagne in bronze at the Musée Carnavalet, Paris. Previously thought to be of much later date, experts now believe that it may be nearly contemporary with the great king

of possessing a single-track mind. Yet in fact he was a man of varied interests and alert imagination. Helen Waddell, in her lovely book *The Wandering Scholars*, called him 'the Athenian lover of strange things'. He invented new names for the months and for the winds; he wrote a German grammar; he strove to codify the jumbled laws of his Empire; he composed the hymn *Veni creator spiritus*; and he introduced vineyards among the hills of the Rhine and the Moselle, thus benefitting posterity with the gift of wines comparable only to those of France. Even as Napoleon, who would refer to him as 'my great predecessor', Charlemagne had a genius for detail and an amazing memory. He would count the hens in his chicken run and would reprove a choir boy who sang out of tune. His aim was to create a Christian empire, an *imperium christianum*, and he succeeded in this aim. His kingship combined the old Roman idea of despotism, vestiges of ancient Teutonic traditions of communal organisation, with the patriarchal and almost theocratic conception of the Christian King. He certainly believed in the principle of kingship exercised for the benefit of its subjects and would have endorsed the doctrine of *salus publica suprema lex*.

He loved discussing theology and philosophy with learned men; HIS CONTRIBUTION his favourite author was Saint Augustine; he corresponded with Harun- TO CULTURE al Rashid, Caliph of Baghdad, who sent him a water-clock and an elephant which were much admired. He was in fact an intellectual, which in the early ninth century was a very unusual thing for a Frank to be.

His greatest contribution to culture was, however, the untiring and most persistent interest that he took in education. At Aachen he established a school for the instruction of Frankish youths of promise, irrespective of class or income. He gathered round him scholars from every country. There were Paulus of Aquileia and Arno of Salzburg. Alcuin of Northumberland, whose teachers had been pupils of the venerable Bede himself, remained the instructor and intimate friend of Charlemagne for fourteen years. He liked to call this group of scholars his 'academy'. They would read the classics aloud after meals and call each other by pet names. Alcuin, for instance, would always address Charlemagne as 'David', and the Emperor would call Alcuin 'Horatius Flaccus'. It was stated by one of his biographers that the Emperor, although he read voraciously, never learnt to write, and would sign his decrees by inscribing a cruciform mark. It is more probable that he was unable to master the elaborate script of the age, known as 'Carolingian Minuscule', from which later typography was derived. He strongly disap-

Charlemagne presents a model of his church at Aachen to the Virgin Mary. Archbishop Turpin is on his left.

proved of monks who did not work, but merely prayed. It was owing to his insistence that a great body of lettered clerks were set to copy not merely the extant manuscripts of the great classical writers, but also the native folk-songs and ballads. Had it not been for Charlemagne's inquisitive mind we should never have had the myths of Dietrich von Bern, the Ring cycle or legible and quite accurate transcripts of the great classical writers. We owe him much.

CHARLEMAGNE'S
METHODS OF
GOVERNING

The Empire which he won or accumulated stretched from the Ebro to the Baltic, from the Channel to the Danube. He possessed the whole of Italy, apart from a few strips still held by the Byzantine Emperors.

Charlemagne abolished the office of Mayor of the Palace, but his household, or palatines, continued to exercise administrative and even military duties and did not confine themselves to courtly functions. He created something approaching a civil service of clerks under the supervision of a protonotary or chancellor. He instituted a council of optimates, whose advice he could obtain if he desired. In addition he continued the Merovingian system of the popular assembly, or *campus medius*. It consisted mainly of ecclesiastics and barons and the only popular element was composed of their retinues. Charlemagne would discuss

138

Charlemagne's devotion to the Church is illustrated in this plaque of the interior of a cathedral from the great reliquary at Aachen

measures with the higher orders, but would also speak to the retinues and obtain their *consensus* or obedience. More important decisions were taken at the autumn assembly, which was carefully selective, and the resolutions of which were, in theory at least, submitted for the consent of the more democratic May assembly. The Emperor retained firm hold of the Church and no bishop could be elected without his consent.

His provinces were governed on his behalf by Dukes, Marquesses or Counts, who were frequently of native origin. He was supreme ruler both of Church and State, managing the Church through his Arch-Chaplain, and entrusting secular business to the Chancellor and the Count Palatine. He was interested in agriculture and did much to improve the primitive methods then employed; he was a pioneer economist, sought to establish a trade treaty with Offa of Mercia, and imposed a uniform currency from Metz to Venice. He derived his own revenues, not from direct taxation, but from his vast crown estates and from a profitable percentage of fines.

He was resolute in his defence of widows, orphans and the oppressed. His commissars or *Missi Dominici* would tour the provinces to receive complaints, and report on all cases of corruption or oppression. The provincial governors whom he appointed were chosen solely for their ability or good character; their titles were not hereditary and they were often chosen from the peasant class. Much of his legislation, as well as his instructions to provincial governors, took the form of 'Capitularies' or circular rescripts, many of which have survived. It is from them, rather than from the official and unreliable biographies of Einhard and the Monk of Saint Gall, that we can best judge his tremendous energy and the quality of his achievement. He was not merely devout; he was inspired with real religious fervour; he loved learning and hated injustice; he was the first autocrat since the days of Augustus to insist that a ruler was responsible for the safety, happiness and well being of all his subjects. 'He was the supreme example in human history of the Christian King...,' writes Douglas Woodruff. 'Men recognised that in him kingship had touched a higher level, and through the long centuries his memory remained, transmuted into an immortal figure of strength and wisdom, matchless, majestic, benign, of more than mortal strength, the anointed and chosen of God, the pledge and symbol of Christendom faithful and secure.'

CORONATION OF
CHARLEMAGNE

In 795 Pope Adrian died. His successor Leo III was unpopular and the nobles urged him to abdicate, which he refused to do. He was then set upon in the streets of Rome, thrown from his mule, and almost blinded and battered to death. He was thereafter confined in a monastery from which, with the aid of his former chamberlain, he managed to escape. He was accused of murder, adultery, simony and perjury. Charles summoned him to Paderborn where he was submitted to a commission of enquiry, the verdict being non proven. Charles sent him back to Rome with an escort and on his arrival a more formal investigation was instituted of the charges against him. He was acquitted on all counts and restored to the papal throne. In November 800 Charles journeyed to Rome and paid his respects to the now vindicated Pope.

On Christmas Day 800 he attended high mass in the basilica of St Peter's. He received the communion and bent before the altar in devout prayer. Seeing him thus crouched the Pope snatched a crown that had been concealed behind the candlesticks and placed it on the head of the King of the Franks, proclaiming him as Augustus and Emperor of the West. The congregation acclaimed him with a mighty shout of 'To Charles Augustus, crowned by God, the great and peace-giving Emperor, be life and victory'. 'In that shout,' writes James Bryce, 'was pronounced the union, so long in preparation, so mighty

The coronation of Charlemagne by Pope Leo III in St Peter's, Rome. From a fourteenth-century manuscript

in its consequences, of the Roman and the Teuton, of the memories and the civilization of the South with the fresh energy of the North, and from that moment modern history begins.'

Einhard his biographer pretends that Charlemagne had been totally unaware of the Pope's intention and that he lamented afterwards that His Holiness should have played this trick upon him. He is represented as exclaiming 'Would that I had not entered St Peter's on Christmas day'. It is however inconceivable that a Pope, indebted as he was to Charlemagne, and in a church crowded with Frankish warriors, would in so important a matter have acted without the King's knowledge and consent. It is more probable that, although Charles had decided to proclaim himself Emperor, he did not wish to receive his crown from the Pope's hands and before he had made some diplomatic arrangement with the Basileus at Constantinople. The impression remains that the Pope perpetrated a nasty trick. It is regrettable to add that, once Charles had been anointed Holy Roman Emperor, he insisted on his Palatines, courtiers, counts and bishops performing the kow-tow before him and even on their kissing his shoe. I am sorry about that.

On 28 January 814 Charlemagne died of pleurisy and was buried in a sarcophagus in the cathedral that he had built at Aachen. His Empire was further partitioned between his grandsons under the Treaty of Verdun in 843. The Carolingian dynasty survived until 987, when almost by chance, Hugues Capet, the ancestor of a long line of famous French kings, succeeded.

The legend of Charlemagne inspired poets and composers until the twentieth century. Although he knew it not, he was the founder of modern Europe and the champion of a new conception of kingship.

The Emperor Lothair, grandson of Charlemagne and inheritor of a third of his empire. A fourteenth-century portrait

EIGHT

Feudal Kingship

FEUDALISM WAS BASED ON the conception of the State as a pyramid, in which each layer of society obtained protection from, and owed obligations to, the layer immediately above it. The king was at the apex of this pyramid and it was to him directly or indirectly, that every layer owed loyalty. In strict theory the king was the sole landowner, the others being land-holders only. Powerful kings, such as William the Conqueror, Henry I, Philippe Auguste and Edward I, were able to give effect to this theory. Under weak, absentee or unpopular kings, such as Stephen, Richard and John, the theory broke down completely and civil war or anarchy ensued. In the then rudimentary condition of communications it was physically impossible for the king to be present in person in all the areas where trouble arose. He was obliged to delegate much of his authority to his counts and barons and, once fiefs became hereditary, it was inevitable that an exclusive baronial class should be constituted and that the local magnates should assert their independence of the central authority. By the thirteenth century, however, it was the principles of centralisation and security that triumphed.

The feudal theory was of mixed and ancient origin. Even before the Frankish invasion of Gaul, the Roman system of client and patron, the *patronicium*, had become well established. The Franks brought with them the Teutonic institution of the *comitatus*, or *Gefolgschaft*, namely the practice of free warriors pledging themselves to the service of a local chieftain. Each local chief, according to Tacitus, had his retinue of sturdy youths who ' were in peace an ornament and in war a protection ' (*in pace decus, in bello praesidium*). The teutonic *comites* owed to their chief the obligation ' to protect and defend him and to devote their prowess to his glory. The chief fights for victory, the *comites* fight for their chief '. Tacitus makes no mention of the reciprocal benefits which the *comites* obtained for their vassalage.

LORD AND VASSAL
During the period of anarchy that coincided with the Merovingian *rois fainéants*, when security could not be expected from the State, free men sought security by becoming the vassals of some local lord and castle-owner, capable of giving them at least local protection. The word ' vassal ' derives from the Celtic *gwas*, signifying ' boy ' or ' servant '. The act by which a free man placed himself under the *mundium* or *maimbour* of a seigneur was the *commendatio*. The lord promised his vassal food, clothing and protection in return for life-long obedience. It became customary for the lord also to accord his vassal a benefice in the form of land. The vassal would kneel before his lord and pledge fidelity and homage, swearing an oath of fealty; the lord would take the hands of the vassal between his own hands (*immixtio manuum*) and kiss him on the cheek. Thenceforward the contract between them became indissoluble; in the early days of feudalism neither the benefice (or fief), nor the vassalage, was hereditary. The bond was personal and sacred.

By the twelfth century the feudal system had become the basis of local government, of the administration of justice, of legislation and of all executive and military power. The theory was that all land, with its attendant obligations, was received from the Crown. The king was surrounded by an inner circle of tenants-in-chief - dukes, counts, barons and ecclesiastical dignitaries and houses - bound to furnish certain specified services in return for their lands. Their main obligation was to provide a specified quota of armed knights serving without pay for a specified period. They were also supposed to provide occasional ' aids ' or money payments and to attend the king's court as assessors. They owed to the king both loyalty (*fidelitas*) and honour (*obsequium*). The Monarch on his side was supposed to consult his tenants-in-chief in matters of major policy, to arbitrate in the quarrels which

Right: *Philip VI of France with his council in 1332. The Council's decisions were not binding on French kings*

incessantly arose between them, and to protect their rights and properties. At a later date the main towns and ports acquired charters giving them the rights possessed by tenants-in-chief.

Under the firm rule of Charlemagne, the tenants-in-chief were kept under some degree of discipline by his *missi dominici* or royal commissars, but on the break-up of the Carolingian Empire the counts and barons began to assert their independence of the central authority and to carve out almost independent principalities of their own. Once the lands and offices granted by the king became hereditary, the chain of personal allegiance snapped into its component links. Even quite small barons built their own fortresses, collected their own armed vassals around them, and became local tyrants and robbers. The workers were degraded to the status of slaves or villeins or serfs, bound to the land, and possessing no social or political rights whatever. Under weak monarchies, or when the supply of feudal levies declined and the central government were obliged to enlist mercenaries, the Crown would sell 'immunities' to religious houses and rich barons in order to obtain the necessary finance. By this process the power of the king was seriously diminished and anarchy increased.

ESTABLISHMENT OF ORDER

In the popular mind, however, the theory persisted that kingship represented the old Roman conception of order and justice and was the sole protection possessed by the little man against the local robber in the castle. By the thirteenth century, feudalism had ceased to be a stable political or military system; in its place the Royal Council or *curia regis* became the focus of government and was able to replace private by public law, to introduce an orderly and institutionalised Exchequer, to obliterate many of the castles erected by local chieftains, and to spread the idea that true security could only be found in the strength of kingship. Thereafter, under strong monarchs, the fear of tyranny became stronger than the yearning for order and security. The Angevins were suspected of seeking to establish absolutism, although in fact the word can have signified little to the mediaeval conscience. What in fact these able rulers were aiming at was order, security, stable administration, justice and therefore centralisation. During the long and various struggles between the king and barons, the mass of the people, the towns and the merchants were generally on the side of kingship, regarding a centralised tyranny as less capricious than a tangle of local tyrannies. In general also, the Church favoured the monarchy, which it regarded both as its champion and its servant. Essentially however the feudal system was an anarchical system; the pyramid did not possess a sufficiently wide base. It was bound in time to crack and topple.

One of the most curious examples of feudal monarchy was that established in the Latin kingdom of Jerusalem by Godfrey de Bouillon. It extended at the summit of its power from Beirut to the borders of Egypt. The fact that the crusading barons were the first to seize, occupy and fortify territories led them to regard themselves as the equals of their king and as such justified in expecting from him the defence of their rights and privileges rather than any assertion of his own supremacy. The first three kings were actually elected by the barons; but the theory that the king himself held his kingdom as a fief led to the feudal law of succession by heredity being applied to the monarchy. The real sovereign in Jerusalem was the High Court of Barons to the rulings of which the King was subject. He could claim to be souzerain only over the four great baronies and the twelve minor fiefs of his kingdom. The body of tenants-in-chief constituted the real sovereign power and their consent was necessary for all legislation. The possession by the barons of fortresses, such as the Krak des Chevaliers near the port of Tripoli, increased their independence, and adventurers such as Raynald de Chatillon, were able to use this mighty castle as a base for their raids on passing caravans.

Two great courts of Justice, the high court of the nobles and the court of the burgesses, were established in Jerusalem and dominated the central authority. The kings of Jerusalem, hampered as they were by extreme feudalism, and threatened as they were by the ever-increasing strength of Moslem hostility, did not long survive either the strain of government or the relaxation of what became a harem indulgence. Within a century Jerusalem, until its fall, witnessed the accession and death of as many as eleven kings. It is not surprising that this ramshackle and decentralised kingdom should have proved unable to withstand the holy war of Saladin and should within less than a century, have allowed the city of Jerusalem and the whole kingdom to slip from its grasp.

In France, during the feudal period, there was little sense of nationality. Although the poets of the *Chansons de Geste* would write all too frequently about *la doulce France*, although among the people there lingered a sentimental legend of the Christian kingship and the efficiency of Charlemagne, in fact there existed small sense of national unity. Even the language was not common to all the inhabitants. In Boulogne men used a teutonic dialect, in Brittany they spoke breton, in Gascony

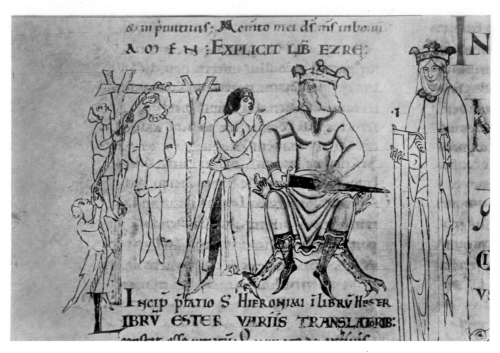

'*La Justice du Roi*', *from a twelfth-century manuscript at Dijon. This illustration to the Book of Esther (the handing of Hamon) demonstrates the mediaeval artist's idea of the strong king as the ultimate power in the land*

the language of the people was basque. A Frenchman living in the frontier provinces could not tell you whether he owed fealty to the kings of France or to the German emperors. The great territorial magnates (the Dukes of Normandy, Aquitaine, and Burgundy, the Counts of Flanders, Blois, Chartres and Anjou) were in fact independent princelings, owing but the vaguest loyalty to the Crown of France. Yet the Capetian kings, although in practice they exercised little authority outside the Ile de France, did retain a shadow of supremacy owing to the support of the Church and to their formal coronation at Rheims. The fact that they had been recognised as the successors of Charlemagne, above all the fact that they had been anointed from the *sainte ampoule*, did much to preserve their supernatural essence, and their myth. As I have said, it was for long believed that the king and the king alone possessed the divine power of healing and that the royal touch could cure a child from the then prevalent affliction of scrofula.

In France under the later Carolingians the kings were poorer and less powerful than the vassals and were obliged to confirm them in their rights by a succession of surrenders, or capitularies. On the death of Louis V, the last of the Carolingians, the Assembly at Senlis passed over his rightful heir, Charles of Lorraine, and elected Hugh Capet in his place. The early Capets were obliged to follow the conciliatory policy of the later Carolingians. Louis VI, known as 'Louis the Fat', who succeeded to the throne in 1108, was determined to enlarge his small Royal domain and to keep the road from Orléans to Paris clear of robber barons. With the aid of his gifted adviser, Suger, Abbot of St Denis, and after thirty-four years of constant fighting, he secured this objective and was able even to repulse an invasion attempted by the German Emperor, Henry V, in 1125. His successor Louis VII lost most of what Louis the Fat had secured and, had it not been for the constant support of the Church, the French monarchy might have become a vassal to the Angevin Empire of England. Fortunately his son Philippe Auguste was a man of political genius who by his campaigns and above all by his diplomatic combinations, restored and fortified the prestige of monarchy in France. He acquired Normandy, Anjou, Touraine, Maine and Poitou, created a royal army better equipped and disciplined than the old feudal levies, and founded the admirable civil service which to this day has remained one of the glories of France. His son, Louis VIII, died three years after his succession, leaving his remarkable widow Blanche of Castile as regent to their infant son Louis IX, known to posterity as 'Saint Louis'. The world-wide veneration felt SAINT LOUIS for this saintly monarch gave a new aspect to feudal monarchy. The King, by his virtue, his protection of the middle classes and the poor, by his hatred of war and brigandage, gave real meaning to the phrase 'The King's peace' and prepared the way for the destruction of feudalism and its replacement by a strong centralised monarchy. In the thirteenth century, under Philip the Fair, the central administration was fortified by the introduction of a unified system of law, based on Roman law and protected and administered by the *parlements* of Paris and the provinces. Yet the tradition of feudalism, or more accurately of regionalism, continued to subsist until the sixteenth century, when Francois I established absolutism and dominance of the royal will as the principle of French monarchy.

It was French kingship, owing largely to the constant support of the Church, that succeeded in imposing feudal monarchy in its strongest form. The great vassals were too powerful in their own territories to desire any cooperation with their rivals in contesting the subtly increasing power of the Crown. In England the conditions of the time deprived the feudal monarchy of its strength. Whereas the Capetians always produced male heirs to the Crown, thus avoiding disputed successions,

The funeral procession of Edward the Confessor at Westminster, 1066. From the Bayeux tapestry

England was again and again riven by the conflict of rival claimants. Owing to the wisdom of William the Conqueror the great vassals in England were less territorially concentrated than were the mighty vassals in France. When an unreliable monarch, such as King John, flagrantly violated his own feudal contracts, and first quarrelled with, and then subjected himself to, the Pope of Rome, the barons combined to impose on him the surrender of Magna Carta. In France it was centralised monarchy that triumphed in the end: in England, from the day of Magna Carta onwards, absolutism was more difficult to establish. Feudalism always contained within itself the elements of anarchy and it was above all in England that these elements prevented the triumph of absolutism.

In England, even after the conquest, the feudal system assumed a more native form. William the Conqueror, being an astute statesman, realised that such a thing as English nationalism existed and that his conquest and his autocracy would be less difficult to enforce if he could convince the conquered people that he was the legitimate successor of Edward the Confessor and determined to respect the customs of the realm. He thus maintained the unified system of taxation which had persisted since the days of the Danegeld, even as he maintained the Anglo-Saxon fyrd or militia. He also, at least in theory, allowed the old Witenagemot to survive, although he transformed it into a grand council of tenants-in-chief subservient to his own authority and demands.

William, Duke of Normandy, embarks for the invasion of England. From the Bayeux tapestry

The Saxon system of shires and hundreds was not abolished although it was reconstituted so as to become the instrument of the central authority rather than a focus of local opposition. The Conqueror, moreover, realising from experience how independent or rebellious a local magnate could become, took care that none of his dukes and counts obtained too much property in a single geographical area, and saw to it that the manors and estates that he so lavishly accorded to them were sprinkled throughout the shires and not concentrated in the counties which they administered. In preserving the old Saxon traditions and institutions, the Normans rendered their autocracy both more acceptable to the conquered people and more organic. Thus the Grand Council, developing as it did from the old gathering of tribal elders, the Witenagemot, became an organic development rather than a constitutional device. Whereas the English Council before long developed into a representative Parliament, the French States General never, even after 1789, became much more than what H. W. C. Davis has termed 'an ornamental feature in the French constitution'.

On August 1 1086 the Conqueror summoned all free tenants to a huge assembly at Salisbury and imposed upon them an oath of loyalty directly to himself. No Capetian king would have dared thus to cut across the oaths taken by tenants to their immediate seigneurs. The Salisbury Assembly marked an important difference between the English and the French systems. 'On that day,' writes Freeman, 'England became for ever a kingdom, one and indivisible, which since that day no man has dreamed of parting asunder'. It was different in France. Had it not been for the alliance of the Church, the magic of the coronation, the *sainte ampoule* and the fierce jealousies of the dukes, counts and barons, the French monarchy would not have survived.

ORIGIN OF THE
EXCHEQUER

There were other Anglo-Saxon institutions and customs which the shrewd Conqueror found it convenient to preserve. He continued to collect the Danegeld through the Sheriffs, who in France would have been called 'Vicomtes'. The money so collected was at first kept in chests in the King's bedroom at Winchester, but it soon became obvious that trained accountants must be employed. They did their receipt and expenditure notes on a chess board, similar to the abacus today so deftly used by a Chinese money changer at Nanking, and the public accounts department thus became known as the *Curia Regis ad scaccarium*, a Latin word subsequently anglicised into 'Exchequer'. The accounts themselves were preserved in what were called 'pipe rolls'. Thus the King, in his own bedroom, acquired control of finance.

In order to provide himself with an army, the Conqueror, while maintaining the old English fyrd, or militia, while granting rich lands to those who had accompanied him to Senlac and those who thereafter flocked across from Normandy to England, insisted on imposing the continental system whereby each vassal, and even the bishops and abbots, were obliged to provide a certain number of armed knights or pay a specified fee, or scutage, for exemption.

In England, as distinct from France, the king could rely for the most part on the support of an ever-increasing mercantile class. All that these city merchants desired was peace and stable government. They had learnt the sad lesson that under a weak or corrupt king public security deteriorated. 'Good governement in the middle ages,' wrote H. W. C. Davis, 'was only another name for a public spirited and powerful monarchy'. What the bourgeoisie dreaded more than anything was a disputed succession and civil war. Yet during the reigns of the Normans and Angevins automatic succession by primogeniture was not, as it later became, an axiom of kingship. A powerful king could oblige the barons to recognise, and swear fealty to, his eldest son and could persuade the Church to anoint the prince as 'king designate'. But a weak king could do nothing to secure the peaceful accession of his heir, since there persisted a sharp difference of opinion on the correct

Henry II and Eleanor of Aquitaine, from the twelfth-century church of Notre Dame du Bourg, Langon, France

principle. The Court jurists contended that the king was an absolute monarch by grace of God. The Church insisted on the fiction that the monarch was elected by 'the community of the realm', and that it was only after he had been crowned and anointed by the Archbishop, as Saul and David had been anointed, that he could claim the allegiance of his subjects. By this device they strove to preserve the theory that the Church alone could render legitimate the rule of any sovereign. Thus Stephen on his coronation proclaimed himself as 'by the grace of God, with the consent of the clergy and the people, elected King of England, consecrated by William Archbishop of Canterbury and confirmed by Innocent the Pontiff'. Yet Henry II, in his famous charter, styled himself merely as 'King by the Grace of God'.

Fortunately we possess an essay on mediaeval kingship composed by the remarkable man John of Salisbury and entitled *Policraticus*. John, although born at Old Sarum, was a cosmopolitan and a scholar. He was educated in Paris and at Chartres and crossed the Alps on visits to Rome no less than ten times. He was moderate and austere ('cruel only to himself') exercised great influence over his contemporaries, was a close friend of Thomas à Becket, had to escape into exile after the quarrel between Henry II and the Archbishop, was present at the murder in the Cathedral, retired to Rheims, and died in 1180.

THE ABSOLUTE
MONARCH
John of Salisbury took the organic view of the State. The limbs of the body politic were provided by workers; the administration, and especially the financial administration, represented the stomach, and were as such subject to acute bouts of indigestion: the councillors represented the heart; the king was the head; the Church the soul. Kingship, he contended, was not an indispensable institution, although a strong and public-spirited king was useful to the body politic. He alone could enforce the Law of God and it was this power which gave him a sacred character. The monarch thereby became the image of God on earth and treachery towards him should for this reason be punishable by death. Yet it was from the Church that he had received the sword of temporal power; he was both the representative and the guardian of the Church; if he acted against the holy faith, or disregarded the interests of the ecclesiastical hierarchy, his subjects were bound in duty to depose or even to assassinate him. John of Salisbury did not regard succession by primogeniture as an essential in the body politic. Yet candidates for the throne should preferably be chosen from among the members of the royal family and should, on their election, be approved by the Church. John of Salisbury had no conception of the king as the first servant of his people; once elected and anointed he must reign as an absolute monarch, limited only by his duty to defend the Church. A monarch who defied the Church or was too weak to preserve its rights and interests could no longer command the loyalty or allegiance of his subjects. All kings therefore owed their crowns to Rome.

By the barons and the mass of the people mediaeval kingship was in England regarded as limited only by the coronation oath. The Anglo-Saxon kings, from Edgar to Edward the Confessor, had, before being anointed, sworn to preserve the laws and customs of the realm. The oath taken was generally in the following prescribed form:

In the name of the Holy Trinity, I promise three things to the Christian people and my subjects. First, that God's Church and all Christian people of my dominions hold true peace; secondly that I forbid robbery and all unrighteous things to all orders; and thirdly that I promise and enjoin in all dooms, justice and mercy, that the Everlasting God of his everlasting mercy may forgive us all who liveth and reigneth.

It was in this form that the oath was administered by St Dunstan to King Ethelred; it was in this form that it was repeated by William the

The head of King John's beautiful effigy in Worcester Cathedral, to which he bequeathed his body

Conqueror. A breach of this contract was regarded as freeing the royal vassals from their oaths of allegiance. If an interdict were pronounced on the realm, or if the king were excommunicated, then his subjects were released from the duty of obedience. It was only with the expansion and intensification of national consciousness that the people as a whole came to resent papal intervention. Shakespeare was surely committing an anachronism when he placed in the mouth of King John a patriotic speech which, in 1215, would not have been framed in such flamboyant and selfconfident terms. 'What earthy name,' thundered King John to the papal legate:

> What earthy name to interrogatories
> Can task the free breath of a sacred king?
> Thou canst not, cardinal, devise a name
> So slight, unworthy and ridiculous,
> To charge me to an answer as The Pope.
> Tell him this tale; and from the mouth of England
> And this much more, that no Italian priest
> Shall tithe or toll in our dominions;
> But as we, under heaven, are supreme head,
> So under Him that great supremacy,
> Where we do reign, we will alone uphold,
> Without the assistance of a mortal hand;
> So tell the Pope, all reverence set apart
> To him and his usurp'd authority.

These are brave words, but they bear but slight relation, either to King John's subsequent recantation, or indeed to the mediaeval condition of public thought or feeling.

Mediaeval kingship, both in England and on the continent, followed more or less the same pattern, namely that of a recurrent struggle between anarchy and centralisation. The British flatter themselves that in their isolated island the passion for liberty was so endemic that it survived in the shires and the hundreds, rendering it difficult for the Norman conquerors to impose autocracy throughout the land. 'The survival,' writes Winston Churchill, 'of the hundred, the county court and the sheriff marks the great difference between English and continental feudalism . . . '. It was in the rural nobility and their 'untitled descendants', justices of the peace and knights of the shire that opposition to despotism survived. It might be more accurate to contend that the Normans and the Angevins were shrewd enough to realise that in these elements of rural organization, in these germs of local self-government, they possessed a machinery adapted to check the tendency of the barons to establish regional principalities, to keep the sheriffs up to standard, and to furnish the Crown with valuable instruments for their surveys and investigations. Yet, owing to our good fortune in having three kings of strength and statesmanship, - William the Conqueror, Henry I and Henry II - the local magnates did not in England succeed in defying the central authority to the outrageous extent that the French dukes asserted their independence. Under a weak king, as during 'the nineteen long winters' of Stephen's ineptitude, the local barons defied the royal discipline. They struck their own coinage, they imposed their own courts of justice, they levied fines and taxation, and in defiance of the royal prohibition they erected as many as 1,115 baronial castles of their own. When the central authority succeeded in enforcing its sanctions, in imposing its writ, as happened under Henry II, the turbulence of the feudal barons was checked and the King's writ became respected, sought for, and obeyed throughout the realm. Apart from kingship there were few other checks on the pretensions and depradations of the feudal barons.

It is true that even in the eleventh century the Church sought to mitigate the state of rapine and murder by proclaiming from time to time 'the Truce of God'. Under this edict ecclesiastics, peasants and noncombatants were to be left to pursue their avocations in peace; the fields were not to be laid waste nor the cattle abducted; and there were certain

The effigy of Henry II at Fontevrault Abbey, France. He gave England the soundest and freest government in Europe

seasons of the year, such as Lent, when the barons were forbidden to fight each other. One such Truce went so far as to proclaim that no fighting could be allowed except on Mondays and Tuesdays. This edict was disobeyed.

Another mitigating influence upon the brutal barons was the doctrine of chivalry. The orders of knighthood were at first not hereditary and the oaths that a young knight swore were personal as between himself, his master and his God. A knight would as a child serve for six or seven years as a menial or valet or squire in the castle of his prospective master. He would serve the meals, tidy the rooms, air the linen, and wash his lord. He would meanwhile receive his first lessons in horsemanship and the handling of sword, lance and shield. On reaching the age of eighteen he would undergo the ceremony of knighthood. He would be given a lustral bath and girded by his lord with the knightly sword. He was then 'dubbed' kneeling before his lord and being struck sharply on the neck by the baronial fist, a blow which in French chivalry was called the *colée* or accolade. To this very day the recipient of an English knighthood kneels on a little prayer-stool before his Sovereign and is dubbed firmly with a sword, first upon his right shoulder and then upon his left. He then rises from the stool and, if he be a practised or uninhibited courtier, kisses the hand of the monarch in token of fealty. As the institution of knighthood became even more formalised, the Church decided to intervene. The prospective knight was obliged to place his sword upon the altar and to undergo the 'vigil of arms' kneeling all night naked in prayer. The next day the young man would take a solemn oath to obey the orders of the Church, to defend the weak, to fulfil his feudal obligations towards his lord, not to tell lies, to be generous in distributing alms, to combat the infidel, and to fight always for the right against evil and injustice.

The age of chivalry, owing to the troubadours and the writers of romance, has acquired a glamour which it assuredly did not merit. Most of the young knights were riotous, cruel, conceited and delinquent; the much advertised idealization of womanhood, known as *le fin amour*, was often degraded into promiscuity; and the creation of a class of militant knights perpetuated an unhealthy caste system. I do not regard the *preux chevalier* of the twelfth century as an ideal type of manhood.

In theory at least chivalry was an elevating convention. The young knight was told that not only must he venerate the Church and protect priests from any form of persecution, but that it was bad form to sneer at the weak or the ill-favoured. 'It is,' wrote Chrétien de Troyes, 'a low born thing to laugh at someone else' (*Vilenie est d'autrui gaber*). A perfect knight, moreover, should be gay, and enjoy his adventures. *Jouyr loyalement de son estre* was a motto of chivalry, even as one should endeavour to render one's love affairs refined rather than brutal:

> A la joie appartient
> D'aimer moult finement.

Thus the young squire who rides with his father from Southwark to Canterbury singing songs along the pilgrim's way, was 'as fresh as is the month of Maye' and withal modest and prepared to help:

> Courteys he was, lowly and servisable
> And carf biform his fader at the table.

I suspect that Chaucer took as sentimental a view of chivalry as Shakespeare took of patriotism. I doubt whether *le fin amour* was always so squeamish, or whether the knights were always so chivalrous as our romantic poets have surmised. I suspect that Eustache Deschamps' description of the coarseness, the murders and the thefts, of chivalry was closer to the real thing:

> Las! Que j'ay veu de turbulacion.
> De grands orgeuils et de grands vanitez
> De traisons et de crudelitez!

Right: An illustration to Chrétien de Troyes' story of the Holy Grail, which symbolised the knightly virtues

telle maniere que nulz denlz, nauoit pou
oir de parler ains se regardoient auffi
comme cilz fussent tons bestes mues.
Lors entre leans le sainc graal couvert
dun blanc same mais il ny ot oncques
cellui qui peust veoir qui le portoit Si vint
par mi leurant huys du palais.

Et maintenant quil vfut entrez,
fu le palais remplie de si bonne
odeuvre que si toutes les espices

But let us take it that the ideals of chivalry did do something to curb the violence of the feudal age and to accord to woman the reverence that is her due. In the end, however, chivalry, even as its parent feudalism, declined into anarchy and, as Eustache Deschamps lamented, the old ideal of prowess became highway robbery:

> Chevalerie cesse
> Et valliance veult estre larronnesse.

A further check upon feudal kingship was exercised, or sought to be exercised, by the Pope of Rome. The forged documents that were supposed to justify the papal claim to temporal power, such as the Donation of Constantine and the False Decretals, were not, to any large extent, cited as justifying these claims. The theory was rather that Christ had handed his Church to St Peter, that St Peter had delegated it to the Bishop of Rome, and that the need to unite Christendom against the infidels and the heretics was primarily a papal responsibility. The earliest controversy between Church and State arose from the insistence of the Vatican on being the sole authority capable of consecrating bishops: this 'conflict of investiture' lasted for many generations and embarrassed many English and continental Kings. The great Pope Gregory VII went so far, in his *dictatus papae* of 1078, as to claim that he could if he wished depose the Emperor and release feudal vassals from their oaths of allegiance. As will be seen later, this mighty champion of ecclesiastical supremacy, having forced the Emperor to make obeisance to him at Canossa, died in exile at Salerno in 1085. In England an extreme conflict with the papacy was at first avoided by the tact of William I who was careful only to appoint bishops who would be agreeable to Rome. A compromise was reached over investiture under which the bishops were only chosen by the canons with royal aproval, and did homage to the king as his vassals. At the same time the ring and crozier, symbolising spiritual authority, could only be conferred upon them by the Pope. The Capetians, whose authority was always being challenged by the feudal magnates, found it necessary to manifest unconditional subservience to Rome. In England, where since the conquest the monarchy was self-reliant, the king felt able to assert the right to be independent in secular affairs. Henry I in 1101 had the courage to write to the Pope stating that 'the dignities and customs of the realm of England shall not be diminished in my life-time. Even if I should subject myself to this humiliation, which may God forbid, my barons and the people of England would not permit it'. It was indeed unfortunate that King

John, when embarking on his unneccssary quarrel with the Pope and thereby exposing himself to overt humiliation, did not bear this admirable precept in mind.

England on the whole benefitted much from her Norman and Angevin kings. William the Conqueror enforced royal authority by methods which, except in Yorkshire, were not too brutal. Henry I established the theory that the king was the Viceregent of God on earth and that for his people he was the guardian of peace and the champion of justice. By instituting the system of itinerant justices he rendered ' the king's law ' superior to baronial jurisdictions. The *Curia Regis* gradually acquired the prestige of a central government and high court. Henry II, possessing as he did rich dominions on the continent, was able to defy the English barons and to establish a central administration, so efficient and so powerful as to replace the by then rotting pyramid of the feudal system. ' A merely English King, ' writes H. W. C. Davis, ' could hardly have succeeded in bridling English feudalism with an administrative system so efficient, so impartial and so rigorous '. His purpose from the moment of his accession was to establish the rule of law, to curtail privilege, and to render the Crown supreme from the Tweed to the Pyrenees. By his ' Inquest of Sheriffs ' he put an end to the corruption of provincial satraps and replaced them by competent civil servants of his own choice and training. Kingship as an institution owes much to this

The effigy of Richard I, Coeur de Lion, at Fontevrault Abbey, France. More than any other English king, he epitomised the ideal of chivalry

hot-tempered, restless, red-headed, bandy-legged and resolute man. 'It is due to him,' writes Winston Churchill, 'that the English-speaking race all over the world is governed by the English common law rather than by the Roman'. It was he who introduced the jury system, thereby abolishing the old baronial jurisdictions and the absurd method of trial by ordeal of battle. Richard I, although he was in England only five months in a reign of nine and a half years, and mulcted his subjects in taxation for his foreign wars and his eventual ransom, did much to enhance the romantic glamour of monarchy and achieved the perhaps ill-deserved prestige of the superb crusader and the perfect knight. He was succeeded by his brother John who, as we shall see, was clever, competent, tricky and very much disliked.

KING JOHN OF ENGLAND

It was customary, when I was young, to represent King John as a monster of iniquity who fully merited what Bishop Stubbs called 'the deep and desperate humiliation' of having to sign Magna Carta on the meadow of the little island of Runnymede near Staines. The black portrait of King John is mainly due to the prejudices of two monks of St Albans, Roger Wendover and Matthew Paris. Modern research, while admitting his cruelty, his treachery and his morbid suspicions, suggests that he was unfortunate rather than ill-intentioned, and emphasises his great work as administrator, financier and founder of the British Navy. His fault was that, although a cunning tactician, both in war and peace, he was a deplorable strategist. He never seems to have foreseen the ultimate consequences of his impetuous manoeuvres. He was a suspicious, and therefore very mean, dwarf. Although he gained transitory popularity by his refusal to recognise the right of Pope Innocent III to intervene in what he regarded as the domestic affairs of England, he sacrificed that popularity by his final abasement to the papacy and by his transference of the realm to the Holy See as a papal fief. He antagonised the Church by the seizure of ecclesiastical properties; he outraged the barons by selling his 'Goodwill' for money, by his employment of alien adventurers and his invasion of their feudal rights; he turned the merchant class and the mass of the public against him by the taxation he exacted to support his wars and expeditions; and he lost all prestige by his defeats in France. The whole nation was shocked by his murder, in a fit of drunken Angevin rage, of his nephew Arthur. The barons were not without reason afraid that the mercenary army he was collecting for the ostensible purpose of regaining his French dominions would be used against themselves.

King John hunting stags. From the Cotton manuscripts in the British Museum, thirteenth century

At the feast of the Epiphany in 1214 the barons appeared in full armour and demanded to be accorded the Charter of Henry I. King John begged them to accord him a truce until Easter and spent the interval in searching for allies. He induced Innocent III to denounce the rebellion of the barons as 'factious and conspiratorial'; he exacted an oath of homage from the whole body of freemen; he sought to acquire the support of the monks and churchmen by promising them the right to elect their own ecclesiastical superiors. It was of no avail. The barons, the knights and the burgesses remained united in demanding what they called 'Henry's Charter', meaning thereby the liberties that 'the Lion of Justice' had at his coronation in 1100 promised and assured. The barons, accompanied by two thousand knights, met at Stamford and

163

The great seal of King John, affixed to a grant of lands to the Abbey of Bec, dated 31 March 1203, now in the possession of Eton College. It was with a seal similar to this that King Jhon signified his agreement to the Magna Carta in 1215, thus establishing the theory of the king's subjection to the law of the land

marched on London, which they entered on May 17. The King, who had bolted to Wiltshire, begged the barons to accept the arbitration of the Pope. They refused to make any concession, and on 17 June 1215 King John, mastering his Angevin rage, was obliged to capitulate and to sign the charter that was laid before him.

Professional historians, who take it as a duty to puncture the bubbles of popular myth, have told us that, so far from being a charter of democratic liberty, Magna Carta was no more than a contract between the King and his armed warriors under which he guaranteed the pretensions of a privileged class. It is true that, whereas the clauses dealing with the rights and privileges of the barons are explicit and detailed, those which accord rights to other classes of the community are curt and vague. Bishop Stubbs, the greatest authority on royal charters, asserted that it was a mistake to dismiss Magna Carta as doing no more than confirm the 'selfish exactions' of the barons, but that 'clause by clause the rights of the commons were provided for as well as the rights of the nobles'. Yet the Great Charter certainly does little to accord rights to the towns or the burgesses of the merchant class, whereas it does nothing specific to emancipate the serfs or to provide them with social and political justice.

It is not so much the text of Magna Carta that we should scrutinize as the force of the myth or legend it created. It became the talisman of succeeding generations of lawyers and statesmen who insisted in reading into it statements and promises of principle, which, in the conditions and language of 1215, were neither stated nor encouraged. It may be a myth to contend that Magna Carta laid the foundations of such democratic institutions as Habeas Corpus, trial by jury, no arbitrary arrest, no taxation without representation, and the equality of all, even the King, before the law. But it is certainly a historical fact that the interpretation given to the Magna Carta by succeeding generations both stimulated and justified the conceptions on which these mighty principles were based. That authoritative lawyer, Sir Edward Coke, in his *Commentaries* of 1629, laid it down when discussing Chapter 29 of the Charter that 'Upon this Charter, as out of a root, many fruitful branches of the Law of England have sprung'. He realised that the myth of Magna Carta had by then become more potent even than the actual text of the several chapters. 'Take we heed,' he said, 'what we yield unto: Magna Carta is such a fellow that he will have no sovereign'. Even Mr W. L. Warren, whose recent book on King John is so balanced and scholarly, admits that the legend of Magna Carta is not entirely baseless and that it has, not only when exploited in the seventeenth century, exercised a potent influence on English constitutional practice and theory. He writes:

> It was a code of law... established by royal charter at the prompting of the king's subjects. As such it opened the way to periodic revisions of custom and law and implied that the government should not be conducted to the damage of the governed. Moreover, by merely existing, it was a standing condemnation of the rule of arbitrary will.

The fact that the Pope had denounced the Charter as 'null and void of all validity for ever', and that this denunciation had been ignored, fortifies its character as a dominant national document. 'Many,' writes Mr Warren, 'who knew little and cared less about the contents of the Charter have, in nearly all ages, invoked its name, and with good cause, for it meant more than it said.'

To the contemporary world the surrender of Runnymede certainly appeared as an overt humiliation of kingship and a resounding assertion that the king himself was subject to the law of the land. Neither the king nor the Barons in fact intended to abide by the Charter. King John obtained the support of the Pope and began to enlist a mercenary army; the barons called up their knights in armour and allied themselves with France. Had not John died within the year from a surfeit of peaches and cider, civil war would have resulted and Great Britain might even have become an apanage of France. But John was succeeded by a child

King Edward I of England (1272-1307) in council with his bishops and attendants. The scribes, represented much smaller to signify their relative unimportance, sit in front

of nine, and the seething disturbance subsided under papal pressure and a prudent regency.

It was Edward I, with his conception of popular kingship, who finally abolished the feudal system in England and laid the foundations of the constitutional monarchy which took us more than four hundred and fifty years finally to establish.

NINE

Elective Monarchy

ONE OF THE STRANGEST ELEMENTS in monarchy is the almost magnetic attraction exercised by the hereditary principle. In primitive times the descendants of the medicine-men, or shamans, claimed to have inherited from their forefathers a fabulous gift which placed them in a specially intimate relation with the gods of fertility and which was transmissible to their children. In Egypt, and under other theocratic systems, the Pharaoh and his family were regarded as supernatural and as representing some divine incarnation. We have seen what elaborate myths and fictions were contrived by the Roman Emperors to preserve the principle of continuity and the almost mystic element of legitimacy. The magic aspect of monarchy became enshrined in the formula ' The Divine Right of Kings ' and was associated with the Old Testament dogmas regarding ' The Lord's Anointed '.

In the nineteenth century, after the fall of Napoleon, the principle of legitimacy was revived in order to reconcile public opinion to the restoration of the Bourbons. Louis Philippe, on assuming the crown, found himself severely hampered by the fact that he was utterly devoid of regal magic, and that his claim to be a ' citizen king ' was taken all too literally by the cartoonists and pamphleteers of his reign. Even in our own days the fabulous respect for royalty survives in its glamour and a certain sanctity; it is considered irreverent and almost blasphemous to make jokes in public about the royal family; and we are all conscious, when in the presence of the Sovereign, of a certain tension which is akin to awe. The feeling, for instance, which is shared by all members of the Commonwealth, that the Queen is both a universal and a private symbol of unity is a mystical rather than a rational emotion. Expedient though this feeling may be, it can in fact be traced to pre-historic times when the medicine-men were worshipped with fear. Superstitious affection - the sense that in some magic manner the Queen is the personal possession of all her subjects - has replaced anxiety. The Crown has long since become the symbol of unity rather than a symbol of discipline and order. The fact that the glamour of royalty survives as a feeling rather than as a thought, as a sentimental emotion rather than as a logical concept, does not diminish its efficacy. In the United Kingdom and in the British Commonwealth the fable of monarchy is often exaggerated to a degree that is irrational and sometimes nauseating. Yet it remains potent, widespread and beloved.

KINGS OR PRESIDENTS

Logically, of course, the presidential principle, whereby an individual is elected on his merits, is more defensible. It is improbable, as I have already said, that any dynasty will produce a succession of heirs, generation by generation, possessed of equal virtue or a compelling sense of responsibility. Yet, when Parliament is in fact the supreme sovereign in a State, it is possible, even if painful, to depose an unsatisfactory monarch and to maintain continuity by transferring the crown to his heir. The glamour, even if slightly tarnished, can be repolished and can shine anew. The processes by which a corrupt or ailing President can be removed are more complicated and may lead to internal dissension. Presidents are not addicted to voluntary abdication and it often requires a revolution to turn them out. It is the rational dread of interregnums, rival candidates, and civil wars which, more than anything else, has caused the hereditary principle, however illogical it may be, to survive for all these centuries. Yet it would assuredly not have survived had not all executive power been taken from the hereditary monarch and transferred to an elected Parliament. In Great Britain at least we have achieved the best of both worlds.

Among the Teutonic and Scandinavian tribes, to whom we owe so many of our institutions, so many of our social and political traditions, the rulers were elected on a restricted system. The Teutonic warriors, unlike the praetorians of the Roman Empire, could not elect anybody

An allegory of the arts and sciences, otherwise called ' the philosophical allegory of the Catholic Religion', by Gaddi in the Spanish Chapel of Santa Maria Novella in Florence. A beautiful evocation of the foundations of Renaissance monarchy

they thought of, even their own admired colonel. Their choice was confined to a male member of the ' royal ' family, namely an individual in whose arteries throbbed the blood of the former chieftain and who could claim to be in some manner the descendant of Wotan or Thor. The most suitable member having been chosen, he was ' acclaimed ' by' the warriors, yelling their approval and raising the chosen leader on their shields. Even so did the phalanx ' acclaim ' the King of Macedon by shouting their acceptance. To this day, as can be shown, in the ritual of the British Coronation service, the Sovereign undergoes the twin ceremonies of ' recognition ' and ' acclamation ', the former being conducted by the Archbishop of Canterbury and the shouting being done uniformly by the boys of Westminster School. Yet under the Teutonic system so many occasions arose when an uncle refused to acclaim his nephew as chief of the tribe, or when two brothers fought each other ferociously, that gradually, and not without frequent disputes and murders, the principle of primogeniture became established under which the heir to the throne succeded automatically once his father died.

THE BURDEN
OF KINGSHIP

Thus, in place of the disturbing methods of choice or election, legitimate succession became the rule. With all its possible disadvantages, it has its merits. The heir to the Crown, being destined from birth to fill his high position, can be trained and educated for his destiny. He acquires the habit of being able to recognize and remember people who, to the ordinary citizen, are just dull indistinguishable faces; he learns that it is his duty to obey the Government and to suffer fools with patience; he learns how to endure ceremony without manifesting overt signs of boredom; to learn how to be discreet in utterance and pleasing in appearance; he learns dignity; he learns humility under grandeur. Realising that for the vast majority of his subjects he represents the enhancement and idealization of the national character, his domestic life will be an example of constancy, austerity and self-denial. Subjected as he will be to ' that fierce light that beats upon a throne ', he will be aware that the slightest indiscretion, the momentary display of petulance or exhaustion, will be observed, reported and magnified. He will know that he is condemned, under the glare of arc-lights, to a life-sentence of hard labour; if he possesses the required reservoirs and aqueducts of duty, he will bow his head obediently to this cruel fate. He must be careful even not to take overt pleasure in pastimes that do not appeal to the common man; he must never indulge in irony or in the facile jokes that serve as the lubricants of social intercourse; he must laugh loudly when not amused and never laugh at some incident that would not be regarded by his subjects as a fit subject for hilarity. In fact he must surrender his personality to the exigencies of his task. He is bound in the process to become something of an automaton. I accord him my reverence and compassion.

Such is the fate of constitutional monarchs who are born to their high altitude. Yet, in fact, the elective system, logical though it may

Right: *The Emperor Otto receiving the homage of the nations. From a manuscript at the Musée Condé at Chantilly*

seem, has not in Europe proved a success. Let me take as examples the Holy Roman Empire and the Polish Constitution.

The late Lord Bryce, in his classic work upon *The Holy Roman Empire*, does not agree with those who contend that his coronation in St Peter's on Christmas Day 800 was sprung upon Charlemagne by a Pope desiring to establish the principle that he alone possessed the right to create Emperors. Lord Bryce argues that Charlemagne in the eyes of his contemporaries had justified his claim to be the Defender of the Church and that the paladins, knights and warriors would have regarded his coronation, not as a sacerdotal trick but as 'natural and right'. To them it appeared logical that, even as the Visible Catholic Church, uniform in faith and ritual, should exercise undisputed authority over the spiritual lives of men, so also should there exist a Roman Empire protecting and safeguarding both the Church herself and the unity of the Christian world. To them the coronation of Charlemagne was no sudden innovation but the continuance of the Empire founded by Augustus. They regarded Charlemagne as the sixty-eighth successor of Augustus Caesar, and as the true inheritor of Rome. To them the mighty name of Rome still signified solidity, unity, justice, peace and order.

In later centuries this simple theory was blurred by partisan interpretations. The Swabian Emperors claimed that the Crown had been secured by military conquest and that the Bishop of Rome had no right to intervene. The ecclesiastical party contended that no man could claim to be Emperor unless accepted, crowned and anointed by God's Vicar on earth. And the populace and nobles of Rome argued that only by the vote of the SPQR could an Emperor claim to have been legally installed. Bryce denies these claims. 'Charles,' he writes, 'did not conquer; nor the Pope give; nor the people elect.' In practice Charlemagne regarded himself as the visible and autocratic head of Christendom, as the judge and ruler of all his subjects. He controlled the ecclesiastical body and again and again in his capitularies did he emphasize his almost theocratic status.

With the death of Charlemagne and the ensuing partition and disintegration of his Empire, the conception of the Emperor of Christendom, wielding both spiritual and temporal despotism, became inapplicable. By 888 the Carolingian Empire had dissolved into anarchy and fell a prey to Viking, Hungarian and Moslem invaders. It was Otto I, justly called Otto the Great, who suppressed the rebellious German princelings, defeated the Hungarian invaders, allied himself with the Pope, assumed

A twelfth-century fresco in the church of Santi Quattro Incoronati, Rome, illustrates the legend that the Emperor Constantine bestowed temporal authority on the Papacy. Constantine kneels before Pope Sylvester I and hands him the cap of authority

the title of King of the Lombards, and was crowned by Pope John XII as Holy Roman Emperor on 2 February 962.

The mediaeval world, although not given to political speculation, was content with the dual conception of a world-church and a world-monarchy, so closely knit together in purpose and interests that they constituted between them an indissoluble line of continuity. The Church was regarded as the soul and the Empire as the body, each dependent on the other. To the Pope, the visible head of the eternal Church, was entrusted the care of souls; the Emperor, being human and temporal, was the guardian of men's bodies and acts. This theory of dual rule was but rarely expressed in practice. The churchmen came to contend that the Pope was in fact the head of Christendom and that only through him could the Emperor derive his authority. The Emperor was regarded as the 'Defender and Advocate of the Christian Church'. A mosaic in the Lateran depicts St Peter handing to the Pope the keys of heaven and hell and to the Emperor the banner of the Christian army. Yet the Papacy during the years of anarchy lost prestige owing to the dissolute habits of successive Popes and became more and more dependent upon the support of the Emperor's armies.

Otto the Great was at one and the same time Holy Roman Emperor and autocrat of all the Germanies. When the feudal system penetrated into Germany, the Emperor came to be regarded as the Lord Paramount of Europe ' holding the world from God '. Gradually the great offices of the Household (those of cup-bearer, seneschal, and marshal of Empire) were distributed among the regional dukes and margraves, who, as they increased in power and importance, developed into the ' electors ' who chose the Emperor from a limited number of royal houses.

Otto well realised that his function as Holy Roman Emperor and his function as King of the Germanies, his feudal position as Lord Paramount and his national status as a German autocrat, were not compatible. He felt that great issues in politics are determined, not by theories or even traditions, but by the possession of overwhelming force. Thus when Pope John XII was discovered to be intriguing with the Hungarian barbarians and adhering to the Emperor's enemies, Otto descended as a whirlwind upon Rome, deposed the Pope, abolished the republican institutions of the Roman aristocracy and populace, and obtained from his nominee Leo III the concession that in future the Emperor had the right to veto a papal election.

A conflict between the Emperor and the Papacy had become inevitable, and when, under the reforms of Hildebrand, who became Pope Gregory VII, the papacy recovered its prestige, a fierce battle ensued between the Pope and the Emperor Henry IV.

THE CLAIM OF PAPAL SUPREMACY

The clergy based their claim for papal supremacy on two series of forged documents. There was in the first place the *Donation of Constantine* under which the first Emperor of the East was held to have granted to Pope Sylvester, not only spiritual dominion over the patriarchates and in all matters of faith and worship, but also temporal dominion over Rome, Italy, and ' the provinces, places and cities of the western regions '. This document, which served as the foundation of the Pope's claim to temporal power, was accepted without question by the mediaeval world. It was not until 1440 with the approach of the Renaissance that the scholar Laurentius Valla questioned its authenticity. It is now dismissed as a forgery perpetrated about 775 by a clerk in the Roman curia. By the *False Decretals* composed by Isidore in 850 the Popes

Henry IV waits outside the gates of Canossa. From Fox's Book of Martyrs, 1563

claimed unlimited authority throughout Christendom in all cases affecting the clergy or included under canon law.

Hildebrand himself never doubted the authenticity either of the *Donation* or of the *Decretals*. He was convinced that it was his mission to restore to the Church its purity, its discipline and its power. He began by fighting against simony, feeling that too many of the high offices of the Church had been secured by corrupt means. He then proceeded to insist upon the celibacy of the clergy. However much the clergy themselves may have resented these reforms, it was not for the Emperor as the Defender of the Catholic Church to oppose them. But Hildebrand, with his Lombard tactlessness, was resolved to go further. He launchep the 'Battle of Investiture' decreeing that it was a sin for any cleric to obtain preferment from lay hands or to hold any benefice to which secular obligations were attached. In so decreeing, he was assailing the inner keep of feudalism. Half of the wealth and land of Germany was in those days in the hands of bishops or abbots, and to release them from their feudal obligations was to assail the rights and powers of the territorial rulers. Henry IV as Lord Paramount refused to authorize this decree. He was summoned to appear in Rome and to be judged for his misdemeanours. The Emperor replied by convoking a Synod which was instructed to depose Gregory VII. Thus challenged the Pope replied

176

by excommunicating the Emperor and by threatening to place all imperial territories under an interdict. To such a threat the Emperor was obliged to surrender. He journeyed to the castle of Canossa in the Appenines, where Gregory VII was then in residence, and stood in the snow of the courtyard, bare-footed and clad in the brown shirt of a penitent craving forgiveness. This was grudgingly granted, but the quarrel was not healed during the reigns of Henry IV or Gregory VII. Henry V, when he succeeded his father, was more ruthless. He went so far as to imprison Pope Paschal II when he refused to crown the new Emperor unless he formally admitted papal supremacy. In the end an agreement was reached in the Concordat of Worms of 1122, by which the Emperor renounced the right of investiture and the Pope admitted the right of the Emperor to demand feudal service from ecclesiastics possessing fiefs within the Empire. But the spirit of nationalism had by then been aroused. German patriotism thereafter centred around opposition to what they called 'Italian priestcraft'.

This summary account of the struggle between the Emperor and the Pope is essential to any understanding of the stages by which the Emperor became less and less Roman and more and more German. The controversy flamed anew under Frederick I, the mighty Barbarossa, and after twenty years of violence an agreement was negotiated by the mediation of the Doge, Sebastiano Ziani, and Pope and Emperor publicly embraced each other in the Porch of St Mark's at Venice. In the interval the rivals had each strengthened his position. The Pope had gained the alliance of the Lombard cities who resented being bullied and taxed by a German Prince. The Emperor had been fortified by the revived study of Roman

FREDERICK
BARBAROSSA

Frederick Barbarossa drowned in Cilicia in 1190. From the ' Sachsischen Weltchronik '

law. He was hailed as 'the living law upon earth'. In the end, Barbarossa was defeated by the Lombard League at Legnano, and by the Peace of Constance he surrendered all but titular control of the Lombard cities. He died in 1189 when on the Crusade, being drowned when bathing in the Kalykadnus, a river of Cilicia. But the German legend insists that he lives on, hidden and asleep in a cavern of the Kyffhauser, waiting to be aroused to battle by the appeal of his countrymen. He continued none the less to slumber under the mountains of Thuringia in 1918 and again in 1945.

GERMAN PRINCES
OF THE EMPIRE

By the twelfth century, when all fiefs had become hereditary and the great feudal magnates had established their independence and power, the idea gained ground that the Empire was not the family possession of the Emperor but belonged to the totality of the German princes and barons. It thereafter seemed fitting that the choice of Emperor should rest with the leading feudal magnates. As early as 1156 the expression 'Prince Electors' gained currency. When in 1268 the Emperor disappeared, Conradin was captured, like Cicero, at Astura, and beheaded by his rival, Charles of Anjou. The Emperor lost all connection with Rome, and even with Italy. The electors would have been prudent in deciding that the Holy Roman Emperor had fulfilled his function and that, with the extinction of the Hohenstaufen dynasty, the vain title of Holy Roman Emperor should be abandoned. Instead of coming to this sensible conclusion they proceeded to elect Richard Plantagenet, Earl of Cornwall, and brother of King Henry III of England, as Holy Roman Emperor. Richard refused to pay to the electors the huge bribes that they expected and they therefore cancelled the election and chose in his place Alfonso of Castille. Richard Plantagenet died and Alfonso remained at Toledo, studying astronomical works of reference. A period followed when there was no Emperor and which goes by the name of the 'Interregnum'. With no feudal superior to control them, the German

An Augustale of Frederick II from Brindisi

Charles V presiding over the Diet of Augsburg in 1530. On the Emperor's left are the three spiritual electors, the Archbishops of Mainz, Cologne and Trier (the latter's throne vacant); on his right, the temporal electors of Saxony, Brandenburg and the Elector Palatine

princelings became robber barons and the country was exposed to chaos. The Pope, distressed by the anarchy which ensued, insisted that an Emperor should be chosen. The electors, more or less in despair, and not wishing to place above them any princeling of superior military power, chose Rudolph, the founder of the Hapsburg dynasty. From 1437 to 1806, with but few intermissions, the imperial crown remained a perquisite of the Hapsburg dynasty.

Is it correct to describe the Holy Roman Emperor as elected or as succeeding by hereditary right? Was the Empire a *Wahlreich* or an *Erbreich?* The answer is that it was both. The electors were obliged, owing to the mystic glamour of royal blood, or *Gebluthsrecht*, to choose the candidates from a limited circle. On the other hand nobody could claim to be Emperor unless he had been chosen and designated by the electors. The elective formula was in fact adopted as an alternative to the papal claim that the Church alone could nominate an Emperor. When Pope Clement VI demanded that the Emperor Lewis should

The Emperor Charles V enters Bologna for his coronation by Pope Clement, who is seen accompanying him. A detail from a fresco at the Palazzo Ridolfi at Verona

admit that the Empire was a fief of the Holy See, the Diet of Frankfurt replied by issuing a declaration in 1337 to the effect that the Empire was held from God alone, and that an Emperor, once he had been duly elected by the Princes, needed no confirmation or approval from the Bishop of Rome. The freedom of the electors was also limited by what was known as the 'Salic Law', under which no woman could succeed to a monarchy. In fact the Salic Law was not a political document but a penal code, deriving from Merovingian and Frankish times, and assessing the fines and penalties for criminal offences. In one sector it happened to contain a chapter relating to the inheritance of private property in which it was laid down that daughters cannot inherit land. This proviso, by a transference which seemed perfectly logical to the feudal mind, became interpreted as the exclusion of all females from the royal succession. This was a misinterpretation, or in any case an extension, which caused much constitutional and political controversy in later centuries.

For example, when in 1711 the Emperor Joseph I died without male issue, his successor Charles VI endeavoured to provide under his 'Pragmatic Sanction' that the Salic rule should be reversed and that his daughter, Maria Theresa, should on his death succeed to all the Austrian possessions. He sought to obtain international recognition for this succession law and the Pragmatic Sanction was in fact accepted by the nine Great Powers. Yet on the death of Charles VI in October

1740, Frederick II of Prussia repudiated his promise and launched upon the War of the Austrian Succession. Maria Theresa, being admittedly disqualified from succession to the Empire, remained ruler of the Austrian territories and was accepted by Hungary. Her husband, Francis of Lorraine, was crowned Holy Roman Emperor as Francis I in 1745. His enlightened but unfortunate son succeeded him as Joseph II.

It was, as I have said, the continued and recurrent pressure of the papacy to secure the adoption of the ecclesiastical theory that the Emperor could be chosen as well as crowned by the Pope, that led the German princes to insist that the office of Emperor was too holy to be transmissible by descent and that the leading bishops and magnates of the Germanies should be empowered by God, and without the intervention of the Pope, to choose their own Emperor. An electoral college was constituted. A group of leading bishops and princes would draw up a list of suitable candidates and the names agreed to were then presented to the nobles for a final vote. This short list of candidates was known as the 'Praetaxation', and it was the magnates who were recognised as having the right to draw up the list who gradually became the electoral college. It later became the rule to dispense with the vote of the lesser nobles and to leave the choice of Emperor to the electoral college. In the early ordinance, the *Sachsenspiegel*, the electoral college consisted of six magnates, namely the archbishops of Mainz, Treves and Cologne together with the Palatine of the Rhine, the Duke of Saxony, and the King of Bohemia. To these was added the Margrave of Brandenburg and eventually the Duke of Brunswick, the King of Hanover. The body of these eight electors became immensely powerful and insisted on receiving, in return for their votes, all manner of concessions, called *Wahlcapitulation*, from prospective candidates. Each of these was able in the end to obtain the title of 'King' and to establish his own dynasty. In the process of successive surrenders to the electoral body, the *Kurfürstenverein*, the Emperor lost power and prestige. Thus, whereas England, France, Denmark, Hungary, Poland, Italy and Burgundy had thrown off even the fiction of allegiance to the Holy Roman Empire, and when the Emperor himself had lost his Italian possessions and could no longer appeal to the magic name of Rome, the Empire became in fact a purely German institution, a generally accepted privilege of the House of Hapsburg. Yet the Austrian Emperors, although for the most part men of ability and good will, were inclined to subordinate the interests of the Germanies as a whole to the interests

CHOICE OF
THE EMPEROR'S
SUCCESSOR

of the House of Hapsburg. The spirit of criticism and realism that developed during the Renaissance tended to diminish the magic of the Roman name, and to confine the authority of the Emperor to juridical questions, as represented by the *Reichskammergericht*. The Reformation split the Germanies into the two factions of Protestant and Catholic and the claim of the Hapsburgs to have authority over all German subjects became questionable.

The Empire by the eighteenth century had declined into a very loose confederation of German princes under the presidency of the Hapsburgs. The title of Holy Roman Emperor was by then little more than a ' convenient legal conception ', and the Diet, to a man of Frederick the Great's acute realism, represented no more than ' dogs in the yard, baying at the moon '. It was Frederick the Great who demonstrated that a small Power, if it possessed an excellent army and was led with genius, could successfully defy the Emperor, France and Russia combined. His foundation of the *Fürstenband* checked the ambitions and dreams of Joseph II and by the end of the eighteenth century ' strings of resounding titles were all that was left of the Empire that Charles had founded, and Frederick had adorned, and Dante had sung '. It perished because it failed to recognize that sovereignty, if it is to be effective, must be founded on ultimate superiority of force.

On 6 August 1806, the Emperor Francis II, fearing that Napoleon would claim to be Holy Roman Emperor as successor to Charlemagne, resigned the title. From the day that Leo had crowned Charlemagne in St Peter's, the title of Holy Roman Emperor had lasted for 1006 years.

WEAKNESS OF
THE POLISH
CONSTITUTION

A more tragic example of how sovereignty can be reduced to impotence by an illogical constitution, is provided by the history of Poland. A mighty nation can be lured to destruction when sovereignty is too widely distributed and when individual dissidents can, while remaining within the law, challenge the authority of the central government and force it to cease its function. The predatory enemies of Poland, scenting its coming dissolution, soared like vultures above its sick body, waiting for the end.

We should remember that in the seventeenth century, Poland was, after Russia, the largest country in Europe, and contained a population of eleven-and-a-half million, greater than that of France, Spain, England or the German Empire. Its people were industrious and highly intelligent. Yet its whole constitution was founded on the theory of the Contractual State, the relations between the central authority and the

Archbishop Peter Aichspalt of Mainz, who presided over the electoral college of the Emperors, with King John of Bohemia, the Emperor Henry VII and the Emperor Ludwig of Bavaria

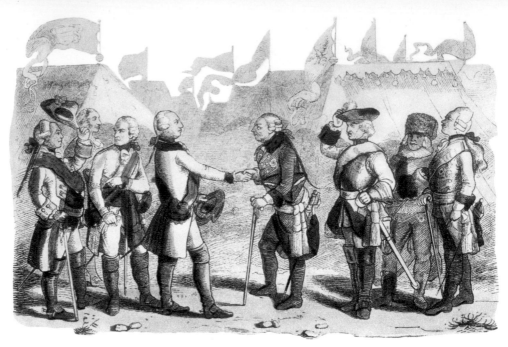

The Emperor Joseph II won the esteem and admiration of his great adversary, Frederick II, before Neustadt in Moravia. The Emperor is accompanied by the Field Marshals Laudon and Lascy, and Prince Kaunitz, the Minister of State; while the King of Prussia is attended by his generals Dessauer, Ziethen and Schwerin

component parts being governed by pacts and convenants which destroyed the authority of each. These contracts, or *Pacta Conventa* as they were called, were entered into whenever a new king was elected. As the electors gained in power they strove still further to diminish the central authority of the monarchy, and with every new accession the number of contracts increased. Thus the obligations imposed on his accession upon Stanislas Poniatowski in 1764 were many times more numerous and compulsive than those that had been extracted from Henri de Valois in 1573. If the King failed, in the opinion of the Diet, to execute his engagements under the contract, then all Polish subjects were freed from their allegiance. The King was not merely a puppet in the hands of the Polish nobility and gentry, but his subservience was openly acknowledged and published in his coronation oath.

No constitution ever devised by the ingenuity or selfishness of man, not even the very worst constitution of ancient Greece, could be compared in ineptitude to that with which the Polish landowners saddled their unhappy country. By the seventeenth century the monarchy had been stripped of all executive power and reduced to purely representative functions. It was elective and not hereditary, with the result not only that on the death of the monarch the country was exposed to long interregnums and the consequent emergence of rival claims, but that opportunity was accorded to foreign Powers to intrigue, bribe and threaten, in the hope of securing their own candidate's election.

Legislative and executive power passed to the Crown Diet, composed of a Senate consisting of archbishops, bishops and leading officials and a House of Deputies composed of, and elected by, the gentry. It contained no representatives of the cities or the Church. A totally illogical provision in the constitution, and one which abolished all continuity of government, was the fantastic institution of the free veto, or *liberum veto*. According to this provision, any deputy or senator had merely to rise in his place and to pronounce the words *nie pozwulam*, or ' I protest ', not only to secure the defeat of any measure before the Diet, but also to cancel any previous legislation passed by that Diet, and to ' explode ' the Diet, or in other words to force a dissolution. Since there were as many as 182 deputies from the gentry, it was abundantly possible for vested interests, or a foreign ambassador, to buy the vote of a poor deputy to bring all government to a standstill.

INSTITUTION OF THE FREE VETO

The absurdity of this provision was recognised by all Polish patriots and again and again endeavours were made to abolish it. In 1768, for instance, a reform was introduced, whereby the veto applied. to certain specified branches of legislation, the majority vote prevailing in regard to other branches. But, since the legislation embodying this reform was in itself subject to the veto, and since the expectant vultures did not desire any change in the existing suicidal constitution, the reforms came to nothing. The Administration itself was a further check on central authority. No civil servant could be dismissed, and the administration therefore came to regard itself as an independent body, secure in its opposition to the government.

As time passed, it became widely recognised that, whatever may have been the purpose of the original framers of the Constitution, it had since become warped, or what Professor Skwarczynski charitably called ' deformed ', by sectional interests and ambitions. The Four Years Diet of 1788-1792 strove desperately to introduce a new Constitution under which the contractual principle was to be abandoned. The monarchy was to be rendered hereditary and accorded greater powers, the cities were to be given self-government and the peasants were to be protected against oppression. These reforms were opposed by Russia, whose representative at Warsaw, Prince Repnin, assumed the authority of a Russian satrap or governor.

In 1772 the vultures had descended on their prey and by the first partition had torn the dying body into three sections. They at the same

time accorded a new constitution to what remained of a lacerated Poland. Both the elective monarchy and the *liberum veto*, as guarantees that Poland would remain weak and disunited, were retained in this constitution. Russia refused to permit the constitution drafted by the Four Years Diet. Russian troops entered Polish territory and resistance was offered by the small Polish army under Kosciuszko. But King Stanislas, a patriotic and enlightened man, feeling it hopeless to resist the might of Russia, disbanded his army, and agreed to abolish the constitution drafted by the Four Years Diet as being a 'dangerous novelty'. The second partition occurred in September 1793. Kosciuszko appealed for a national resistance and after many initial successes was eventually defeated and captured by the Russian armies. Stanislas Poniatowski was denounced as 'an intruder and usurper' and retired to St Petersburg, the origin of his strange fortune, where he died. In 1796 the third partition was perpetrated, and Poland was wiped off the map of Europe.

Napoleon, with his creation of The Grand Duchy of Warsaw, did something to repair this international crime and the Congress of Vienna created a small independent state under Russian protection known as 'Congress Poland'. The risings of 1830 and 1863 were suppressed by Russian troops, and until the liberation of 1918, Poland became little more than a Russian province, which, in effect, it has since again become.

THE COLLAPSE OF POLAND

Historians have often discussed whether the fall of Poland was due to its monarchy being elective and not hereditary, or whether it was due mainly to the selfishness of the gentry and the institution of the *liberum veto*. The fact that those neighbouring monarchs and statesmen who desired the disintegration of the country and who aimed at partitioning it between themselves, always insisted that the veto should be retained and the monarchy remain elective, shows that these two elements in the constitution effectively hampered national unity and prevented national resistance. Whereas France and England, under hereditary monarchies, had become powerful, independent States, and could enforce their will upon their rivals, the Holy Roman Empire and Poland became little more than geographical expressions, unable to resist the rapacity of their neighbours. History, if it teaches us anything, teaches us that hereditary monarchy may be illogical, but proves, in certain stages of civilization, by far the best method of preserving national unity and power.

Left: *A cartoon by Moreau le Jeune on the partition of Poland in 1772, showing Catherine the Great, Stanislaus II of Poland, the Emperor Joseph II and Frederick the Great*

TEN

The Divine Right of Kings

IN CHAPTER TWO I CONSIDERED the stages by which the medicine-man of primitive tribes became the king-priest of the community. Once hunting ceased to be the sole method of obtaining food, once pastoral and agricultural methods provided the means of subsistence, the king-priest came to be regarded as possessing some magic contact with the forces of nature and was venerated as the incarnation of the gods of fertility. So close was this identification, that the king, once his physical powers waned and he ceased in any overt way to personify fertility, was liable to be put to death and to be replaced by a younger and more vigorous successor. Yet the theory remained that the magic communication between the king and the gods, the magic gift of being able to invoke fertility, was in some manner hereditary and transmitted from generation to generation. The royal family became in this manner sacred and even divine: although it took many centuries before the system of primogeniture was accepted as the most convenient method of succession, it was generally believed that only members of the royal blood inherited magical properties, including the gift of healing, and that if a king were to be elected, he must at least pretend to be descended from royal ancestors.

In some cases, notably in the Far East, the qualities of king and priest continued to be mystically combined and the Chinese Emperors or the Japanese Mikados, although not to the same extent as the Dalai Lamas, obtained the status of theocrats. Yet since the hereditary principle cannot always produce an unbroken succession of competent sovereigns, a system was evolved whereby the magic properties of the priest remained in the sacred royal family, while the executive properties of the king were transferred to more dependable hands. Thus in Japan executive powers were wielded by the Shoguns, and were transferred under the Merovingian *rois fainéants* to the Mayors of the Palace. The kings and the Mikados were accorded ceremonial functions only, presiding at religious festivals and possessing only hierophantic prestige.

In Europe, where the tradition of imperial unity and order survived from Roman times, a dichotomy developed between the idea of religious unity and the conception of secular unity. The Pope, as head of the Church, symbolised the unity of Christendom: the Emperor, as the inheritor of Roman empire, was at least supposed to symbolise the unity and order of the lay world. For centuries this dichotomy of theory, this partition of allegiance, produced a conflict of policy. The Pope claimed that he was supreme ruler of the secular as well as the religious world, owing to the inheritance of St Peter and such fraudulent concessions as the Donation of Constantine. The Emperors and the kings felt obliged to fortify their claims to supremacy or independence by inventing a supernatural sanction of their own. It was thus that there arose the myth of the 'Divine Right of Kings'.

ORIGIN OF THE MYTH

The contention of the more unbiassed theologians was that God, in the desire to further and to protect the cause of Christendom, had chosen two equal vicars to rule the world, the Pope to regulate ecclesiastical matters and the Emperor to defend the Christian States against the infidels and to prevent internecine strife. Yet the theologians of the middle ages were not unbiassed. The clergy claimed that the Pope, as the heir to St Peter, possessed complete power (*plenitudo potestatis*) even in secular affairs, and that any sovereign who resisted the commands of the Papacy was guilty of defying 'the ordinance of God'. The upholders of national and secular independence, often in the course of this everlasting controversy denounced as 'Erastians' or 'Imperialists', relied upon such scriptural texts as 'Render unto Caesar' and 'My kingdom is not of this world', to contend that St Peter and his successors had no right to claim such predominance. They were much assisted in imposing this theory by the growing tide of nationalism, and by

Dante Alighieri, a portrait by Andrea del Castagno at the Convent of Sant' Apollonia, Florence. 'What could be accomplished by one man,' wrote Dante, 'is better done by a single ruler than by many rulers'

the counter-theory that no Italian priest should be allowed to interfere in the internal affairs of sovereign states. In asserting or denying these two opposing theories of Church or State supremacy, the theological and political controversialists of the period did much to concentrate men's thoughts upon the nature of sovereignty and the basis of kingship.

Dante, who had suffered atrociously from the rivalries and vengeance of the Italian city-states and their pugnacious factions, dreamt of a totalitarian world in which, under imperial discipline and even despotism, the individual citizen could enjoy security and pursue happiness. While admitting that the Pope should possess supreme authority in spiritual matters, he contended that the Emperor should be supreme in all secular matters and should dominate all those whom he called the

Latini, namely that section of human society that derived from the Roman Empire and in which the Latin language was the common tongue. He thereby excluded from his examination the Eastern Empire and the infidels.

Within what we should now call 'the free world', the Emperor should be recognised as an autocrat, who, in that he was possessed of everything desirable, would have no ambition to obtain the possessions of anyone else. Peace and order were the supreme needs of men and a single Emperor was more likely than any other ruler to establish on earth that serene order that we all so much admire in the constellations. 'What could be accomplished by one man,' Dante wrote in his *De Monarchia* of 1310, 'is better done by a single ruler than by many rulers' (*quod potest fieri per unum melius est per unum fieri quam per plura*). It was the 'manifest will' of God that a German Emperor should rule Europe, even as it had been his 'manifest will' that the Roman Empire should impose on all the habits of peace. Had it not been that God warmly approved of the Roman Empire, he would not have chosen as the birth place of his son one of the most obscure corners of the mighty commonwealth.

It was only by being subject to a single ruler that the several sections of humanity could be adapted to an organic whole. Unlimited monarchy was essential to the welfare of mankind and ordained by God. The Emperor therefore did not derive his authority from the Pope: he derived it directly from God himself. Man, being partly composed of corruptible and partly of incorruptible elements, must aim both at blessedness during his life on earth and blessedness in the life hereafter. The first could be achieved by expressing in one's daily life what was best in one's own faculties (*in operatione propriae virtutis*): the second, which transcends human reason or calculation, can only be achieved through Faith, Hope and Charity. It was the secular arm that could alone enable the individual to achieve security and self-expression. The Pope could guide us towards eternal life, but should not intervene in matters pertaining to life upon this earth: 'The authority of temporal kingship derives directly from the fountain of universal kingship'.

A specially British aspect of this controversy is given us by John Wycliff, the translator of the Bible and the clergyman who went so far as to condemn the Papacy as 'anti-Christ'. At Balliol, of which he later became Master, he absorbed those dreams of a Free Church in a Free State which since his day became one of the traditions and the

191

A wood-engraving from Fox's Book of Martyrs showing Wycliff's bones being burned and the ashes cast into the River Avon. Wycliff was a great upholder of the legend of the Divine Right of Kings

glories of that enlightened college. Being a progressive, he was supposed to have inspired the Lollard movement. After his death his body was dug up by Richard Fleming, Bishop of Lincoln, his bones incinerated and the ashes cast into the Avon:

> The Avon to the Severn runs
> The Severn to the sea
> And Wycliff's dust shall spread abroad,
> Wide as the waters be.

The Severn certainly gave to the Danube the inspiration of the Hussite movement. Wycliff was assuredly a formidable Erastian and his *Tractatus de Officio Regis* amounted to a declaration of war against the Pope.

In this remarkable pamphlet Wycliff proved that God favoured kingship, since three kings had been designated to visit the manger at Bethlehem. The king must be honoured as the vicar of God (*rex enim est dei vicarius*) and our awe of the king is a reflection of our fear of God. The king possesses 'palpable' (*sensibilis*) dignity, whereas the dignity of the Church is impalpable. Thus even a bad king should be revered owing to the office and titles that he holds. The priest should own no possessions or titles, since Christ himself was poor. A king should be intelligent but not necessarily a cultured intellectual. If he be a stupid man, then the community has lost 'its finest pearl'. If he be an evil man, then the whole realm suffers in his person. The king was above the law while respecting it and only violating it in emergencies. He should study theology and suppress heresy. He governs for the good of his people and should seek to reflect divine justice. He possesses full jurisdiction over the clergy of his realm, and should exact an oath of allegiance from all foreign priests who enter the kingdom. If the Pope asserted his right to diminish or control the secular power of the king, he should be denounced as anti-Christ. Is it surprising that so outspoken an Erastian should have been exhumed by the founder of Lincoln College and his ashes cast into the stream?

The historians inform us that it is an error to suppose that the doctrine of the Divine Right of Kings, which aroused such argument between the eleventh and the seventeenth centuries, was directly derived from the primitive fertility myth that monarchs were incarnate gods. It was, we are told, a political formula invented by those who contested the papal claim to universal supremacy. Yet it is evident from the language employed during this long-drawn controversy that something at least of the old magic superstitions survived. Bossuet openly assured the kings of France that they were of divine origin, and James I, in his *Basilikon Doron*, could inform his son that he was born 'a little god, destined to sit on his throne and to rule men'. A justification for this claim was sought in the words of Psalm 82 v 6, 'Ye are gods, and all of you are children of the most high. But ye shall die like men and fall like one of the princes'. The superstition lingered on.

MAGICAL ELEMENT IN DIVINE RIGHT

The Anglo-Saxon kings had been elected by the Witan from among the adult males of the royal family. It is strange to realise that our present Queen is descended directly, although not always through the male line, from King Egbert who was Bretwalda of the West Saxons from 802 to 839. The Norman conquest interrupted this family tradition but did not abolish it. In spite of Canute, Hardicanute, Edward the Confessor and the house of Godwin, the ancient theory persisted that a king should have inherited some strain at least of the old royal blood. What the Normans did was to establish the principle of succession through primogeniture on the analogy of the rule governing the inheritance of fiefs. Although this principle was not invariably observed, it was certainly regarded as the normal form of succession and as such justifying the claim to legitimacy.

Primogeniture itself was believed to possess some sacred sanction as implied in the motto 'Only God can make an heir'. Opinion was for long divided between those who asserted that the heir to the throne succeeded automatically the moment that his father died, and those who asserted that no king could claim to be legitimate until he had been anointed with the holy oil. The extreme monarchists rejected the latter theory, since it was the Church that administered the unction and claimed therefore that the ecclesiastical authority was superior to the secular. Yet there were many theologians (and we must remember that until as late as the eighteenth century theology and politics were inextricably intertwined) who contended that a king could not become 'the Vicar of God' unless he had received unction and that his anointing rendered his sovereignty indefeasible. Shakespeare was correct in attributing such ideas to King Richard II, who asserted,

> Not all the water in the rough rude sea
> Can wash the balm from an anointed King.

LATER VERSIONS OF DIVINE RIGHT
Less mystical theories were in subsequent centuries adduced to justify monarchy. There was the patriarchal theory of government, under which kings ruled as 'the fathers of their people'. And there was the theory advanced by Sir Robert Filmer in his *Patriarcha* of 1679 that monarchy was a 'natural' institution and therefore of divine origin. Filmer put forward the syllogism, 'What is natural to man exists by divine right. Kingship is natural to man. Therefore kingship exists by divine right'. This syllogism did not, after the execution of Charles I, appeal to the logicians; they detected in it an undistributed middle.

The pure doctrine of Divine Right has never been more succinctly expressed than in the address presented to King Charles II by the University of Cambridge (a very precise seat of learning) in 1681.

'We still believe and maintain,' proclaimed the elders of Cambridge, 'that our Kings derive not their title from the people, but from God; that to Him only they are accountable; that it belongs not to subjects either to create or censure, but to honour and obey their sovereign, who comes to be so by a fundamental hereditary right of succession, which no religion, no law, no fault or forfeiture can alter or diminish.'

Implicit in this definition were the three principles that the king was above the law, that the phrase 'limited monarchy' was a contradiction in terms, and that it was the moral duty of subjects not to resist their sovereign but to regard obedience as an act of conscience.

The heads of the English usurper, King Henry IV, and his Queen, from their tomb in Canterbury Cathedral

The imperialists would adduce the argument that a community that had two heads, one spiritual and one temporal, was condemned to dissolution. 'A society,' wrote William of Ockham in his *Dialogus*, 'approaches desolation and ruin when divided against itself' (*Illa societas est propinqua desolationi et ruinae quae est contra se divisa*).

Wycliff in the *De Officio Regis* went even further. He advanced the difficult idea that the king was superior to the Church since he reflected the godhead of Christ, whereas the priest reflected His manhood only. He argued that the king was above the law (*solutus legibus*) and that it was the moral duty of the citizen to obey the authority of the crown in every circumstance. Richard II was deeply imbued with Wycliff's teaching and asserted that 'the laws were in his mouth or in his breast and he alone could change the statutes of the realm'. In his opposition to papal interference in English affairs he represented the feelings of his people; but his attempts to establish a secular autocracy met with popular opposition and in 1399 he was deposed and his cousin, the usurper Bolingbroke, ascended the throne in his stead. But when Parliament recognised Bolingbroke as Henry IV they were careful to maintain the fiction of Divine Right by asserting that he had succeeded 'through the right God had given him by conquest'.

Edward VI's 'Device for the succession', a statement of how the English throne should pass in default of a male heir

The Tudors, who were obliged by circumstances to abandon the doctrine of legitimacy and Divine Right as justifying their usurpation, relied on the public need of unity and security. They ruled by force. Even Queen Elizabeth, whose legitimacy was questionable, discarded hereditary primogeniture as the 'fundamental law' and proclaimed that Parliament possessed the right to alter the succession. Then came the Glorious Revolution and the Declaration of Rights, which for ever destroyed the doctrine of Divine Right, of hereditary succession and the duty of passive obedience. 'Henceforward,' writes Mr Figgis, 'the Divine Right of Kings is an expression of regretful aspirations and in no sense an actual fact. Pity for the unfortunate and loyalty to a forlorn hope were now the main elements of the faith'.

It is questionable whether, even if it had not been that the legitimate dynasty was expelled, the doctrine of Divine Right would have survived the Rationalism of the eighteenth century. Already Milton had argued that 'to say that the King is accountable to none but God is the overturning of all law and all government'. Bolingbroke in his *Patriot King* stated that 'a Divine Right to govern ill is an absur-

Left: Henry VIII of England presiding over his Parliament. From Sir Thomas Wriothesley's manuscript in the Royal Library, Windsor

dity: to assert it blasphemy '. The theological arguments, which had already been discarded by Hobbes, were finally rejected by Locke and Rousseau. The conception of the Social Contract, which is the antithesis of Divine Right, came to dominate and eventually to destroy the Age of Reason. Today the doctrine of Divine Right is dismissed as a sentimental fiction. Yet it certainly became the watchword by which, both in England and France, the civil authority asserted its independence of Rome; it thereby marked the transition between the mediaeval and the modern world.

MONARCHY
BECOMES AN
INSTITUTION

The conflict between the Papacy and the Empire, between Church and State, is well outside the scope of this study. Yet, in that it obliged both theologians and practical statesmen to consider and to define their conceptions of kingship, it provides us with many interesting examples of shifting views. Monarchy today, although it has certainly not lost myth or glamour, is defined in institutional terms. We are accustomed to consider the nature of sovereignty in legal and realistic language. ' Sovereignty, ' wrote Laski, ' is no more than the name we give to a certain special will that can count upon unwonted strength for its purposes '. Yet where does that will reside in the modern pluralistic State? Assuredly not in the Crown; only questionably in the Cabinet; not in Parliament exclusively; not in the Trade Unions; but presumably in the will of the electorate on those intermittent occasions when the people are moved to exercise their will. Rousseau contended that the British people could only be defined as ' free ' on the recurrent occasions of a General Election. This was typical of his illogical thought; public opinion, if sufficiently stirred, can always bring about the fall of any Government without waiting for an Election. Which amounts to little more than to say that, except in totalitarian states, modern sovereignty is dispersed rather than concentrated, a dispersal that safeguards the security and encourages the self-expression of the individual. Kingship, as the centuries passed, ceased to be a matter of principle and became a matter of convenience. Monarchy ceased to be regarded as a supernatural gift from God and became an institution devised by man for the convenience of the governed.

It is curious to observe how for generations the mystical or religious conception of kingship existed simultaneously with the practical or materialistic conception. As early as the second half of the fourteenth century we have poems and pamphlets, such as *Piers Plowman* and *Mum and the Sothsegger* which imply some contractual basis of kingship. The

Title-page of the 'Leviathan', 1651, in which Thomas Hobbes argued the case for a powerful king

author of *Mum* regarded monarchy as the best form of governance, since under a strong monarch security and unity could be imposed. He felt that under a weak king such as Richard II the barons had ' privily plucked the royal power away ' until ' the Crown was cracked '. Weak government was harmful to all those who desired ' pees and reste ' and a weak king could rightly be deposed and a more efficient successor chosen. A generation earlier William of Ockham had preached a national monarchy conditioned by a national law. This conception of kingship as a human, rather than as a divine, institution was reinforced by the volumes on *The Republic* published by Jean Bodin in 1576 and much discussed in the colleges of Cambridge and Oxford. Bodin contended that kingship was derived, not from God, but from human needs. Monarchy was essential to an ordered State and the good monarch was as a father to his people. Bodin also evolved some interesting generalisations regarding the influence of climate on national character. The North produced stupid but vigorous men who were not gifted with any habit of obedience; the South produced men who were intelligent but lazy and for this reason passive; it was the middle climate, notably that of France, which produced men who were both intelligent and temperate and who were ideally suited to a benevolent monarchy. History has not confirmed the generalisations of Jean Bodin.

JAMES I
DEFENDS
DIVINE RIGHT

Only three years after the death of Jean Bodin, King James VI of Scotland and our own King James I produced his defence of the Divine Right which he entitled the *Basilikon Doron* and which he dedicated to his ' dearest sonne, Henry the Prince '. His ideas on kingship are so confused and contradictory that it is difficult to decide in what terms he considered his own constitutional position. At one moment he assured his son that he should learn to love God ' for that he made you a little God to sitte on his throne and rule over other men '. At the same time a Prince should realise that his exalted position does not give him a license to behave worse than other men, but on the contrary magnifies his slightest fault. ' A blemish in another, ' writes the King, ' is a leprous byle unto you '. The ' glistering worldly glorie of Kings ' is accorded to them in order that they may become ' bright lampes of godliness and virtue '. Since his subjects will seek to ' counterfeite (like apes) their Prince's maners ', a king must set a shining example of temperance and good behaviour. Only a tyrant considers his ' unrulie privace affections '; a virtuous king regards it as his primary duty to make and to preserve good laws. In private life the Prince should eat

A ryal (a gold coin worth thirty shillings) of James I, one-and-a-half times its actual size

sparingly of healthy food, avoiding sauces which are ' a filthy vice of delicacie '. His table manners should not be ' affectatlie mignarde, like a daintie dame ' but he should feed himself in a ' manly, rounder and onest fashion '. He should dress simply and without effeminacy; he should speak distinctly and manfully. He should take physical exercise for the sake of his health, but should avoid such ' rough and violent exercises as the foot-ball '. Rather should he prefer the more elegant ' caitche or tennise and the palle maillé '. It could scarcely be said that King James in his own private life followed these austere principles.

In the administration of justice the Prince should mingle firmness with clemency. Certain crimes, such as witchcraft, murder, incest, and sodomy, poisoning, ' false coyne ', and slandering a man's parents are unpardonable: lesser crimes should be treated according to the circumstances. A prince should mistrust those who believe in the natural equality of men, since ' paritie is the mother of confusion and an enemy to Unitie which is the Mother of Order '. He should be specially wary of the puritans who represent ' very pestes in the Church and commonwele, brething nothing but sedition and calimnies '. A Prince should pay honour to the nobility, but should insist that even the richest magnate must be subject to the law. He should be careful to see that the commons refrain from speaking ' rashelie ' of their superiors. The poor should be kept contented by good laws and by ' honest feasting and merrinesse, by lawful gaimes in Maie and by good cheere at Chiristmasse '. The Prince should be conciliatory towards the middle class of merchants, since if they once feel neglected or insulted ' up goes the blew blanket '. He should choose his ministers and advisers from the nobility and should avoid employing foreigners or self-made men or ' start-ups '.

The constitutional principles of James I were as confused and shambling as his diction and physical gait. At some moments he appeared to proclaim the doctrine of Divine Right, stating that his subjects should regard their king with 'mystical reverence' as being above the law and the Vicar of God. Yet he was well aware that he could not act in defiance of the common law of the land without provoking a revolution, an event which he ardently wished to avoid. At one moment he informed the House of Commons that 'they were not to meddle with anything concerning our government or deep matters of State'. He refused to accept the principle that Members of Parliament enjoyed immunity from arrest and imprisonment. 'We think ourselves free', he stated, 'and able to punish any man's misdemeanours in Parliament, as well as during their sitting and after'. He often used the term 'absolute prerogative' but neither he nor his Ministers had any clear conception of what those two words conveyed. On the other hand he never explicitly claimed to possess a divine right to be above the law of the land. In a message to Parliament in 1610 he acknowledged 'that he had no power to make laws of himself or to exact any subsidies *de jure* without the consent of the three estates'. Yet he contended that the rights of the Commons had been granted to them by 'the grace and permission of our ancestors', and he reserved for himself the right, if occasion arose, to 'retrench them of their privileges'. Thus although he did not claim the right to legislate he did claim the right to break the law 'for the public good'. Since he was himself the sole judge of where that good resided, this qualifying clause had no significance.

Henry VIII had certainly regarded himself as an autocrat; Elizabeth also held dictatorial views; yet acts of arbitrary sovereign will, which the country allowed in the Tudors, were less acceptable under the Stuarts. The misfortune of that unfortunate dynasty was that they were unable to adjust themselves to the wind of change. Harold Laski considered that it was fortunate for Great Britain that James I was so muddle-headed and did not even have the sense to be guided by men of high intelligence and low morals, such as Francis Bacon. Had he been a more expert political theorist he might have established a 'Byzantine type' of kingship. 'It is at least certain,' wrote Laski, 'that his incapacity laid the secure foundations of constitutional government'. For this bold paradox there is some justification.

The lack of lucid thought, the apparent absence of consistent conviction, that blurred and congested the muddled mind of James I can be recog-

The frontispiece of Charles I's 'Eikon Basilike', his apologia published on the day of his funeral

nised in many of the political theorists of the early seventeenth century. The vacillations of the sainted Charles I can be attributed, not so much to his duplicity and unstable character, as to uncertainty regarding the ends that he desired and the means by which these ends should be secured. Charles I did not lay claim to any divine right; he honestly believed that he was continuing the constitutional system established by his father and the Tudor dynasty. It was this obstinate illusion that led to the abominable scene in Whitehall on the early afternoon of 30 January 1649. His demeanour on that occasion was so gentle and dignified that a powerful reaction developed in his favour. The publication on the day of his funeral of his pathetic apologia, the *Eikon Basilike*, crystallised this almost superstitious belief that he had suffered a martyr's death; even in this century there are many who regard the injustice of Charles I's trial and execution as a slur upon parliamentary democracy. Yet, however virtuous he may have been in his private life, his political conduct was from the outset marred by weakness and treachery.

It is beyond the scope of this study to examine the intricate and still controversial proceedings that culminated on the scaffold at White-hall. Parliament, who were in general supported by what Richard Baxter called 'the country nobility and gentry', considered themselves to be the natural defenders of Magna Carta and the champions of 'the ancient and undoubted birthright and inheritance of the subjects of England'. Milton, in his *Tenure of Kings and Magistrates*, contended that 'it is lawful and hath been held so through all ages for anyone who has the power to call to account a Tyrant or wicked King, and after due conviction to depose and put him to death'. Charles may have been false and double dealing, but he was assuredly not wicked. Nor could his trial at the hands of his pledged enemies be described as in any manner legal or just. Moreover those who have faith in the established Church contend that it was in defence of Anglican Orthodoxy that the King sacrificed his life. 'Had Charles,' wrote Bishop Creighton in 1895, 'been willing to abandon the Church and give up episcopacy, he might have saved his throne and his life. But on this point Charles stood firm, for this he died and by dying saved it for the future'. This view was upheld by Newman, Keble and Gladstone. 'It was for the Church,' wrote Gladstone, 'that Charles shed his blood upon the scaffold.'

THE BELIEFS OF CHARLES I   Charles certainly believed, if not in divine right, then in the sanctity of certain royal prerogatives, which he had inherited from his predecessors and which it was his bounden duty to transmit undamaged and undiminished to his successors. We cannot blame him for such illusions, since they at that date formed an element in all political thought. Even those philosophers and theorists who, like Francis Bacon, did not believe in absolutism, did believe that the State should be governed by what they called 'wisdom', meaning thereby the knowledge, experience and foresight of highly cultivated men. Bacon did not regard Parliament as containing the oligarchy of intellect that he desired; he despised the Members of the House of Commons as being ignorant, hysterical and governed by prejudices or affections that were either wholly selfish or else excitable, transitory and emotional. Walter Raleigh was a firm believer in the Divine Right of Kings. He believed that monarchs were chosen 'by God and by the law divine'. 'No Prince,' he contended 'can be said to be subject to the laws'. Even acts of tyranny and injustice should be accepted by a subject with reverent subservience. That was a most Elizabethan idea and not one which

Francis Bacon, Lord Chancellor to James I   *Charles I at his trial, by Sir Edward Bower*

would have commended itself to Pym. Archbishop Laud, who stated that he 'was never such a fool as to embrace arbitrary government', continued to regard the King as 'God's viceregent' and to assert that 'the most high and sacred order of kings is of divine right, being the ordinance of God himself'.

Edward Forset, whose *A Comparative Discourse of the Bodies Natural and Politique* was published in 1606 and exercised great influence on contemporary political theory, contended that kingship was above the law. He argued that the 'resplendence and power of sovereignty' derived from the will of God. Whether a king came to the throne by legitimate descent, by election, or by conquest, it was still God's will that he should have been invested with this glory and thus rebellion was for him 'the deadliest and most detestable of sins'.

Such were the doctrines which the unhappy Charles inherited and absorbed. He had as a child suffered much from ill-health; his growth was stunted and, as often happens with very short men, he tended to become suspicious; his most consistent principle was to defend, as a personal inheritance, the prerogatives bequeathed to him by his father. Had he followed this task with even average firmness and honesty he might well have triumphed over his enemies, since respect for kingship was still alive throughout the realm. He forfeited respect by his duplicity. The compassion with which he is today regarded is mainly sentimental; we cannot seriously claim that he was a credit to the cause of kingship.

ELEVEN

The Sun-King

CONCURRENTLY WITH THE MYTH of the Divine Right of Kings, there grew up the more practical conception of the Sovereign as the symbol of national unity and the personification of national prestige and glory. He was expected to be authoritarian and magnificent. Those who preserved the old-fashioned theory of kingship did not expect their monarchs to be particularly gifted or resolute: it was sufficient if they were legitimately anointed and if they maintained and safeguarded the customs and traditions of the realm. The later and more realistic conception of the functions of monarchy implied that the king or prince should be a man of high intelligence and strong will; no weakling or idiot could symbolise the grandeur of the State or impose discipline and order upon the barons and the commons. What they required was an intelligent and vigorous man of iron will; they did not worry much about his virtue or his humanity.

The prophet of this realistic conception of kingship was the Florentine Nicolo Machiavelli who lived from 1469 to 1527, and who in 1513 published his *Il Principe* and in 1519 his *Discorsi*, each of which exercised immense influence on the contemporary theory and practice of kingship. The *Principe* has become the bible of all autocratic systems since the sixteenth century.

Right: *Louis XIV receiving the Persian ambassadors (detail) by Coypel (1661-1722)*

When I was an undergraduate I was taught that Machiavelli was an evil prophet, whose cynicism should be denounced by all right-thinking Whigs. Since then, with the progress of *Realpolitik*, even Machiavelli has found his champions and disciples. It has been pointed out that his purposes were noble purposes. His dream was to secure the unification of Italy, the cessation of wars between city and city, and the creation of a national army which would replace the local condottieri and mercenaries and exist only for the defence of the national homeland against foreign invasions. Machiavelli, who had long experience of the internecine squabbles of Italy, who deplored the wastage of regional conflict and party dissension, realised that unity and peace could only be vouchsafed to Italy under the rule of a single despot powerful enough to suppress local conflict or partisan fanaticism, and resolute and cunning enough to maintain himself in power. His own experience at the court of Cesare Borgia (who in my Oxford days was not held up to us as an ideal statesman), convinced him that only by strength and cunning could any despot seize power and survive.

It was contended by the defenders of Machiavelli that democrati THE RIGHT TO LEAD liberalism must always prove a weakness in the State; that if party animosities were not to divide and debilitate the will-power of the nation, if complete national unity and strength were to be achieved, it was essential to have the whole force of the nation directed by a single master mind. Such an autocrat or dictator could not maintain his power if hampered by moral or even humane scruples: he must be prepared to be both ruthless and cunning: he must be able to deceive. Therefore, it was argued by those who defended the principle of autocracy or ' leadership ', that the Führers and the Duces of this world must be men of fanatical will-power able to rouse their peoples to hysterical enthusiasm and to impel them to discard reason in favour of heroic recklessness. To such defenders of the dictatorial system, the mystic element in monarchy was a devitalising sentiment; the only right they recognised was the right to lead; and to them inevitably Machiavelli was the prophet of *Realpolitik* and the champion, not of the unified State only, but of the unitarian State. He was lauded as the supreme realist, and we who still clung to the tattered velvets of whig liberalism, were derided as antiquated humbugs who refuse to recognise the wind of change or the realities of modern world politics.

I was impressed by such arguments and read Machiavelli again, dismissing the idea that he was the complete cynic and adopting the

Nicolo Machiavelli who, in 'Il Principe' - the textbook of Renaissance princes and of all autocrats - advocated the principles of dictatorship, the antithesis of true kingship: a fifteenth century terracotta bust

assumption that his aim was a noble one, that he was a premature Cavour or Garibaldi, and that it was Victorian of us to dismiss his theories as 'cynical' or, as the term went, 'machiavellian'. On rereading his works with some attention I was impressed by the strength and beauty of his style, which ripples like the muscles of a long-distance runner, and by the outrightness of his argument. As a guide to politics, his analysis was admittedly more useful than the less practical theories of Bentham or Rousseau. I was impressed by his assertion that his aim in writing his great book was to 'write something useful'. 'I have found it more convenient,' he asserted, 'to go straight to the essential point and not to waste time by making imaginative remarks about the ideal'. This surely, at a date when political theory was inextricably entangled in theology, was an excellent assertion.

I am prepared to admit that, in the age of the Borgias, reform could only be achieved by violence, and order only imposed by fear. Yet, being a congenital liberal, and regarding fear as among the most terrible of human ills, I cannot for one moment admit that the theory of Machiavelli is anything but evil, leading as it does directly to dictatorships and all the lying and brutality by which alone such systems can be maintained. No patriot king, I feel, would have surrendered the state to authoritarianism, as Hindenburg surrendered to Hitler and Victor Emanuel to Mussolini. Machiavelli, as Hitler, misconceived the unity of average virtue; failed to foresee the eventual refusal of mankind to be coerced into false opinions; and ignored the wave of revolt that is bound to arise when a whole nation is conditioned forcibly and told lies. To me, the cynicism of Machiavelli is repulsive: it cannot be defended either by the integrity of his purpose or the splendid muscles of his style.

He believed that a ruler should be feared rather than loved: that force was more potent than law; and that a Prince who relied on law rather than on fear would fail to survive. Of course it was necessary for a ruler to *pretend* that he venerated and practised all the virtues. He should appear to his subjects as pious, trustworthy, religious, righteous and humane. But he must know that in practice it would often be necessary to be treacherous or cruel, and to act rapidly in defiance of religion and morals. Above all, a ruler must be possessed of iron will. 'It is possible,' writes Machiavelli with his usual incisiveness, 'for a weak prince to maintain himself if he succeeds a strong prince: but no rule can survive if a weak prince has a weak successor'. 'It happens rarely, or almost never,' he writes again, 'that a man of humble origin rises to power without duplicity and strength of will. Strength is never sufficient without cunning.' Strength implies the capacity to come to rapid decisions. The prince who hesitates convinces his people that he lacks *Virtù*. What, to Machiavelli, is the meaning of that strange word *Virtù*? Inflexible will, quick powers of decision, and a capacity to act with ruthlessness and speed. Napoleon and Frederick II possessed this *Virtù*: Mr Gladstone and Mr Asquith, I am glad to say, did not.

The major contribution made by the Italian despots and oligarchies of the Renaissance to European civilization was the stimulus they gave to culture in all its forms. Machiavelli was but little concerned with

VIRTÙ

this aspect of their achievement. Cruel and arbitrary though their despotisms may have been, they did much to foster the revival of learning and to broaden the narrow intellectual limits of the mediaeval world by spreading humanism throughout the Continent. In scholarship, in literature, in science, and in the plastic arts Europe remains deeply indebted to the Italian Renaissance, and it was the despots and the closed oligarchies that provided the thinkers and the artists of the age with the security they needed for the expansion of their ideas.

Machiavelli's conception of dictatorship is to my mind the very opposite of any true doctrine of kingship. A dictator, even though he may provide great opportunity for his adherents, is always bound in the end to strain the nation beyond its capacity. The principle of dictatorship is dynamism and therefore war; the principle of kingship is stabilisation and peace. We should not, I feel, admire those political philosophers who defend Nicolo Machiavelli. I am glad he was tortured when imprisoned by the Medici. But his tomb is honoured by the Florentines to this day.

DICTATORSHIP
AND KINGSHIP

In ignoring the mystical, or metaphysical, aspects of kingship, Machiavelli had in mind, not so much the institution of hereditary monarchy, as the temporary usurpations of condottieri, war-lords and dictators. His works are more akin to Hitler's *Mein Kampf*, or to Mussolini's excellent article on Fascism in the Italian Encyclopaedia, than they are to Plato, Aristotle or the long line of political philosophers. Yet, whereas Machiavelli was a master of taut style, Hitler's language was that of a Bohemian agitator.

Kingship, as I have said, has little connection with dictatorship, being based on a different ideology. Among the many thoughts and emotions that render kingship a recurrent phenomenon in human governance, are the quite respectable doctrines of legitimacy, continuity, tradition, pageantry and grandeur. The king, being above parties, politics or classes, becomes the symbol of the nation as a whole. He represents national character, cements national unity, and ministers by his grandeur to national vanity.

No monarch in history has fulfilled with such magnificence the symbolic or representative functions of kingship as Louis XIV of France. There exists no word in the English language that comprises the whole spectrum of splendour and ambition conveyed by the French expression *la Gloire*. It ranges from the noblest purples of pride to the pinks of vanity; it ranges from heroism, through sexual ostentation, to ribbons

Left: *Louis XIV on horseback, from Lebrun's studio, probably painted in 1668, the year of Louis' triumphal entry into Douai during the French invasion of the Spanish Netherlands.* Right: *Louis XIV triumphing over the Fronde - the rebellion of the nobility against Cardinal Mazarin during the King's minority: a statue at Versailles by Gilles Guérin*

and brocades. At its best it corresponds to what we mean by 'glory and honour'; at its worst it becomes a petty ambition, snobbish, self-satisfied, *avantageux*, and provocative of selfish and vulgar gestures of ostentation. I confess that I am not displeased that there should be no equivalent for this deleterious word in the English or the American vocabulary. We may be snobbish, we may be shopkeepers, but we do not attach undue importance to *la Gloire*. Louis XIV represented and exaggerated all that is most splendid in this emotion. It brought his country to the very verge of ruin; and himself to a penitent and gloomy old age.

There are historical reasons that explain how it came that Louis XIV should have regarded kingship as a family profession, even as a craft, which (although essentially a stupid man) he perfected and exercised with a skill and concentration that amounted to genius. His parents had endured a sterile marriage for twenty-two years and his sudden appearance was viewed as a supernatural event. He succeeded to the throne at the age of five and his childhod was disciplined and controlled by his mother and her great Minister and paramour, Cardinal Mazarin.

Medal by Varin of (left) *Louis XIV as a child;* Right: *his mother, Anne of Austria, reverse. Louis succeeded to the throne at the age of five. His mother and Cardinal Mazarin ruled during his minority*

The nobles, the lawyers and the Orléans branch of the royal family resented the despotism and avarice of these foreigners and combined in two successive revolts, known in French history as 'the Frondes'. There was the *Parlement fronde* of 1648 and the Princes' *fronde* of 1650. By 1652 the Cardinal, who had been obliged to take refuge abroad, returned to Paris and the rebellions were over. Meanwhile the baby king had constantly been bundled away from Paris and taken for safety to some provincial capital or palace. On one occasion, when the politicians and nobles heard and credited a rumour that he had been abducted by Mazarin, they insisted on penetrating into the Louvre and pushing into his bedroom, and on filing past the great bed from which the little boy watched them as they slouched past staring. He glowered at this indignity in childish rage.

From that moment he conceived a hatred of the Louvre, at that date a grim fortress with a few splendid apartments such as the Gallery of Apollo, but almost uninhabitable owing to the stench that rose from the middens and the latrines. One of the curious things about Louis XIV was that he transferred his loathing of the Louvre to his own capital city. Between 1666 and 1715 he never spent a night in Paris and in the last twenty-eight years of his reign he only visited the capital eight times. His last visit to Paris was in 1706 when he was persuaded to inspect the magnificent church of the Invalides which had just been completed. In the remaining nineteen years of his reign he never once set foot in the capital. Now that Paris has become the centre and symbol of French glory it is strange to reflect that the Roi Soleil persisted in his dislike and absenteeism.

The experience of the Frondes, the lessons in statecraft which Cardinal Mazarin had inculcated, convinced Louis XIV that if the Crown were to retain its authority and prerogative it was essential to deprive the aristocracy of all executive powers and to keep them under close and constant surveillance. On the death of Mazarin in 1661 the King, although only twenty-two years of age, proclaimed to a startled world that henceforward he would govern by himself. For the remaining fifty-five years of his reign his authority remained unquestioned.

The basis of his system was to draw a sharp distinction between 'power' and 'grandeur'. As ministers and executive officers he chose men of ability from the middle classes, such as Colbert, Louvois and Pomponne, who were entirely dependent for their continuance in office on his own good-will. They were accorded great powers in their several departments, subject only to his supervising autocracy. The nobles on the other hand were allowed no administrative functions, but were loaded with all manner of decorative honours. This system was repeated throughout the realm. The provincial governors were drawn from the aristocracy and given large salaries, lavish expense accounts, and splendid pomp. The real administrative work was performed by the *intendants* who were appointed from the civil servant class.

DISTINCTION
BETWEEN
POWER AND
GRANDEUR

The first 'Lit de Justice' held by Louis XIV in 1643. The King could overrule the Parlement de Paris' *refusal to ratify his edicts by holding a 'Lit de Justice', at which he ratified them himself*

In order to supervise the nobles and to prevent them from acquiring regional influence he obliged them to become members of his Court and regularly to be in attendance on his person. Any member of the landed aristocracy who showed signs of preferring to visit his own estates, or even to reside in Paris, to lolling in the saloons and galleries of Versailles or Marly, was liable to fall into disgrace. 'I do not see him,' the King would grumble, meaning thereby, 'He is not a good courtier and can expect no favours from me'. His phenomenal memory for faces, his astonishing gift of observation, rendered it difficult for any noble to stay away from Versailles without his absence being noted. Since it was not easy in those days for a noble to meet the expenses of his rank from the rents and produce of his own estates, the aristocracy came to rely more and more on the sinecures, pensions, grants, emoluments and presents which could be obtained from the King alone. Nobles with large families, anxious to obtain army commissions for their sons or posts as women of the bedchamber for their daughters, were obliged to stand for hours in the lobbies of the palaces in the hope of catching the King's cold glance. Versailles became for them a concentration camp of crystal and gold and for the most part they lost all touch with their own peasants or with the world outside the palace railings. This system may have prevented another *fronde* from developing, but it certainly shattered all understanding or confidence between the aristocracy and the nation as a whole.

Not only were the courtiers expected to dance unremitting attendance, but they were supposed to avoid all dangerous thoughts and language. There were all too many informers in the galleries of Versailles, and all political discussion was dangerous and in fact forbidden. The courtiers, although often men and women of great intelligence, were obliged to confine their conversation to trivial matters. The men discussed the day's hunting and the women chattered about clothes. It is not surprising that the French aristocracy of the eighteenth century never acquired any sense of serious responsibility. Hilaire Belloc, in spite of his admiration for despotism as a protection against the monied interest, admits that the danger for an autocrat is that 'he may lose that moral sanity which is the fruit of companionship'. There was no free companionship at Versailles; there was only etiquette.

Right: *Bust of Louis XIV by Bernini: executed in the 'grand manner', this bust, though it does not hide the lack of symmetry or the sensuality in the King's features, does give an overriding impression of nobility*

If we are to understand the means by which Louis XIV fabricated this dream world around him, it is necessary to consider in some detail the ritual, the etiquette and the fantasies of the French court in the seventeenth century. Never has the symbolic element in kingship been exploited with such elaboration.

MAJESTY Louis XIV was a tall and portly figure and the personification of majesty in every look and gesture. Even his most powerful ministers, even his most victorious field-marshals, felt inferior in his presence. 'At Court,' wrote La Bruyère, 'even the great ones are made to look small.' '*Le monde en le voyant*,' wrote Racine, '*reconnut son maître*.' The ordinary courtier, even a proud woman of letters such as Mme de Sévigné, would tolerate hours of boredom, weeks of abasement, if they could be rewarded with but one glance of recognition from that imperial eye. Saint Simon recounts how, on one occasion, Louis XIV, walking from the palace to enter his coach, actually turned round to address a word to a chamberlain behind him. In general he would walk undeviatingly forward without even glancing behind him. The majesty of such direct gait has to be seen in order to impress the memory. I have never forgotten once, in the regal palace at Madrid, seeing King Alfonso XIII and his lovely Queen walking hand in hand together through a double row of ambassadors and grandees without looking either to right or left. 'This,' I thought to myself, 'is authentic grandeur.' Similarly the chamberlains of Napoleon III would recount to their grandchildren how Queen Victoria, attending a gala performance at the Paris opera, without a glance below or behind, took her seat in the armchair, confident from long practice of royal seating that it had been placed exactly at the right place and at the right distance. One could tell she was an Empress by the way she walked.

Louis XIV was anything but an intellectual. He considered the habit of reading as a waste of time. He had some taste in music and would often hum to himself a passage from Lulli, in a gentle little voice that was never out of tune. He had a passion for architecture and garden design and it was his reckless extravagance that has bequeathed to posterity some of the most superb buildings, apartments and architectural gardens that exist in the world. And although, as I have said, he took small interest in literature, the impulse and energy communicated by his grandeur inspired the greatest writers that France has ever known. Charles Maurras has well written that 'he gave life to all the ideas of his age. His grandeur was *fertile* grandeur'.

Versailles as it was during the last years of Louis XIV's reign. Painted by Pierre-Denis Martin in 1722, this picture commemorates the return of the court to Versailles, which it had left on Louis' death

His religion was that of a child. He would say his prayers with the utmost regularity, never missed mass, and would take a number of relics to bed with him as a protection against evil spirits. He believed in the devil as an animate being with horns and tail. He was much influenced by Michel Le Tellier, his Jesuit confessor, and when austerity was introduced into his life by Mme de Maintenon, he became obsessed by thoughts of original sin. Yet he placed his own glory and grandeur even above his religious reverence. La Bruyère has recorded that when in chapel he would not allow the courtiers to turn their backs upon him. Thus whereas he, in his box, faced the altar, they of the congregation turned their backs on the altar. 'They appeared,' writes La Bruyère, 'to worship the King while the King worshipped God.' Such

'*Le Lever du Roi*': the '*petit lever*' and '*première entrée*' in their comparative privacy are over, and the '*grand lever*', the first public scene of the daily ceremonial pageant at the court of Louis XIV, now begins

overt gestures of magnificence were not by any means the only means by which he imposed his supremacy and displayed his glory.

There was the exactitude of his time-table, the routine of his daily life, which were as precise as the great gold clocks that ticked away upon the marble chimney-pieces of the saloons. Those who had been granted the exceptional honour of private audiences were expected to arrive always a few minutes before the appointed time. To one Minister, who appeared exactly as the clock was striking, the King remarked in cold displeasure, 'I almost had to wait' (*J'ai failli attendre*). It was said that a Frenchman who 'knew his court' would, even if he were stranded in the Gobi desert, tell you exactly what the King was doing at 3.30 on that Tuesday afternoon. Even Mme de Maintenon found this time-table excessive in its rigidity. 'We shall all die,' she once remarked, 'from symmetry.' Yet his punctuality spread a disciplinary effect.

Every morning he would be woken at 8.30 by his first valet drawing the curtains of his vast bed and murmuring the words, 'Sire, it is time.' The valet would then cover the disordered sheets by spreading over them a magnificent counterpane embroidered with the royal arms with little inserts at each corner depicting the arms of the cities that the great monarch had besieged and captured. Then, so long as she lived, his old nurse would enter and give His Majesty a morning kiss. Then entered the ' blue valets ', so called because of their blue liveries, accompanied by the palace doctors and surgeons.

While the King was still between the sheets, the doors would be opened to admit those entitled to the private *entrée*, namely the immediate members of the royal family, the Grand Chamberlain, the four Gentlemen of the Chamber, the Grand Master of the Wardrobe, and a few specially favoured courtiers such as Marshal Boufflers. The first valet would then pour some spirits of wine over the King's hands and dry them with a napkin. Although Louis XIV would have a bath sometimes for medicinal purposes, he never washed his teeth. After wiping his hands on the napkin, the King would, while still lying in bed, indulge for fifteen long minutes in silent prayer, while his courtiers stood beyond the barrier waiting for the next manoeuvre in the parade.

The King would rise from his bed, put on his slippers, and be helped by the Grand Chamberlain into a sumptuous dressing gown. The court barber would then take off the King's night-cap, brush his hair, and put on the ' morning wig ' which was smaller than the vast bob-wig that he wore for the rest of the day. The King would then give the order for the public *lever* to begin. The great doors would be flung open and the remaining members of the household would enter, accompanied by those officials or visitors who had been granted the signal honour of morning audience. Once every other day the King, who had a stiff beard, would be shaved by the barber. He would then put on his trousers and buckle his shoes. Two of the blue valets or pages would hold silk screens in front of him while this was proceeding. He would then be handed his shirt by the Dauphin or some other close relation, the first valet guiding his arm into the right-hand sleeve, and the second valet guiding his arm into the left-hand sleeve. The discarded night-gown and the relics that he had kept under his pillows were reverently taken to the anteroom. The Chef de Gobelet then advanced and kneeling before the King handed him a cup of sage tea, which had previously been tasted by the royal taster to make sure that it contained no poison. The Dauphin then handed the King a napkin, half damp and half dry, with which he wiped his lips. His Majesty then donned his coat, his blue ribbon and his sword. He chose a handkerchief from several offered to him on a golden platter and received from the Grand Master of the Wardrobe his hat, his cane and his gloves. Although the

THE
GRAND LEVER

courtiers were all supposed to dress lavishly in satin coats and waistcoats and with diamond orders, thus increasing their expenses and their consequent dependence on the royal bounty, the King himself dressed comparatively simply in black or brown velvet, his only jewels being his shoe buckles of diamonds and the diamond clasp that held the ostrich feather in his hat.

Thus arrayed, the King would dip his fingers in holy water and for a prescribed number of minutes would recite further prayers with his chaplain. He would then enter his study, give his orders for the day, and discuss the most recent architectural or garden plans with Mansard or d'Antin. The procession to Mass followed and the courtiers packed in the Gallérie des Glaces would take the occasion to catch his eye and beg for an invitation to Marly. '*Marly, Sire?,*' they would murmur bowing deep. 'I'll think it over,' the King would answer, and in the course of the day they would be told whether they were to be asked to Marly or not. It was not considered intrusive to tout for such invitations: in fact a courtier who never begged to be asked to Marly was regarded as somewhat *frondeur* and suspect. It was an incidental humiliation.

CABINET
COUNCIL:
DINNER RITUAL

After chapel came the Cabinet council. Each day was devoted to a special department, foreign affairs, finance, home affairs, army and navy, or religious matters. After the council the King, accompanied by the royal family and the high officers of the household, would go to stool, seating himself on a *chaise percée* of mother of pearl with chinoiserie panels and receiving petitions. At 1 pm precisely dinner would be served when he would lunch alone at a square table set in the window. The courtiers would group themselves around him and the Chef de Gobelet or the Grand Chamberlain would hand him his dishes and his wine. Louis XIV was abstemious as regards alcohol and would always mix his Burgundy with water. On the other hand, he ate voraciously, and to the despair of his house-doctor, Dr Fagon, would consume vast quantities of veal and capon and cakes. When the meal was over, he would again wipe his lips with a napkin handed him by the Dauphin and retire to his study where he would amuse himself by talking to his bastards and handing little biscuits to his pet dogs.

Louis XIV was an ardent sportsman and almost every afternoon he would go hunting or shooting in the surrounding parks and forests. On occasions he would fish with cormorants bearing gold chains round their necks. His stables were vast and his horses magnificent: he employed

The King in Council: an engraving of the Revocation of the Edict of Nantes in 1685 by Jan Luiken

some 3000 huntsmen and grooms; there were more than a thousand hounds in his packs. He would hunt in all weathers, forcing the ladies of his court to accompany him in snow and rain. On his return to the palace the charade would begin over again with what was called the ceremony of the *débotté* or 'boots-off'. Once again the courtiers would be admitted in relays while the King took off his heavy hunting boots and changed his wig. He would then work with his Ministers and at 10 pm would come supper in the Oeil de Boeuf, at which he would sit at a small table surrounded by the royal family and the household. If there was no ball, no ballet, no concert or opera that evening, the King would play billiards with his bastards while the courtiers gambled at cards. Then followed the *grand coucher*. The King would kneel at his bedside with the chaplain and say his prayers. He would then designate the high officer of state, or even the foreign ambassador, to whom that night would be accorded the honour of holding his bedroom candle-stick. Having again put on his dressing-gown he would make a slight inclination of his head, signifying that only those who had the privilege of attending the *petit coucher* should now remain. The elect of the household remained round him, while he sat on his

A royal audience: Louis XIV receiving Cardinal Chigi, the Papal Legate of Pope Alexander VII, in audience at Fontainebleau in 1664. A Gobelin tapestry

chaise percée and at last retired to rest with his relics tucked under his pillow. Silence would then descend on the palace.

Louis XIV, who was a shrewd judge of human nature, realised that his courtiers might become restless unless provided with constant ceremonial functions to compensate them for the absence of all serious employment. He thus created an apparatus of etiquette, requiring industrious study to master its intricacies, and constant alertness in following its regulations. He believed that the rigidity of class distinctions preserved discipline. 'Nothing,' he wrote in the Memoir of Instructions addressed to his son and heir, 'moves well bred souls so much as distinctions of rank. They are the first motive of all human action and above all the noblest and greatest. Moreover, it is one of the most visible signs of my power that I can accord value to a person who, in himself, is nothing.' He knew that he could cause despair or ecstasy by witholding or according to some court lady the right to sit upon a footstool or even to have a cushion when she sat on the floor. He knew that he could give pain or pleasure to some aristocrat by not inviting him, or inviting him, for the week-end at Marly. The gradations by which he expressed his favour or disfavour were calculated with scientific precision. A man could detect whether he was to expect advancement from a glance of the King's eye or from the angle at which he raised his hat in acknowledging obeisance. One of the most absurd details of etiquette concerned what they called *le pour*. The Master of the Household would at Marly write in chalk upon the door panels the names of the occupants of the several bedrooms. In general he merely wrote the name of the person thus billetted; but if he added the word *pour* before the name, then a very high distinction had been accorded. The Princesse des Ursins, on visiting Marly, and finding that on her door panel the Master of the Household had writen '*pour Mme des Ursins*', instead of just '*Princesse des Ursins*', actually fainted with joy and had to be given salts. Such was the ecstasy conveyed by a single preposition scribbled in chalk upon a bedroom door.

As we may well imagine, the importance given in the course of this eternal charade to precedence or *place à table*, was greater than that accorded to great victories in Flanders or the acquisition of frontier provinces. When the Marquise de Torcy, wife of the Foreign Minister and niece of the great Colbert, inadvertently sat down in front of the Duchesse de Duras, the King grew purple in the face with rage. Chairs figured disproportionately in this struggle for precedence. Only reigning monarchs and their consorts were allowed to sit in an armchair and it was in fact the privilege granted to Mme de Maintenon of using an

The Palace of Fontainebleau, Louis XIV's hunting-lodge, which stands in the forest of Fontainebleau. The older château was used in the twelfth century by Louis VII, and Francis I built most of the Cour Ovale

armchair that convinced the courtiers that she really must have married the King. The Duchesse d'Orléans, the King's sister-in-law, was forbidden to visit her foreign relations, since a controversy arose as to whether, when they met, the Electress should be given a foot-stool only, or accorded a *chaise à dos*.

In the end the intricacy of court etiquette, the elaboration of protocol and precedence, created satiety. In these hot and often smelly saloons, the courtiers would cluster like a swarm of bees around the monarch as he passed. For years, for generations even, they continued to believe in the gigantic allegories that had been invented. Yet as the years passed the glitter of ten thousand candles became dimmed; even a man as obsessed with rank as was Saint Simon must sometimes have asked himself whether, amid war and famine, precedence was in fact so overwhelmingly important. Even the most frivolous or ambitious courtier must sometimes have asked himself whether his whole future, and that of his family, really depended on the chalking of the word *pour* upon his bedroom door. The moment the courtiers started to question whether the fantasy with which they were surrounded, whether the false values that were adduced to stimulate and divert their ambitions, were in fact the most excellent aims of life, appalling boredom resulted. Hour after hour did these men and women magnificently arrayed have to wait in the galleries in case His Majesty might pass. Once they became bored by grandeur, once they came to lose confidence in the values of court life, they ceased to cherish their own dignity or to execute the functions of their class. Even the King became bored by his own magnificence. ' What torture it is, ' wrote Mme de Maintenon, 'to have to amuse a man who is unamusable. ' Dark clouds indeed accompanied the setting of the Roi Soleil.

DIVINE RIGHT   The King himself probably retained some theory of his Divine Right. He certainly retained the feudal conception of the monarch as head of a vast family. He believed that to him alone was granted the right of approving or forbidding the marriage of any member of the nobility. He was convinced that obedience was the first duty of the subject. Even a bad monarch, he wrote, had the right to demand obedience. He had deep compassion for those fellow monarchs, such as James II, whose autocracy was limited by ' the discretion of a mob calling itself an Assembly '.

Yet in spite of his insistence on his own unique majesty, he was readily accessible to all and sundry. 'I give to my subjects,' he wrote, 'without distinction the opportunity to speak to me at any hour.' He

*Louis XIV in
theatrical costume
as Le Roi Soleil*

would dine in public when the tourists would file past the table and stare at him while he ate. The Tuileries gardens were open to the public daily and in fact were used as a Parisian latrine. Louis XIV was so convinced of his own sanctity that he took few precautions to avoid assassination. He was not surrounded by security officers or secret police.

THE ROYAL
HOUSEHOLD

The expenses of this vast apparatus were immense. He had a domestic staff of some 6,000 people. Every member of the royal family maintained at the King's expense his own household and his own kitchens and staff. When the court moved from Saint Germain to Fontainebleau, or from Versailles to Marly, the tapestries and chandeliers and mirrors were taken with them. His camp-train comprised 30,000 horses, splendidly harnessed in coloured leather and gold. The gardens at the Trianon contained some two million china urns and vases, the plants in which were bedded out anew twice every day. At Marly he would not allow common animals to be seen in the clipped groves; every sparrow was killed and the rabbits slaughtered. The formal beds were planted with eighteen million tulips. Even the carp in the ponds were specially trained and bred, wearing gold collars and being given pet names, such as 'Topaze' or 'Proserpine'.

He lavished fortunes on his mistresses and their relations. Yet he claimed that he never allowed his love affairs to interfere with the duties of kingship. In his instructions to the Dauphin he asserted that women should never be permitted to discuss politics. Not only would such interference have diminished his own repute but would have aroused public criticism against the women whom he loved. 'The moment,' he wrote, 'that you allow a woman to talk to you about important matters it is inevitable that she will lead you astray.' Moreover no woman was ever able to keep a secret. Thus women must be kept for pleasure only, 'since my primary object has always been to preserve my glory and my authority.'

To an eccentric such as Hilaire Belloc, who regarded Louis XIV as the perfect example of kingship, in that he possessed 'miraculous will' and protected his subjects from class government 'which is the opposite of kingship and its death,' the glory of France was in fact to be identified with that of the Roi Soleil.

His system was imitated by all the minor courts of Europe. An even more elaborate type of etiquette was imposed on the Spanish Court under the Catholic monarchy of Philip II and his successors. The Spanish

Louis XIV with his heirs, by Largillière. Left to right: *Madame de Maintenon, the Duc de Bretagne, the Dauphin, Louis XIV, and the Duc de Bourgogne. All three died of small-pox, and his younger great-grandson, the Duc d'Anjou, succeeded*

etiquette was grim and rigid in its formality and was in the end adopted at Vienna. When George V, as Prince of Wales, paid a state visit to the Emperor Francis Joseph he was subjected to the icy blast of Austrian etiquette. When, after standing for hours enduring *cercle* in one of the Hofburg galleries, he retired exhausted to his private apartments, he sighed for the calmer, warmer, formality of Buckingham Palace or Windsor. 'My goodness,' he wrote in his diary, 'this Court is stiff.'

Even in my own day, as I have said, the King and Queen of Spain, seated in the throne-room at Madrid, above the golden lions of Aragon and Castile, would pay no attention whatsoever to the grandees, the courtiers, the diplomatists, and the Cortes deputies, who slowly filed past them, bowing low. Aloof, abstracted and super-human, they would gaze out of the windows opposite the throne as if lesser mortals were unworthy of their attention.

The last Tsar of Russia, was a shy and simple man. Rarely would he leave the domesticity of Tsarskoe Selo for the splendours of his mighty capital. He would appear for the New Year reception at the Winter Palace, or for the ' blessing of the waters ' on the quay beside the Neva, dressed in the simplest of uniforms and accompanied only by two or three of his Cossack Guard. The courtiers and the Metropolitans would form an obsequious circle around him and he himself would twitch nervously from group to group exchanging a few embarrassed but amicable words. The Tsaritsa beside him would incline her head sadly, not desiring to appear taller than her husband. Already there was an aspect of tragedy in her tired eyes, as if she foresaw the massacre in the house of the engineer Ipatiev at Ekaterinburg. The guns would boom a salute from the fortress of St Peter and St Paul, the Tsar would muster a few polite words to the assembled ambassadors and their staffs, the pages of the *Corps des Pages* would conduct their Imperial Majesties to the Red Square: the ceremony left us with the impression of a diffident little man with his anguished consort returning for a very English tea at Tsarskoe Selo. No sense of power remained behind them.

GRANDEUR AND
THE NATION

In spite of Louis XIV's highly centralised grandeur there existed in France a considerable element of provincial self-government and even independence. Richelieu had complained that in France ' every village is a centre of power '. Even Colbert failed to impose a uniform currency or a uniform system of weights and measures. In appearance, the despotism of Louis XIV was absolute, universal, and unquestionable. In practice, it was limited by regional custom. To this day, in France, there is a unity known as ' the Nation ' which is, perhaps fortunately, more continuous and more independent than cabinets or politicians. In the consciousness of the Nation there still remains a vivid memory of the grandeur and glory of the *Grand Siècle*. Nor is General de Gaulle's ideal of *la Gloire* so very different from, although not as expensive as, the conception in which Louis XIV believed so fervently and which he inculcated into his subjects. In the end the extravagance of his egoism led to disaster. But, so long as success attended it, there is little doubt that the ideal of kingship realised by Louis XIV was a potent force in the development of civilisation and ideas. Such grandeur will not be seen again upon this earth.

TWELVE

Caliphate

THE MIRACLE OF MOHAMMED THE PROPHET is one that only mystics can fully comprehend. He was not a great soldier and in fact his enemies on more than one occasion accused him of cowardice. He was not a martyr to his faith, and at one dangerous moment he repudiated his central doctrine that there was no God but Allah. He was not an ethical teacher, and even the most devout could scarcely claim that the Koran can be compared to the Bible for moral precepts and examples. He was not an intellectual, being almost wholly illiterate and indifferent to art and poetry. He was assuredly no saint, his conduct being marred by treachery, cruelty and lasciviousness. He was shrewd and self-assertive. He managed, by constantly insisting on his idea, to convince his disciples and the Moslem world that he was in fact the Messenger and Interpreter of the only God. His successors, armed with the sword of Islam, created an Empire that stretched from the Atlantic to the China seas. To western thought there is nothing supernatural about Mohammed. He seems to us an ordinary Arab, possessed of all the faults and virtues of his race, who invented little that was original and nothing that was sublime. It is indeed a miracle that this tenuous and inconsistent doctrine should have generated such compelling force.

The Great Mosque at Meccah. In the centre of the courtyard stands the Ka'bah, a pre-Islamic temple, which was the chief sanctuary of Meccah and a privileged holy place long before the time of Mohammed. He preserved the tawaf *(sevenfold circuit of the sanctuary) and the kissing of the sacred black stone*

Mohammed, son of Abdulla and Aminah of the tribe of Kuraish, was born in Mecca about 570 and died in 632. His parents died when he was an infant and he was brought up by his uncle Abu Talib. He received but little education and started life as a camel driver and a conductor of merchant caravans. At the age of thirty-nine he married a rich widow of the name of Khadija, who owned many camels and a grocery shop in Meccah town. At the age of forty he was visited by the Angel Gabriel who informed him that he had been chosen as the Messenger of the only God. He had always been subject to epilepsy and he was henceforward able artificially to induce epileptic states during which Allah dictated to him the messages and aphorisms which, when collected, compose the jumbled *surahs* of the Koran.

He would, in the blazing heat of southern Arabia, creep under two blankets, emerge scarlet with perspiration and intone the revelations which he received. His aim was to supersede the paganism and idolatry then constituting the Meccan religion by the monotheism of Abraham. His earlier revelations are concerned almost exclusively with the repetition of the message that there is no God but Allah, who is all-powerful, all-knowing and occasionally merciful. Gradually this developed into the Moslem formula that there is no God but Allah and that Mohammed is his prophet (*Mohammed rasul Allah*). In many of the later *surahs* and pronouncements eternal felicity (in the form of a brothel paradise) is promised to the faithful, whereas those who refuse to accept the message delivered to Mohammed are condemned to everlasting fire. Yet most of the revelations that he embodied into his *surahs* were little more than what Margoliouth calls ' pleasing effusions '. It seems strange to us that millions of brave men should have been prepared to die in defence of the platitudes embodied in the Koran.

Mohammed was a superstitious man. He believed in omens, in lucky or unlucky names and dates, in the evil eye and portents, in imps or Jinns. He would spend ecstatic hours with his thick lips glued to the magic stone inserted in the Ka'bah or central shrine of Mecca. Although his disciples continually urged him when he had achieved full power to destroy the Ka'bah as the sanctuary of idolatry, he refused to do so. In fact he allowed himself to receive a revelation instructing all Moslems no longer to turn towards Jerusalem when they prayed, but to align their prayer rugs in the direction of the Ka'bah. It is to this high rectangle, covered with its black Kiswa with inscriptions in gold thread, that devout Moslems turn to this day and which remains the object of their pilgrimages. Strange that a prophet whose mission was to abolish paganism should have chosen this palaeolithic symbol as the cynosure of his faith.

Mohammed, although extremely voluble, was not an orator, still less a dialectician. His sermons were repetitive and glutted by a rush of words. In a tone of inspired frenzy, he would say the same thing over and over again, which, according to Hitler, is the best means of indoctrinating the masses. He was not of particularly impressive appearance. He was of middle height, very square and stout, with a thick beard and large mouth. His hands were enormous and soft. He was particular about his appearance, made up his eyes with cosmetics, drenched himself in scent, and wore fine Syrian clothes. He disliked bad smells and forbade the use of garlic or onion. He had a special prejudice against decayed teeth, and would use his own toothpick with such assiduity and violence that his gums poured with blood.

His self-confidence at moments degenerated into vaunting; he stimulated his followers by the exaggeration of his boastfulness. So convinced was he of his divine mission that he managed to impart an equal conviction to his disciples. There was little compassion in his teaching; only an insistence on positive belief. He was subject to uncontrolled bouts of rage. His *surahs* contain nothing of the poetic beauty of Christ's teaching. Although later Arabs reached such eminent standards in poetry, philosophy and science, there is but little elevation in the Koran. I repeat that it seems incredible to us that these shallow aphorisms should still inspire three hundred million earnest and intelligent men.

ALLAH
PROCLAIMED

Having achieved economic security by his marriage to a rich widow and a share in her camels and her grocery store, he was able to devote himself exclusively to his communications with Allah and Gabriel. At first (since he was a very cautious man) he kept his mission secret, communicating his revelations to his wife only, to his cousin Ali and to his devoted friend Abu Bekr. In or about the year 613 he decided that he must announce his gospel publicly, and in the Temple court of Meccah he proclaimed the one and only God and denounced the pagan goddesses who were worshipped by his fellow townsmen.

The Meccans were a tolerant folk and averse from shedding blood. For the next eight years they were content to boycott Mohammed and his followers and to expose them to minor indignities. Yet as his adherents, who came mostly from the lower classes, increased in number, there were repeated riots and gang-outrages in the streets of the city.

Life became so inconvenient to the Moslems that many of them emigrated to Ethiopia, where the Negus, under the impression that they were a persecuted sect of Christians, accorded them hospitality and protection. Among the early converts to Islam was Omar, a man ten years younger than Mohammed, and famous for his physical strength and daring. 'If Satan met Omar,' said Mohammed, 'he would get out of Omar's way.' The Meccans, and all those who had a vested interest in the cult of the ancient idols, became alarmed at the spread of the Moslem heresy, and issued a decree forbidding all converts to Islam to have access to the Ka'bah. Mohammed, being as I have said a highly superstitious man, was terrified by this excommunication. He agreed to a compromise under which the ban would be lifted on condition that he would experience a revelation recognising the Meccan goddesses, Al-Lat and Al-Uzza, as 'intercessors', and as such more or less the equals of Allah. Omar, who was more fanatical than his master, was furious at this apostasy; he begged Mohammed to experience

235

The Great Mosque at Medina (Yathrib), from a Dutch print by C. Philips Jacobé, 1774

a further revelation by which the compromise would be repudiated. He accordingly crept under his blanket and emerged, sweating profusely, to assert that the former revelation recognising Al-Lat and Al-Uzza had been dictated to him, not by Allah or by Gabriel, but by the Devil himself. It must henceforward be expunged from the Koran.

MOHAMMED
MOVES TO
MEDINA

Meanwhile his wife Khadijah and his uncle and protector Abu Talib, head of the Kuraish tribe, had both died, and Mohammed felt it wiser to escape from Meccah for a while and retired to Taif. He was informed that the Meccan reactionary party had decided to kidnap and to murder him, so he took refuge in a cave on Mount Thaour, accompanied only by his dogged disciple, Abu Bekr. He was then invited by the leading men of Yathrib, where there were already many Moslem refugees established and where conflict had broken out between the

The Dome of the Rock and the Mosque of Omar at Jerusalem

native population and the rich Jewish community, to accept the office of arbiter or *podestà*, and to restore order and concord. He accepted this mission and moved to Yathrib, which he subsequently renamed 'the City' or 'Medina' on 20 September 622. It is from this day that the Moslems calculate what they call the *hijrah*, and wc call the *hegira*, and which has occasioned some confusion in Moslem chronology.

At Yathrib, where he was from the first regarded as a holy man, Mohammed had little difficulty in establishing a theocratic despotism. He hoped at first that the Jews, with whose religion his own had such a close affinity, would recognize him as a prophet. But the rabbis refused to accept the mission of any man who was unable to speak Hebrew. Being more intelligent than the local Arabs, they began to make mock of Mohammed's revelations, pointing out how inconsistent they were and how conveniently they coincided with the prophet's personal advantage. In the end he became violently anti-semitic and forbade his disciples to copy any Jewish customs even to the manner in which they cut their hair. In the place of celebrating the Day of Atonement, he introduced the fast of Ramadan; Friday, not Saturday, became the sacred day of the week; and the faithful when they prayed were instructed to turn, not towards Jerusalem, but towards Meccah. As his power in Medina increased, he was able to banish the Jewish clan of the Banu Kainuka and to confiscate their possessions to the enrichment of his own treasury.

At Yathrib, or Medina, he constructed a mosque shaped like a barn and roofed with palm leaves that let in the rain. Since there were no clocks in Yathrib he employed the disciple with the loudest voice, Bilal, the first of the muezzins, to summon the faithful to prayer from the roof of the tabernacle. To the west of this mission house were grouped the huts in which Mohammed kept his family. By then he had, at the age of fifty-three, married Abu Bekr's daughter Ayesha, then a child of nine, who grew up to be the most formidable of his many wives. He was accepted in Medina as a saint and ruler and adopted almost regal state. The water in which he washed came to be regarded as so holy that he caused it to be bottled and distributed among the converted.

Being totally ignorant of the nature of palm cultivation, as of the mysteries of fertilisation, Mohammed committed the error of forbidding the propagation of the female palm tree, with the result that there occurred in the Medina district an acute shortage of dates. The prophet and his disciples became so impoverished that they were short of food and their clothes disintegrated into rags. It was essential to obtain some money somehow, and the prophet, with his early experience of the caravan trade, decided that it would be profitable to become a highway robber and to raid caravans.

SACRED MONTHS In Arabia in the seventh century murder was a common occurrence and was mitigated only by an elaborate system of blood money and blood feuds. The flow of commerce was facilitated by a general agreement to set aside specified months of the year as ' sacred months ' during which no robbery or act of violence could be perpetrated. Since the rich caravans that passed by Medina on their way from Meccah to Syria chose these sacred months for their journeys, and travelled without armed protection, Mohammed ignored the sacred month and seized and looted a rich caravan in the parched defiles near Medina. During the

Mohammed assisting at a siege, perhaps of Taif, which resisted him when he was intent on destroying idols, but later capitulated

struggle that arose, a Meccan of the name of Amr, of the Hadramite tribe, lost his life. A blood feud was thereby established and Abu Sufyan, the commander-in-chief of the Meccan levies, decided that revenge must be exacted for the violation of the sacred month and the death of Amr.

In March 624 a rich caravan left Meccah escorted by some nine THE BATTLE hundred men-at-arms. Mohammed's own supporters numbered only three OF BADR hundred men. The opposing forces engaged each other at Badr on March 17 and a fierce battle followed. Mohammed himself fainted at the outset of the battle and on recovering consciousness threw a few pebbles at the Meccan army and then relapsed into ecstatic prayer. Several of the Meccan generals were killed in the early stages of the battle and the main body of the Meccan army turned and fled, leaving behind them seventy corpses and seventy captives. The Moslems had only seventeen men killed.

Mohammed subsequently described the Battle of Badr, when a small force of Moslems had routed a Meccan force three times stronger than themselves, as a miracle accorded to the true faith by Gabriel and Allah. He would describe the survivors of the battle as 'the Badris' and would thereafter accord them special honours and a major share of any spoil that might be captured or any ransoms that might be obtained. Proclaiming 17 March 624, as 'the Day of Deliverance' he returned to Medina in triumph and felt strong enough to assassinate those of the citizens of Medina who had ventured to criticise him and his disciples. His disciple Ali, who had obtained two camels as his share

The Mosque El Aqsa (the Distant Mosque) at Jerusalem, on the site of the palace of King David

of the spoil of Badr, started to trade with the goods confiscated from the Jews. He was intercepted by the prophet's uncle Hamsah, who killed the two camels and devoured them at a feast at which he himself became revoltingly drunk. Mohammed was so shocked by this episode that he experienced a revelation prohibiting the sale and consumption of intoxicants. He himself was specifically exempted from this prohibition.

The Meccans resolved to avenge their defeat at Badr. Gathering allies from the surrounding tribes, they attacked the Moslems at Uhud and inflicted on them a resounding defeat. Abu Bekr, Omar and Ali were all wounded; Hamsah was killed; and the prophet himself was obliged to escape from the battle and to hide in a cave. On his return to Medina, he blamed his discomfiture on the incompetence of his subordinates and had a series of revelations assuring him that the battle of Uhud had in fact been a moral success and that the failure of the Meccan leader, Abu Safyan, to follow up his victory was due entirely to divine intervention. He continued to persecute the Jews and those citizens of Medina whom he called 'the hypocrites' in that they obstinately refused to recognise him as the prophet of Allah. The next few years were devoted to robber raids based on Medina, when many caravans were attacked and camels, sheep and women looted. The little vixen Ayesha had by then reached the age of puberty and was accused by the rest of the harem of having committed adultery with a handsome young Bedouin. Mohammed had an urgent revelation, proclaiming the innocence of Ayesha and denouncing those who had slandered the girl. The scandal-mongers were severely chastised and comparative peace restored in the ever-increasing harem of the prophet.

In the years that followed he extended his dominion over the Arab tribes and villages surrounding the Medina district. He did not massacre those who refused to accept his religion, but allowed them to become satellites or tributaries under the name of *dhimmis*. By January 630 he felt strong enough to attack Meccah. With a force of ten thousand he advanced on the city, forced Abu Suryan to recognize him as the Messenger of Allah, and entered Meccah in triumph. He destroyed the local idols, but carefully preserved the Ka'bah and the sacred stone. Having occupied Meccah he attacked Taif, and after an initial repulse forced it to capitulate. He came to be regarded as invincible and his authority rapidly extended over the whole of southern Arabia.

His theocracy was supposed to be democratic, in that he asserted that all Moslems were equal in the eyes of God. He sought to abolish the blood feud and all forms of idolatry. He improved the status of women and of slaves and prohibited the ill-treatment of animals. A good Moslem must not strike a horse in the face or call down curses on fighting cocks. Baby girls must not henceforward be buried alive and one should only beat one's wife in the privacy of her own apartment. Considering the time and the place, his legislation was beneficent.

In January 632, his only son by a Coptic concubine, died in infancy. Mohammed was afflicted by this loss and declined rapidly in health. On June 7 he had an apoplectic stroke and died peaceably in the arms of Ayesha and without designating an heir.

The story of Mohammed is the story of a man of almost superhuman force of personality. His aim was to establish monotheism and to obtain recognition of himself as the prophet of Allah. He insisted on unquestioned obedience to his theocracy. 'I have come to you,' he wrote, 'with a sign from your Lord.' He sometimes identified the sign with a sebaceous cyst that he developed between the shoulder blades. 'Therefore be careful of your duty towards Allah and obey me.' The revelations vouchsafed to him through the angel Gabriel were such as to strengthen his theocratic despotism and to excuse his errors and weaknesses. When criticised for practising the sexual promiscuity that he

MOHAMMED'S
THEOCRATIC
DESPOTISM

condemned and prohibited in others, he had recourse to a heartening revelation. ' Surely, ' Allah remarked, ' your Lord best knows who errs from his way... Most surely you conform yourself to sublime morality. '

At times the Koran and the connected ' Sayings ' are precise in their instruction, but generally they fade into a mystic vagueness. The following, from Chapter XCVII, is typical of Koranic mysticism:

In the name of Allah, the Beneficent, the Merciful,
Surely we revealed it on the grand night.
And what will make you comprehend what the grand night is?
The grand night is better than a thousand months.
The Angels and the Inspiration descend in it by permission
Of their Lord for every affair.
Peace it is till the break of morning.

THE WORSHIP
OF THE
ONLY GOD

His main purpose, I repeat, was to destroy the pagan cult of tribal idols and to replace it by the worship of the only God. ' We follow the religion of Abraham, ' he wrote in the Koran, ' the upright one '. He was not one of the polytheists. He would refer to the period when the Arabs worshipped their tribal gods, and the Meccans bowed down before the statues of the goddesses Al-Lat and Al-Uzza, as ' the period of Ignorance. ' Again and again did God reveal his nature and purpose to mankind through the mouths of his messengers or prophets. There had been Adam, Seth, Enoch, Abraham, Moses, David, Jesus and Mohammed. He himself was the last of the series, ' the Seal of the prophets ': after his death there would be no more divine revelations. Of these eight prophets the only one who had been utterly sinless was Jesus Christ, but Christianity was itself heretical in supposing that God could ever have a son and in preaching the doctrine of the Trinity which enjoined on Christians the worship, not of a single God, but of three Gods.

Mohammed was persistently worried by the fact that he was unable to perform miracles. In the end he devised the theory that the victory of Badr was in itself a miracle, and that the fact that he himself was inspired to dictate the Koran in the ' pure Arabic tongue ' showed that he was directly obeying divine guidance. He based his teaching on Old Testament legends, which he frequently muddled or misinterpreted. When challenged for his plagiarism or inaccuracy he would reply that he often regarded his revelations as designed to test the faith of his followers, and even that he adopted them for ' his own comfort and convenience '.

He invented a whole heavenly hierarchy. There were four leading angels, the first shaped like a man, the second like a bull, the third

The Koran is the record of Mohammed's divinely inspired teaching: a copy of the first Koran printed in Meccah

like an eagle, and the fourth like a lion. Gabriel himself was fitted with six hundred wings, with any one of which he could upturn mountains. In addition there were the Seraphim, who sang the praises of God, two secretaries to record the doings of men, a heavenly host charged with the upkeep of the earth, and a crowd of spies or 'observers' to report on the actions of sinful men. In a category below the angels were the imps or Jinns and the fairies or Peri.

When a man dies, he is visited by two black angels with blue eyes called Munkar and Nakir, who examine him as to his faith in Allah and Mohammed. If the examination be unsatisfactory, then the victim is gnawed by dragons and scorpions; if he passes his examination he is relegated to *Al Barzakh* or 'the Interval', there to await the resurrection. Prophets are subject to no interval but on their deaths are immediately received in paradise; the souls of martyrs are during the interval lodged in the crops of green parrots who feed on the trees of paradise. The body of a dead man rots into dust and ashes, except for the single bone, the *Ajb*, which at the resurrection serves as a seed for physical renewal; the resurrection is accompanied by a great rain which covers the whole earth to a depth of twelve cubits, causing every *Ajb* to sprout. The resurrection will be heralded by several portents. The sun will rise in the west; Antichrist will appear, bearing the initials CFR upon his forehead and will be slain at the gate of Ludd by Christ himself, who will have returned to earth near the white tower which stands to the east of Damascus. Jesus will become a Moslem, will marry and beget a family, and will remain on earth for forty years, during which period there will be peace in all the world. Then Gog and Magog will appear and will capture Jerusalem. The Arabs will return to the cult of idols, and a great wind will blow away the souls of the faithful and even the leaves of the Koran. The Ka'bah will be thrown down by the Ethiopians; animals will start to speak with human tongues; until finally a Mahdi, bearing the prophet's own name, will come to restore order and true religion to mankind.

At the resurrection, the faithful will fly to paradise on white winged camels with saddles of gold and will there be provided with seventy-two wives, eighty thousand servants, and the gift of eternal youth. The supremely pious will be granted the privilege of seeing Allah in person once every morning and once every afternoon. The wicked and the unbelievers would be consigned to one of the seven circles of Hell and subjected to a variety of punishments similar to those related in the *Inferno*.

Apart from the main principles of religion and dogma, Mohammed in the Koran and accompanying statements laid down certain rituals and practices which the good Moslem must observe. He must pray five times a day, prostrating himself in the direction of Meccah and repeating the formula, 'There is only one God and Mohammed is his prophet.' He must wash his hands and feet before prayers and must be strict in preserving personal cleanliness and decency. He must fast during the month of Ramadan, must regard Friday as a sacred day, must distribute alms, and may have four wives, provided he accords them completely equal treatment, and as many concubines as he wishes. He must refrain from drinking wine and must avoid the flesh of pigs. He must cultivate fatalism and convince himself that everything that happens, whether it be bad or good, derives from divine will. It was a fine religion certainly, exacting in practice, but comforting in theory. Yet it remains a mystery why it should have swept with sword and fire throughout Asia, Africa and Spain.

The Prophet Mohammed died without designating a successor or leaving heirs male. By universal consent his devoted disciple Abu Bekr took

The tombs of the caliphs, Cairo. These tombs belonged to the Circassian or Burji Mame-lukes, whom Mohammed Ali extinguished

control under the title of Caliph, or 'The Successor of the Apostle of God'. He designated as his heir the mighty warrior Omar who captured Damascus, and subjected Egypt, Mesopotamia and part of Persia. He was murdered by a workman in the mosque at Medina and was succeeded by Uthman who in his turn was assassinated at the age of eighty. Uthman was succeeded by the Caliph Ali, who on being assassinated in 661 left two sons behind him, Hassan and Hussein.

The circle of the prophet's immediate disciples was by then exhausted and Muawiah founded the dynasty of the Umayyed Caliphs who extended the Islamic Empire from Cordova in the west to Kashgar in the east. In 750 the Umayyed dynasty petered out and was succeeded by the Abbasid dynasty, claiming descent from Abbas, uncle of the prophet. The Abbasids established themselves at Baghdad, rendered it a centre of learning and luxury under the name of 'The House of Science', and survived for five centuries. By the tenth century their power had much declined, until their rule was practically confined to the area around Baghdad. The later Abbasid Caliphs resembled the Merovingian *Rois Fainéants*, and were dependent on their Turkish praetorian guard under

245

its commander, the Mayor of the Palace, or *ami-ul-amara*. In 1258 came the capture of Baghdad by the Mongols, and the Caliphate, in so far as it survived at all, was transferred to Cairo. Here again the Caliph became a puppet in the hands of the Mamelukes, or praetorians, and the legend arose that the last of the Egyptian Caliphs transferred his authority to Selim I, the Sultan of Turkey. On capturing Cairo, Selim admittedly took possession of the mantle of the Prophet and of the sword of Omar which he carried off to the mosque of Eyub on the Golden Horn. By then, however, the office of Caliph had lost all prestige and it is doubtful whether Selim would have wished to adopt it. It was rather as *Amir-el-mu'minim* or 'Commander of the faithful' and as guardian of the Holy Places of Mecca and Medina that the Ottoman Sultans came to be accepted as the leaders of Islam.

THE SULTANS REVIVE THE TITLE OF CALIPH

It was not until the eighteenth century that the Sultans created the theory that they were the spiritual chiefs of all Moslems throughout the world. They could not claim to be descended from the sacred tribe of the Kuraish; they could not claim to be successors of the Prophet by Islamic Law; their only justification for calling themselves Caliph was that they represented in fact the strongest military power in the Moslem world. It was not until 1774, when by the Treaty of Kutchuk Kainardji Catherine II of Russia obtained recognition as the protectress of all Christians throughout the Ottoman Empire, that the Sultans formally revived the old title of Caliph and proclaimed themselves 'Sovereign Caliph of all Moslems'. In more recent years the Sultan Abdul Hamid, realising that he was doomed to lose his Christian provinces in Europe, created the fiction of 'Pan-Islamism' with himself as Caliph of all Moslems, whatever might be their political allegiance. He sent embassies as far as Java and China to establish this claim. As late as 26 February 1909, in the Austro-Turkish treaty which recognised the annexation of Bosnia and Herzogovina, it was stipulated that the Sultan of Turkey was still to be prayed for as Caliph in the Bosnian mosques, and that the local priests should remain dependent upon the Sheikh-ul-Islam at Constantinople.

Although Abdul Hamid achieved some success with the formation of the Khilafat movement in India, and although our own India Office regarded this movement as a serious potential menace, his attempt in 1914 to proclaim a holy war as Caliph met with little response. On 1 November 1922 the National Assembly at Ankara declared that the Sultanate was abolished but invested Abdul Mejid as Caliph. He was arrayed with the mantle of the Prophet but not girt with the sword of Omar. In March 1924 the Caliphate itself was abolished and Abdul Mejid packed off into exile on the French Riviera. The Pan-Islamic world accepted this abolition of the Caliphate with scarcely a word of protest.

It was the absence throughout its history of any system of primogeniture that created the great schism of Sunni and Shia in the Moslem world. The majority of Moslems, the Sunni, said to number one hundred and forty-five million, contend that the Caliphate, although preferably confined to members of the Kuraish clan, is essentially an elective office and one that is most conveniently conferred on the ruler who controls the two sacred cities and is best fitted to be the defender of the faith. The fifteen million or so Shiahs, who are mainly concentrated in Iran,

The Mosque of Eyub, Istanbul, last home of the mantle of the Prophet and the sword of Omar

contend that the hereditary principle is all important, that no Caliph who is not descended from the Prophet himself can be regarded as legitimate, and that therefore the successors of Ali, who married the Prophet's daughter Fatima, must be regarded as the legitimate Imams, or Vicars of God on earth. Ali Reza of Meshed was the eighth Imam, and the twelfth Imam disappeared mysteriously and will one day return to earth to secure the unity of Islam and the recognition of Ali and his sons as 'the hands of God'.

The sacred sites of the Shiahs are Rajaf, where Ali was buried, and Kerbela where his son Hussein was murdered and lies in the mosque. Fatima, the daughter of Ali Reza, is buried at Kum near Teheran, where the golden dome that covers her grave twinkles above the green little city set in a waste of stone and sand. To this day the first ten days of the month of Muharrem are devoted by the Shiah world to mourning for the deaths of Ali, Hassan and Hussein. The faithful leave the mosques in processions, shouting the cadence, 'Hassan! Hussein!', and slashing themselves with knives until their white robes are drenched with blood. In the evenings, to the glitter of a thousand candles, are held the passion plays, or *ta'ziwa*, at which the murder of Ali and his sons is enacted in stylised form, during which the audience beat their breasts, sway backwards and forwards, and intone the names of Hassan and Hussein with distraught lamentation.

THE HOUSE
OF OSMAN

No system of kingship has been so intricate or so precarious as that of the Caliph-Sultan despotism of the house of Osman, which exercised unbroken sovereignty for six hundred and fifty years. In theory the Sultan, having been acclaimed at the Gate of Felicity and girded at Eyub with the sword of Omar, was supreme head of religion and unquestioned autocrat in all secular matters. In practice, however, the Sultan was subject to incessant plots, could be deposed by a *fetva* of the Sheikh-ul-Islam and could be imprisoned or murdered. At least half the Sultans of the House of Osman were in some violent manner deposed.

Until the second decade of the nineteenth century the power of the Sultans was hampered by the ever-increasing demands of the corps of Janissaries, who terrorised both the capital and the palace. Originally but a small regiment of trained soldiers composed of Christian slaves and Albanians, specially trained in the profession of arms, their numbers had by the nineteenth century risen to a hundred and thirty-five thousand. Not only did they claim as a right a huge donation at the accession of any new Sultan, but again and again they would set fire to Stamboul as

Young king on his knees in prayer, an early sixteenth-century manuscript in the Kevorkian Collection

a means of enforcing their blackmail. Successive Sultans endeavoured to rid themselves of these praetorians by recruiting and training palace guards of their own. Yet always such attempts were frustrated by the Janissaries who would gather on the Ok Meidan or Hippodrome, threaten to burst through the Gate of Felicity, and to loot and burn the Seraglio itself. Eventually Sultan Mahmoud II resolved that an end must be put to the tyranny of these praetorians. The Janissaries had gathered in front of the palace to enforce their demands, but the Sultan had manned the walls with cannon and the assembled praetorians were bombarded and destroyed. After 10 June 1826 the Janissaries had been liquidated and the Sultan freed.

THE IMPERIAL HAREM

There were, however, other more secret forces that hampered his autocracy. The imperial harem was enormous and the black and white eunuchs who were supposed to maintain discipline were generally weak, incompetent or corrupt. The competition and resulting jealousy between the thousand concubines were incessant and intense. A girl who had the good fortune to attract the Sultan's notice, might end by bearing a son, in which fortunate event she received the title of ' Princess Favourite ', or *Haseki Sultan*. Should her son succeed to the throne she became the first lady in the land, under the title of Queen Mother or *Valide Sultan*.

In view of what Alderson calls ' this dangerous profusion of male heirs ', the Law of Fratricide was passed, permitting the Sultan to murder all his male relations and their wives and children. This law was called the *Kanun Namé* and was issued in 1451 by Sultan Mehmed II. ' And to whomsoever of my sons, ' decreed Mehmed, ' the Sultanate may pass, it is fitting that for the order of the world he shall kill his brothers. ' The law, although drastic, did preserve the Empire from civil war and maintain the dynasty for almost seven hundred years.

These murders were carried out by the Court Executioner assisted by deaf mutes. Since the shedding of blood was believed to be forbidden by the Koran, the victims were strangled quietly with a silken cord, called the Keman-Kirisi. Their bodies were buried decently at Eyub, but their wives or pregnant concubines were sewn up in sacks, the head being left exposed, and the bottom of the sack weighted with large stones. These sacks were dumped into the Bosphorus and were carried down by the current until they formed a regiment of upright sacks, wedged in among the rocks and slime of the Seraglio point, their skulls grinning, and their long black or auburn hair swaying in the

The Seraglio. The sultan's mother ruled over this elaborately organized community; after her ranked the mother of the heir-apparent, then the ladies who had borne the sultan's younger children and, lastly, the odalisques

strong current that runs from the Black Sea into the Marmora. In later years some European divers employed on salvage work were so terrified by this spectacle that they signalled to be pulled up and refused thereafter to enter the water again.

European opinion was shocked by the Law of Fratricide and later Sultans devised a more ingenious method of the ridding themselves of all rivals to the throne. The system was adopted of confining the male members of the House of Osman in *kafes* or cages, where they were consistently debilitated by alcohol, drugs, aphrodisiacs and fornication. The *kafes* were in fact little huts in a concentration camp in which the princes of the blood were imprisoned for life in darkened rooms, until they lost their reason or died. It was this habit of family murder that accounts for the almost panic terror in which most Sultans passed their lives.

I have seen two Caliphs only in my life, the first being Abdul Hamid II, and the second Mohammed V, his successor. I saw Abdul Hamid on two occasions, the first being when he was still the autocrat of the Ottoman Empire, and the second some eighteen years later when he had been deposed and was preserved under strict guard in the palace of Beylerbey upon the Asiatic side of the Bosphorus.

The ceremony of the Selamlik was held on a Friday in the little mosque outside the gates of the Yildiz Kiosk. The square was packed with troops belonging to several different regiments, and foreign visitors were accommodated in a kiosk with many windows and a wide balcony from which they could watch the ceremony. While waiting for the iron gates of Yildiz to swing open, the court officials entertained their foreign visitors with polite conversation, coffee and macaroons. Suddenly the gates of the palace would be flung open and from the shadows of the park would emerge a neat little victoria which dashed across the hundred yards separating the palace from the mosque. Seated inside the victoria and all alone was the bowed figure of Abdul Hamid, dressed as always in a fez and frock coat, slowly raising a white gloved hand in response to the salutes of the soldiery, and having all the appearance of a stricken bird of prey. On reaching the mosque, the Sultan would slowly climb the steps which were flanked by the members of his cabinet in gold lace and decorations. He would then turn his whitened face towards the square, at which the courtiers in the kiosk would make an obeisance and the troops would yell in unison, ' May our Padishah live for many years' . The Sultan would then enter the mosque and for some twenty minutes be absorbed in prayer. On leaving the mosque he would be accompanied by his ministers who, for the short stretch of road that separated the mosque from the palace, would run panting beside the carriage of the Caliph, even as the court officials had run beside the chariot of Diocletian.

My second sight of Abdul Hamid was some eighteen years later when, having been removed from Salonika in the German Embassy yacht lest he fell into the hands of the advancing Greeks, he was imprisoned in the lovely palace of Beylerbey, beside the Bosphorus. In an attempt to defy the current, I was tacking in my sailing boat backwards and forwards across the Bosphorus and on one tack I came close to the marble terrace of the palace. Pacing up and down the terrace, again alone, again in his black frock coat and fez, was the deposed Sultan, unmistakable owing to his dead white face and carrion nose. His warders or jailors kept at some distance from him with their arms crossed

Right: *Abdul Hamid II, Sultan of Turkey from 1876 to 1909. He was deposed and spent his last years as a prisoner*

The Dolmabagché Palace, where the Sultans lived after abandoning the Seraglio in the reign of Abd-ul-Mejid

respectfully, their hands tucked into their sleeves. A police launch at this stage dashed out of the boathouse and drove me away with imprecations. I sped on the opposite tack across the water to the European shore.

My last sight of any Caliph was when I attended a ceremony held in the great hall of Dolmabaghtche Palace by Abdul Hamid's successor, Mohammed V. All his life had been spent in internment, being gorged with food, women and wine. This treatment had, as was intended, exercised a deleterious effect upon his physical and mental powers. The old man gazed around him in piteous bewilderment, shuffling one foot after another across the marble floor, and being poked and pushed by court officials in the direction that he was supposed to follow.

The office of Caliph had by then become little more than an archaic survival. Within a few years the Sultans were to be deprived of the holy cities of Meccah and Medina and could no longer claim to be defenders of the faith. In March 1924 the Caliphate was for ever abolished by the National Assembly at Ankara.

THIRTEEN

Bonapartism

'BONAPARTISM' IS A TERM USED TO define despotism by popular consent. After a period of turmoil, the majority of people want calm to be restored and are ready to surrender their personal liberties to an individual who is strong enough to discipline the political factions, to subdue the city mobs and to impose law and order. This consent is given all the more readily if the despot be a military genius who can provide his people with glory. Once the glory fades, his authority wanes.

Yet before we examine the systems of the two outstanding exemplars of Bonapartism, Napoleon I and Napoleon III, it may be useful to consider the analagous method of paternal despotism, enforced by that extraordinary monarch, King Frederick II of Prussia, rightly called Frederick the Great.

When Frederick succeeded his fierce father in 1740, his accession was hailed by Voltaire and other prophets of the enlightenment as the advent of a philosopher king. It is probable that his testamentary disposition on the art of kingship, known as *Les Matinées du roi de Prusse*, is a forgery concocted by his enemies. The duc de Rovigo, when visiting Sans Souci in the company of Napoleon, claimed to have filched the manuscript of this cynical document from a drawer of Frederick's writing table. In this Frederick is represented as saying that justice is but a

255

Allegorical painting of Frederick the Great imposing the Treaty of Hubertusberg in 1763, which ended the Seven Years War and by which, through his military genius and by exploiting the weaknesses of his enemies, he gained an advantageous peace

relative term and that the art of politics consists in deceiving others. Religion is useful as the opiate of the masses, but a monarch should never be religious, since this is apt to create a conscience, and any ruler who possesses a conscience is 'hampered' in the execution of his duties. Frederick the Great was not a liberal philosopher; he suffered no qualms in repudiating his father's guarantee of the Pragmatic Sanction even as he suffered no qualms in partitioning Poland. His watchword was 'efficiency' rather than 'liberty'.

The legend of this temperate monarch, guided in all his actions by 'virtue' and 'the law of nature', is derived from the pamphlet which he composed, when heir-apparent, under the title of *Anti-Machiavel*. To a certain extent he carried out the precepts of this manifesto when he succeeded to the throne. He introduced complete religious toleration: he abolished torture except for crimes of high treason; he saw to it

Frederick the Great reviewing his soldiers, after David Chodowiecki. Frederick introduced a most rigid and exact system of tactics and drill for infantry, and greatly improved cavalry tactics. Horse artillery was another potent innovation

that there was no delay, class prejudice or corruption in the administration of justice: he did much to promote education: he established agricultural colonies, dredged wide areas of marsh, and insisted that fruit trees should be planted along the main roads of his dominions. He encouraged industry and imported silk-worms and mulberries. He revived the Academy of Sciences and encouraged foreign men of letters to visit Potsdam and to help him to render his capital a centre of culture. He drafted the *Landrecht*, a comprehensive German code of law. When he died he had re-established the finances of his realm by the strictest, the most meticulous, economy. He left seventy million thalers in the public treasury, while being able to increase and maintain an army of 200,000 disciplined men. In his own lifetime he had rendered his disjointed inheritance one of the most compact and formidable Powers in Europe.

In his *Anti-Machiavel* he defined what was to become the guiding principle of his reign. 'The prince,' he wrote, 'is not the absolute master, but only the first servant, of his people.' To this service he devoted his tremendous energies without stint or holiday. He supervised the whole administration with incessant and minute investigation. His Ministers, although chosen because of their integrity and capacity, were reduced to the status of civil service clerks. He would rise at six in the morning and continue to work through the long hours of the night, while his greyhounds twitched and snored in front of the stove and his pages drowsed on narrow benches in the corridor outside. His sole relaxation from civil and military duties were playing the flute at state concerts, indulging in conversation at suppertime, romping with his greyhounds, and composing French verses of questionable quality.

He was certainly cynical in that he believed that people were guided solely by fear or self-interest and he would describe the breed of human beings as *diese verdammte Rasse*. He failed to appreciate the German language, which he himself wrote and spoke no better than an ostler; he refused to provide a university appointment for Lessing and regarded Goethe's *Goetz von Berlichingen* as a vulgar copy of a vulgar English original. But he was nice to his mother and his sister; loyal to men like Keith and his beloved valet Fredersdorff; kind to his dogs; beastly to his miserable wife. He was certainly a man of genius and courage.

MILLER ARNOLD ⟩ One of the peculiarities of this highly gifted king was that he possessed a talent for propaganda unusual in monarchs and was able to project, both to his own subjects and to foreign opinion, an idealised picture of himself. He was not a cleanly man and persuaded people that his dirty clothes were evidence of commendable austerity. He would in public feed on beer and sausages, whereas in his private supper-room at Sans Souci the most exquisite French cuisine and wines were provided. It was ingenious of him to secure such wide publicity for the story of Miller Arnold, whose livelihood had been affected by the construction in the mill-stream of a pleasure pond for some riparian noble. The judges of Custrin had decided against Arnold, whose wife was an obstinate and litigious shrew, who managed by her persistence to attract the King's attention, to have the judgement reversed, and the unjust judges cast into prison. It is true that on King Frederick's death the case was revised and the judges exonerated. It is true also that in strict liberal theory the Monarchy had no right to interfere with the judiciary. Yet the Miller Arnold legend spread throughout Europe and seemed

Sans Souci, retreat of the philosopher-king, Frederick the Great, at Potsdam: the south side of the central pavilion

to justify the despot's claim to be 'the advocate of the poor'. People forgot the doctrine of separation of powers.

Another such sentimental story was the tale of the other miller, who refused to sell his mill at Potsdam to provide for an extension of the terrace at Sans Souci. 'Do you not realise,' thundered the King's land-agent at the obstinate miller, 'that the King can confiscate your property?' 'But haven't we,' the man replied, 'the Court of Justice, the *Kammergericht?*' So he kept his mill, the stump of which, to this day is pointed out to tourists by the Potsdam guides as 'the historical mill', *die historische Mühle*. But little mention is made of the civil servants whom he imprisoned without fair trial, or of the young lieutenants whom he reduced to the ranks.

In spite of heavy taxation, carried out on the hated *régie* system, in spite of continuous war, the Prussian people worshipped their eccentric monarch. They were proud, as well they might be, of his military genius, and glad to surrender themselves to an autocrat who ministered to their vanity and who, before their eyes, was rendering their country a great European Power. The guarantee of all despotic systems is success. Yet Frederick the Great, for all his faith in rigid discipline, did in fact regard himself as the father of his people, and was anxious (having himself been taught a bitter lesson when young) not to render too cruel or capricious the *patria potestas* which he enforced. He believed in autocracy: but he also believed in the rule of law. He stands high in the list of effective and benevolent monarchs.

THE JUSTI-
FICATION OF
BONAPARTISM

The system of paternal despotism, so generously enforced by Frederick the Great, differs only in degree from Bonapartism - or the system of despotism by popular consent. The two historic examples of Bonapartism are Napoleon I and Napoleon III. Each of them doubted the wisdom or efficiency of popular assemblies, being convinced that elected deputies are concerned solely with their own interests and the needs of their own party or constituents and that their actions are clouded by vanity, jealousy and greed. It will be admitted that the intense individualism of the French character does in fact impede party discipline and that their delight in abstract theory does reduce their legislative acts to statements of principle which have to be interpreted in forms of jurisprudence by an army of bureaucrats. An English Act of Parliament is generally as detailed and precise as the parliamentary draughtsmen can render it; the civil servant and the judiciary know where they stand. In France, the legislature is apt to frame its enactments in vague, often in rhetorical, language, with the result that the civil service has wider latitude of interpretation. These vague enunciations of political theory were carried to excess during the Revolution, and Napoleon I, in his desire to 'close the romance of the Revolution', decided that it was preferable to govern by quick sharp edicts than to allow assemblies to legislate emotionally.

He was anything but a theorist or an ideologue. He possessed a remarkably tidy mind and viewed with contempt the chaos that the Revolution and the Directorate had left behind. The majority of the clergy were in open rebellion against the State; education was disorganised; the armed forces lacked discipline and equipment; trade and credit had dwindled. He was resolved to discipline the Church, to reorganize education; to see that the law was respected and obeyed throughout the land; to create a powerful army; and to restore the credit of the country's finances and the prosperity of her commerce. The ideal of individual liberty had been perverted by Robespierre into what Dr Fisher has called 'a cowed and spiritless acceptance of collective control'. Local administration had broken down and there existed no resident provincial class able to restore law and order. The French people were

Napoleon as First Consul (1799-1804) by Gerard, now in the Musée Condé, Chantilly

weary of confusion: Napoleon knew that order could only be recovered by rigorous centralisation; he was forced by circumstances to become a despot. He also knew that, if he were to fuse the old France with post-Revolution France, he must respect certain national prejudices or illusions, while fortifying others.

He was well aware that what the French masses most desired was to retain what they had won from the nobility and the Church. Thus private property, however acquired, must be regarded as sacred and 'a law of nature'. It is strange that the Revolution, partly owing to the distrust felt in their leaders of any form of corporation or trade union, should never have sought to preach or to enforce the principles of socialism. The theorists of the Revolution regarded all corporations, such as the Church and the guilds, as restrictions on individual liberty. Napoleon shared and used these prejudices; to his mind, no interest should be allowed to become dominant, apart from the interest of the State and the interest of the individual. He had an acid contempt for the intrusion of emotion into politics. 'Those who wish to serve me,' he wrote, 'must suppress all passion.' Efficiency alone was to be the watchword. In making the *coup d'état* of Brumaire, his aim was, not

merely to restore confidence by establishing order, but 'to substitute a regular, scientific, civilised administration for a condition of affairs that bordered on anarchy '.

He well realised that religion was necessary for the masses, if only as an opiate. 'The people,' he said, 'must have a religion, but that religion must be in the hands of the government.' Thus, by the Concordat of 1801 the Church was reduced almost to a civil service department, under the Minister of Cults. The clergy were expected to preach the virtues of conscription, to read out the army bulletins from their pulpits and to inculcate veneration for the person of the Emperor. This system might have been accepted by the majority of Catholics, had not Napoleon seized the property of the Papal See and treated the Pope himself with gross indignity. His efforts to conciliate public opinion were again and again rendered abortive by his vulgar tendency to go too far and to rely too confidently on material strength, or what he incessantly referred to as his 'star'.

In internal administration again he restored security and order by centralising the whole system under the government in Paris. It was Napoleon who chose the prefets of the Departments, the sous-prefets in the arrondissements, and even the mayors in the communes. He inspired these officials with his own passion for tidiness and with something of his own supernatural capacity for hard and detailed work. His own memory was prodigious and when he descended on the provinces the knees of the sous-prefets would knock together when scrutinised by that sharp enquiring voice and by the terrifying glance of his grey eyes. Not only did he know what was happening in the Ministry of Interior in Paris, but by his astonishing knowledge and memory of local conditions, he could strike terror into the heart of the sous-prefet of Chalons-sur-Saône.

The educational system of France was also secularised and *gleich geschaltet*. The lycée, and the teacher, were placed directly under the supervision of the University of France which was the equivalent of a Ministry of Education. The boys in the lycées were instructed by the imperial Catechism to view their Emperor as a semi-divine person. Primary education, or the education of the masses, was regarded as highly dangerous. The peasants were allowed to remain mainly illiterate.

EDUCATION
UNDER
NAPOLEON

Left: *Le 18 Brumaire by François Bouchot. On his return from Egypt in 1799, where he had won the Battle of the Pyramids, Napoleon was swept to power by a coup d'état which overthrew the Directory*

Napoleon I did not believe in the three watchwords of the Revolution, Liberty, Equality, Fraternity. With his own eyes he had witnessed the atrocities committed in the name of Liberty, which he regarded as a doctrinaire expression conducive to disorder. Equality seemed to him to be based on an utter disregard of biology, and he substituted for it the doctrine, the admirable doctrine, of equality of opportunity, 'a career open to talent'. Those who, by their service and capacity qualified for promotion, were accorded lavish rewards. Kingdoms, *incentives* principalities, dukedoms and vast riches were at the command of the successful, and the meanest private soldier was supposed to carry a marshal's baton in his knapsack.

CIVIL POMP AND MILITARY GLORY

Napoleon was acutely aware of the importance, in any monarchy, of the elements of pageantry, splendour and display. Even as First Consul he surrounded himself with the apparatus of a court, and as Emperor the etiquette that he imposed was rigid and sumptuous. He rendered his despotism highly decorative, even though, to the surviving members of the old régime (and they were few), it appeared artificial and vulgar. Above all he ministered thoroughly to the national passion for military glory. The pride and excitement that his victories aroused among the people fortified his claim to be the elected despot of the masses. It was only when his victories failed him that the French people began to question the infallibility of the dictator whom they had chosen.

He would himself, in the days of his power, never have questioned his own dictatorial rights. On one occasion, when the elected Assembly had the courage to protest against his despotic system, he turned on them in fury. 'I,' he said, 'represent the people of this country: you represent the arrondissements.' Until 1812 this claim was certainly true.

The 'Code Napoleon' although in many respects a model of tolerant jurisprudence, did not in fact guarantee personal security to the individual. It provided complete religious toleration and instituted the jury system; it paid no regard at all to the rights of women, and, while rigidly protecting the sanctity of private property, it furnished the individual Frenchman with no guarantee against arbitrary arrest and other evil practices of totalitarian systems. The system of *lettres de cachet* was in practice continued by Fouché, the gifted head of the police, who still spied on his fellow citizens and could still, if they

Right: The Coronation Service of Napoleon I by David (1748-1825), now in the Musée du Louvre. Napoleon caused consternation by seizing his crown from the Papal Legate and crowning himself

aroused the slightest suspicion of sedition, have them arrested and packed off to Cayenne.

Napoleon held a poor view of human nature, believing that all the actions of man were determined either by greed or fear. ' My dominion, ' he said, ' is founded on fear. If I abandoned the system I should immediately be dethroned. ' Or again: ' When a king is said to be a kind king, his reign is a failure. ' Such cynical utterances accord ill with the theory of despotism resting on a basis of popular affection. Yet the fact remains that, in spite of his despotic ways, his wild ambitions, and his contempt for all forms of representative government, Napoleon I did really strive to secure the greatest happiness of the greatest number of Frenchmen. ' He was, ' writes Dr Fisher, ' the last (and perhaps the most benevolent) of benevolent despots. '

Napoleon I always asserted that he showed the greatest respect for historical tradition and for those institutions that were part of the organic growth of the State. In France itself he did in fact pay regard to traditional formulas and sought in his administrative system to create the forms of centralisation to which the people had been accustomed since the days of Richelieu. ' He gave France what she wanted, ' writes Dr Fisher, ' and his work has outlasted three Revolutions. ' In Switzerland again he followed tradition and in his Act of Mediation combined cantonal autonomy with the conception of a central democratic State.

NAPOLEON'S RESPECT FOR TRADITION

Yet his treatment of other conquered territories paid but little regard either to the geographical or the political traditions of the subjected populations. The tradition of continuity was violated by his restless habit of drawing frontiers of his own invention across the map of Europe. The democratic aspirations of the Enlightenment were flouted by his suspicion of elected assemblies, and by his elaborate provisions of electoral colleges so chosen as to ' filter ', and in fact to prevent, the free expression of the popular will. So far from according ' liberty ' to the conquered countries, he deprived them of those freedoms which they already possessed. He imposed on them the harshest measures of conscription: his fiscal exactions were tyrannous: he stole from their museums the most treasured examples of art: and he openly proclaimed his contempt for the spirit of nationalism. ' I wish in Poland, ' he remarked to Narbonne, ' to have a camp and not a forum. ' When his brother Louis showed signs of wishing to defend Dutch interests, he was driven from the throne. The satellites and the conquered provinces were fully aware that they were regarded by their master as mere tools

Napoleon and Marie-Louise entering the Tuileries on the day of their marriage, 2 April 1810 by E.B. Garnier now at Versailles

and instruments in his blockade of England. Since he could not invade ' the inviolate island of the sage and free ', he determined to starve us out by his Continental System. Even if this meant ruin to the Dutch and the Hansa towns, he was determined to enforce it ruthlessly. His despotism, outside France, was certainly not exercised with the consent of the populations concerned. His satellites were well aware that they were being exploited and ruined to serve the despot's ambition, and when eventually he fell, they welcomed the disappearance of a tyrant rather than they deplored the removal of a liberator. (It was Napoleon assuredly who cleared much feudal lumber from Europe; it was he, more than any other man, who created the idea of Italian, and even German, unity. But it would be a mistake to assume that Bonapartism was applied to the conquered territories, or that his rigid autocracy was welcomed by his satellites. They were all too conscious that they were being tyrannised solely in French interests.)

The mighty French Empire, resplendent though it seemed, was founded, not on consent, but on resentment. Once the military infallibility of Napoleon had declined, his autocracy was exposed to public obloquy. The 'War of Liberation' was fought, not against the old feudal monarchies of Europe, but against the Great Liberator himself.

Few people accused Bonapartism of corruption or inefficiency. But they did accuse it of ruthless exploitation. They resented also his repudiation of promises that he had overtly made or principles that he had rhetorically expounded. It is strange that a man of his political genius should not have realised, until it was too late, that no man can command acquiescence by brutality. Nor did it ever seem to dawn upon him that untruthfulness arouses suspicions of dishonesty and that dishonesty destroys popular confidence. Napoleon, as other dictators, had but slight regard for truth. 'On a scale unparalleled in history,' writes Dr Fisher, 'he erected mendacity into an art of Empire.' It was not his military ambition only, his insatiable passion for glory that led to his fall: it was also his tricky conduct. Aristotle and Hitler contended that a people could be impressed by 'the magnificent lie': the lies of Napoleon I were anything but magnificent.

THE FAULTS OF BONAPARTISM

He appears, while in exile at Elba, to have reflected on the causes of his failure to keep public opinion on his side, and to have concluded that autocracy by consent was no longer feasible. The Bourbons having,

The battle of Austerlitz, Napoleon's most brilliant victory, 1805. The Emperor can be seen directing the operations himself

Napoleon bids farewell to his staff and troops before leaving for Elba after his first abdication in 1814, after Horace Vernet

in spite of their rallying cry of 'legitimacy', been installed by foreign armies, made no sentimental appeal to public opinion. Napoleon realised while at Elba that there were waves of suspicion, elements of revolt, traversing the French masses. The peasants, anxious as always to preserve the fields that they had won, were terrified lest the Church and the émigrés would deprive them of their stolen goods. The officers who had been placed on half pay longed for the sun of Austerlitz to blaze again. But Napoleon also realised that there existed in France a body of solid liberal opinion which it would be a grave political error henceforward to ignore.

Thus, on regaining the Tuileries, Napoleon sent for Benjamin Constant, who in spite of his unreliable character, was regarded as the martyr, as well as the most gifted exponent, of liberalism. With him he drew up the *Acte Additionel* under which he resoundingly identified himself with the liberal programme. Henceforward the executive was to be controlled by the elected legislature; the Church was to be disestablished; and the Press freed. Henceforward, the Empire would stand for peace and liberal democracy. Bonapartism as a system of military despotism was to be abandoned. But Napoleon had made many promises before and his repudiation of his own system did not inspire any widespread confidence. With the fall of Napoleon I, the world believed that the despotism of his Empire had been removed for ever. Metternich himself expressed the view that there could be no Bonapartism without Napoleon. He was incorrect in this assumption.

The great Napoleon possessed a mind of uncommon shrewdness. He realised at St Helena that a new legend could be created on a foundation of martyrdom. 'Adversity,' he remarked to Las Cases, 'was wanting to my career.' He thus proclaimed, exploited and enhanced his own adversity. He gave to Europe and to posterity the tragic picture of a Prometheus, a lone eagle, chained to a barren rock. To this day the French picture the lovely, equable island of St Helena as a barren antarctic precipice swept by gales. As he dictated his memoirs, restlessly pacing up and down the dining room at Longwood, he built up, with scant regard for historical accuracy, a sentimental picture of himself. He had been the child of the Revolution and the champion of nationality: he had defended the Church, introduced into society the sacred principle of equality of opportunity, and repressed disorder. 'I did not usurp the throne,' he proclaimed; 'I found the crown of France in the gutter and the people of France placed it on my head.' If fate had granted him twenty, instead of but thirteen, years he would have created, not a wide despotism, but the United States of Europe based on popular consent. Throughout the continent he would have established liberal constitutions; Parliaments would be elected directly by the people and accorded complete control of domestic and foreign policy; the Press was to be wholly free; the judges were to be irremovable; any citizen would have the right to prosecute the Government in cases of injustice; all mankind was to be free. If he had been allowed to conquer England, his first act would have been to abolish the House of Lords, and to entrust to Sir Francis Burdett the task of drafting a new and wholly liberal British constitution. These hopes, these high ambitions, had been dashed at Waterloo; and now the lone eagle on his barren rock could but inform the world of the glorious liberal world which they had failed to win.

Marie-Louise painting the Emperor's portrait, by Menjaud at Versailles

This apologia had a powerful effect. Poets such as Victor Hugo, versifiers such as Béranger, spread the romantic legend. In every cottage of France there were engravings of the vanished martyr performing deeds of heroism or loving kindness. The legend of Bonaparte lived on.

Louis Napoleon, nephew of Napoleon I, was the son of Louis Bonaparte, for a short time King of Holland, and Hortense Beauharnais. His version of Bonapartism was founded on the principle of autocracy by popular consent, its harsher outlines being veiled in the mists of the St Helena martyrology. When in 1832 the duc de Reichstadt died in Austrian captivity, Louis Napoleon, then aged twenty-four, became the head of the Bonaparte family. The Government of Louis Philippe made the mistake of asking the Swiss Government to expel him from their territory. In order not to embarrass the federal authorities he voluntarily withdrew to London, from where he issued several pamphlets, designed to perpetuate the Napoleonic legend and to represent himself as a martyr and an exile. He would refer to his illustrious uncle as the 'Emperor who had risen from the ranks' (*L'Empereur plébéen*), and contended that, had he not been defeated at Waterloo, he would have created a liberal France and have accorded independence and unity to Poland, Italy and Germany. In these writings he indicated that there would one day arise a Second Empire, based on the will of the people, 'the only source of what is generous and great'. This second Empire would take up the great work of liberation which had been interrupted by Waterloo. To France it would accord, not the transient glory of military conquests, but '*une gloire civile, plus grande et plus durable*'. To the world it would give a League of Free Nations, united by a common code of law and a common judiciary. The doctrine of nationality would be everywhere triumphant and prosperity and trade would flourish throughout the earth. This had been the true intention of Napoleon I, 'the great Messiah of ideas'. It was he who had first realised that essentially democracy was 'a colossal pyramid, with a wide base and its apex raised on high'. There would be a world government, possessing all the advantages of a Republic without its disadvantages. Peace without conquest would be the motto of this second Empire. It would be ruled and guided by an Emperor elected by a popular vote or plebiscite. In this manner would the voice of the people directly decide the fate and constitution of their country.

The misfortune was that the second Napoleon did not possess the concentration or the magnetism of his uncle. His physical appearance was unimpressive and he spoke French with a German accent. His legs were short and his eyes lacked all animation. Greville, who met him in London, describes him as 'a short, thickish, vulgar-looking man, without the slightest resemblance to his imperial uncle or any intelligence in his countenance'. The French politicians of the time did not, until it was too late, realise that beneath this impassive exterior lurked a shrewd intelligence and a cold ambition. The illusion that Louis Napoleon did not represent a danger and that there was no reason to take him seriously was confirmed by the collapse of the two *coups d'état* which he attempted, the first at Strasbourg in 1836 and the second at Boulogne in 1840. Each of these two adventures was ill-considered and ill-planned. They ended in fiasco and ridicule. After the first escapade the young

LOUIS NAPOLEON'S UNSUCCESSFUL COUPS D'ETAT

273

Napoleon III, Emperor of the French. Louis Napoleon reigned as Emperor for eighteen years from 1852-70

prince was permitted to exile himself to America and then to England. The Boulogne episode was taken more seriously, and Louis Napoleon was condemned to life imprisonment in the fortress of Ham on the Somme. He devoted the years of his confinement to the intensive study of history, botany, and natural science, and to the skilful dissemination of the analogy between the prisoner of Ham and the prisoner of St Helena. In 1847 he managed to escape from his fortress in the disguise of a workman engaged upon some repairs in the jailor's private residence. He just walked out through the gateway dressed in a workman's blouse and carrying a board on his shoulder. He thereafter crossed the frontier and made good his escape to London.

Meanwhile the paternal government of Louis Philippe, the benignant smile upon those pear-shaped features, had begun to strike the French people as too smug to be tolerated. '*La France s'ennuie,*' remarked Lamartine; and the excitement of impending revolution began to animate the working classes of Paris. The King and his Ministers escaped to Newhaven and for a while the mob ran riot in the streets of Paris. The property owning classes, which had much increased in numbers and power under the rule of the bourgeois monarchy, feared that something approaching communism was threatening the stability of the State. But the masses and the industrial workers continued in a state of ferment. They were determined to create a social republic based on universal suffrage and the abolition of private property. To the surprise of all in the Constituent Assembly elected in May 1848, the moderates held a majority. Foreseeing that their dreams of revolution were in jeopardy, the workers launched an insurrection and barricades were constructed in the streets of Paris. The Provisional Government acted with resolution and appointed General Cavaignac as military dictator. The barricades were broken down, the workers decimated, and the leading members of the socialist party deported overseas.

Louis Napoleon had been elected to the Constituent Assembly by as many as five Departments. His first speech to the Assembly was another fiasco. Members were bored by his clichés and amused by his German accent. They continued to regard him as a comic figure who need not be taken seriously. Yet behind their backs he was cautiously plotting the seizure of power.

The constitution, as framed by the Constituent Assembly on 4 November 1848, provided for a single legislative assembly and for an executive to be entrusted, on the American model, to a president to be chosen by a popular vote, or plebiscite. So little did they fear the growing tide of Bonapartism, or the personality of Louis Napoleon, that they omitted to declare ineligible for the presidency any member of a former dynasty. At the ensuing plebiscite Louis Napoleon was elected President by five million votes. He established himself in the Elysée, where his uncle had spent his last night in Paris before retiring to Malmaison and St Helena.

LOUIS NAPOLEON ELECTED PRESIDENT

The next three years were marked by a bitter struggle between the Prince President, as chief of the Executive, and the republican wing of the Chamber. By skilfully playing off the monarchists against the republicans and by winning the support of the Catholics and the army, he succeeded in defeating the republicans under Ledru-Rollin. The Assembly then committed the error of swinging too much to the right. They abolished universal suffrage and imposed a property qualification on electors, so framed as to exclude the industrial workers. They also introduced a severe press law, based on the deposit by all newspaper editors of a 'caution money' to secure their good behaviour. This enabled the Prince President to campaign for the return of universal suffrage and to attack the property qualification. At the same time he frightened the middle classes by representing himself as their champion against an impending communist revolution.

On the night of 2 December 1851, the Prince President suddenly dissolved the Chamber, arrested the opposition leaders, and induced a packed Parliament to decree the extension of his term of office for ten years. The republican leaders were imprisoned in Mazas; Cavaignac was interned in the fortress of Ham; and Victor Hugo slipped across the frontier into Belgium. Two thousand politicians were exiled; ten thousand were shipped to Algeria; and three hundred of the extreme left were deported to Cayenne, which was known as *la guillotine à sec*. The uncle had not exacted similar reprisals after Brumaire. A plebiscite sanctioned these transactions by an enormous majority.

A year later, on 2 December 1852, the Prince President proclaimed a hereditary Empire and assumed the title of Napoleon III. His *coup d'état* was confirmed by a practically unanimous plebiscite. He could henceforward regard himself as Emperor by the wishes of his people. In a manifesto that he issued on assuming the throne, he stated the principles and the policy of Bonapartism. 'The name of Napoleon,' he announced, 'is a programme in itself. It means: at home, order, authority, religion and the well-being of the people. Abroad, it means national dignity. Such is the policy inaugurated by my election, which I desire shall prevail with the support of the Assembly and that of the people.'

NAPOLEON III'S
CONSTITUTION

Taciturn, secretive and timid, Napoleon III did not possess the will or the genius of his illustrious uncle. Under the new constitution that he imposed after his *coup d'état* he sought to create a parliament of experts supporting a business government: what he in fact achieved was to 'combine an omnipotent executive with a paralytic legislature'. He

'*A False Step, or The Road to Ruin.*' *This cartoon, published in 1868, shows Napoleon III with the Prince Imperial. Its forecast was only one year out – the Franco-Prussian War started, in fact, in 1870*

alone could summon the Chamber, and their suggestions were first vetted by a Council of State. Their debates were not to be reported; the results of those debates being conveyed to the public in an official communiqué. Ministers were not permitted to attend the Parliament, and their policies could not be questioned. The motto *Liberté, Egalité, Fraternité*, were erased from the plaster of public buildings and schools. Nor did the public seem to resent this Napoleonic gesture. Although at the time of his ascending the throne he had proclaimed that 'the Empire means peace', he was constantly engaged in wars. There was the Crimean war in 1854; in 1859 the Italian war; in 1866 the Mexican expedition: in 1870 the Franco-Prussian war. None of these wars possessed the glamour or achieved the glory of the great Napoleonic campaigns.

Having failed to obtain the hand of a German or Swedish princess, he in 1853 married the beautiful Spaniard, Eugénie de Montijo. He countered the criticism this aroused in royalist circles by issuing an arrogant decree. ' I am, ' he proclaimed, ' preserving my true character. I am adopting the title of parvenu in the face of all Europe. It is a glorious title when conferred upon one by the free vote of a great people. '

After 1860 the Emperor's health declined, he fell more and more under the influence of his Catholic wife and was assailed by bouts of sullen melancholy. While the Empress and her ladies would giggle in the saloons of Compiègne, or scream with laughter while indulging in pillow fights in the passages, the Emperor, morose, gloomy and secretive, would lock the door of his study and ponder on the fall of Empires. He decided that the time had come to pass from despotism to a liberal system. The press laws were relaxed and the Chamber was accorded the right to debate the Gracious Speech. The Mexican experiment ended in complete disaster. The French army was withdrawn and the Emperor Maximilian was executed, to the sound of the band playing *La Paloma*, at Queretaro; his widow lost her reason and the palaces of Europe echoed to her cries for revenge. When Bismarck declared war on Austria, Napoleon imagined that the campaign would last for more than a year and that in the end France, in return for compensations in the Palatinate and in Hesse, would mediate between the two belligerents and emerge as the honest broker. But Germany defeated Austria within seven weeks; Bismarck published Napoleon's demands for compensation, and France was exposed to shame.

THE END OF BONAPARTISM

For eighteen years Victor Hugo had been hurling denunciations at this ' little Napoleon ', and in the growing atmosphere of failure ' the name of Buonaparte, ' as H. A. L. Fisher wrote, ' had lost its magic even in the barracks . . . '. More and more republicans were elected at ensuing elections and the national finances sank into such disorder that there was not enough money in the Exchequer to carry out the army reforms that were known to be necessary. Napoleon eventually was tricked by Bismarck into the Franco-Prussian war and on 1 September 1870, the Emperor, too ill to mount a horse, drove in a barouche to surrender his person to the King of Prussia.

The Empress Eugénie by Winterhalter: beautiful, charming, elegant, she became the mirror of fashion to all Europe

When the news of Sedan reached Paris, the Empress left the Tuileries in panic, rushed through the galleries of the Louvre and found a cab outside the church of St Germain l'Auxerrois. She drove to the house of her American dentist, with whose help she was able to reach the coast in safety and to embark for England. She survived the Empire for fifty years, retaining in the splendid arch of her eye-brows some vestige of her former beauty. When, on 11 November 1918, she heard the news of Germany's defeat and the escape into exile of William II, the old lady walked down to the mausoleum and in a high imperial voice read the terms of the armistice aloud beside the tombs of the Emperor and the Prince Imperial.

It required the advent of Adolf Hitler before the theory of Bonapartism was revived in Europe.

FOURTEEN

Parliamentary Kingship

THE THEME OF LIMITED OR constitutional monarchy, or what I have called 'parliamentary kingship', can best be examined in terms of British constitutional development. In other countries also constitutions have been granted and kings have submitted themselves to parliamentary control. But it was in Great Britain that the theory received its original definition and that the practice has been most fully developed.

In my own life-time I have witnessed the removal of eight emperors, twelve kings and fifteen minor dynasties. The British monarchy has survived two world wars and a social revolution with its prestige and influence almost unimpaired. It is true that we won each of the two wars and that, had we been defeated, the people might have demanded a new deal such as only a drastic change of structure could provide. Our monarchy survived mainly because it was not identified with failure but associated with success. Yet there are other reasons why British kingship has, except for an unhappy interlude of eleven years, lasted for eleven hundred years. In the first place the British are an illogical race and seldom wish to push their theories to extreme conclusions. In the second place the British monarchy has, on occasions of conflict, generally shown itself ready to recognise the shifting incidence of power and to accept the new forces that have pushed to the front. When, as with Charles I and James II, our monarchs failed rightly to estimate the strength of the opposition, they lost their lives or were obliged to seek safety in flight. In other cases they have had the wisdom to compromise before it was too late.

Thus when King John, in the opinion of the barons, was aiming at the violation of the whole system of feudal contract, he was forced to meet the barons and their retainers on the island at Runnymede and to sign the Magna Carta. The articles of this baronial document were in later centuries misinterpreted and magnified into a charter of popular liberties. It became in fact the foundation of parliamentary kingship, or limited monarchy, in England.

When Charles I attempted, in assertion of his belief in the Divine Right of Kings, to defy Parliament and to establish a personal autocracy, he was defeated by the republicans and lost his head upon the scaffold of Whitehall. When, forty years later, James II was suspected of wishing to impose the Catholic religion upon the realm, he was forced to fly the country and was thereafter decisively defeated by William III at the Battle of the Boyne. Yet the Whig magnates who had contrived the Revolution of 1688 were not willing to take any further risks. They

Divine Right denied: the execution of Charles I (30 January 1649), from a broadsheet

imposed on William and Mary the Declaration of Rights, under which the monarchs pledged themselves not to levy taxes without the consent of Parliament, not to maintain a standing army, not to create their own private courts, and not to issue decrees under which certain individuals or sections could be dispensed from obeying Acts of Parliament or under which the operation of the law could be suspended by royal decree. On the death of the Duke of Gloucester in 1700, the last to survive of Queen Anne's seventeen children, Parliament passed the Act of Settlement under which the Hanoverian dynasty, in accepting the throne, would undertake that ministers should in future be responsible for the acts of the sovereign. This enactment, in that it firmly established the principle of 'responsible government' has become one of the main elements in parliamentary kingship as we know it today.

In Anglo-Saxon times the leader of the tribes, who from 829 became known as the 'Bretwalda' or 'king of the English', was elected by the Witan from members of the royal family. They generally chose for that purpose, among the older males of the family, the one whom they regarded as the most competent. When William the Conqueror established his dynasty the principle was, at least in theory, maintained that the king should be 'recognised' by the *Commune Concilium*, the successor of the Anglo-Saxon Witan. In practice, however, the Normans enforced, whenever they were able to do so, the principle of primogeniture under which the sovereign was automatically succeeded by his eldest son.

PRIMOGENITURE

This system has certain, obvious advantages. On the death of a sovereign, his heir ascends the throne immediately and can claim immediate allegiance. *Le roi est mort. Vive le roi.* The competition of rival claimants was thereby eliminated and in most cases no dynastic or civil wars ensued. Moreover, the accepted heir could be educated from childhood in the task of kingship and would not, when he inherited his responsibilities, be wholly untrained: tradition and continuity would be preserved.

A hereditary monarch, succeeding his father by primogeniture, had certain other advantages which are denied to an elected president or a dictator who seizes power by force. Being born in the purple, he has no political past, and as such has no party followers whom he is supposed

Left: *William III (1689-1702) in armour, with a battle scene in the background, attributed to J. Wyck. William's royal authority was limited under the Declaration of Rights*

to reward and no party antagonists who regard him with disfavour. He is not driven, as dictators are invariably driven, to win popular support by spectacular triumphs or to gain the obedience of the people by inventing some foreign menace. His aim is to personify stability rather than adventure, continuity rather than change. Representing as he does the nation as a whole, he should be in the position to mitigate class antagonism or partisan strife. If he be a man of wisdom and if he reign long enough to become a man of experience, he will come to be regarded as neutral in politics and as the embodiment of the national desire, character, and good sense.

The disadvantages of the hereditary principle are also apparent. It is at least unlikely that any royal family will provide a succession of intelligent and virtuous heirs. There are bound to occur monarchs whose judgement is unreliable, whose balance is uncertain, and whose understanding of the principles of parliamentary kingship is as shallow as their conception of the duty imposed on them in return for their high inheritance. There are bound to occur silly, irresponsible and even debauched kings. Yet under the system of strictly limited monarchy the damage that can be occasioned by such foolish or indulgent persons is also limited. In modern conditions the principle of primogeniture is certainly the best that can be adopted.

THE DOCTRINE OF RESPONSIBILITY

The framers of the Act of Settlement of 1701, in establishing the principle that a Minister responsible to Parliament should be ' responsible ' for the acts of the sovereign, did not in all probability foresee how wide an application would be given to that rule in ensuing centuries. The king, in consenting to do nothing without the approval of his Cabinet, was in fact surrendering to Parliament the whole of his executive powers. The expression ' the king can do no wrong ' came to be interpreted as meaning, not that the king as an individual had been granted the grace of infallibility, but that he could in fact, without ministerial agreement, do nothing at all. The doctrine of responsibility had other implications.

It meant in the first place that no Government could survive unless it remained ' responsible ' to Parliament, or in other words unless it possessed a majority in the House of Commons. In the second place it included ' Cabinet responsibility ', which meant in effect that an

Right: Eighteenth-century print from a manuscript depicting the Parliament of Edward I (1277-1307). He is seated between King Alexander of Scotland and Llewellen, Prince of Wales. It is perhaps the earliest representation of the King in Parliament

Alexander Rex Scotore & Lewellin princeps Wallie

Whereas it hath pleased Almighty God to call to His mercy our late Sovereign Lord King William the Third, of Blessed Memory, by whose Decease the Imperial Crowns of England, Scotland, France and Ireland, are Solely and Rightfully come to the High and Mighty Princess Anne of Denmark: We therefore the Lords Spiritual and Temporal of this Realm, being here Assisted with those of His late Majesties Privy Council, with Numbers of other Principal Gentlemen of Quality, with the Lord Mayor, Aldermen, and Citizens of London, do now hereby with one full Voice and Consent of Tongue and Heart, Publish and Proclaim, That the High and Mighty Princess Anne, is now by the Death of our late Sovereign, of Happy Memory, become our only Lawful and Rightful Liege Lady, Anne, by the Grace of God, Queen of England, Scotland, France and Ireland, Defender of the Faith, &c. To whom we do acknowledge all Faith and constant Obedience, with all hearty and humble Affection: Beseeching God, by whom Kings and Queens do Reign, to Bless the Royal Queen Anne with Long and Happy Years to Reign over us.

Given at the Court at St. *James's*, the Eighth Day of *March*, 1701.

God save Queen Anne.

Somerset *P.*	Carlisle & *M.*	R. Ferrers
N. Wright *C. S.*	Grantham	Ja. Vernon
Devonshire	Weston	Stamford
Bolton	Jersey	Byron
Richmond	Essex	Sommers
Schonberg & Leinster	Pembroke	Cuningesby
Northumberland	Craven	J. Holt
Lindsey *G. C.*	Radnor	Edw. Northey
Berkeley	H. Boyle	Berkeley
Bedford	Manchester	Ranelagh
Ormonde	Denbigh	Rich. Hill.

London, Printed by *Charles Bill*, and the Executrix of *Thomas Newcomb*, deceas'd; Printers to the Queens most Excellent Majesty. 1701.

individual Minister must remain loyal to the Cabinet as a whole and that the Cabinet must remain loyal to him. This doctrine which, in Great Britain, presents so cogent an element in political discipline, is not as compulsive abroad. The French Assembly, with its many competitive parties, with the variations and permutations which this condition creates, was in pre-de Gaulle days rendered almost ineffective by the absence of central responsibility. The same disadvantage was noticeable in the Reichstag of the Weimar Republic, where the absence of a two-party system rendered the German Parliament and the German Cabinets incapable of constructive leadership.

The doctrine of responsibility has had in Great Britain a third useful effect. The Opposition is obliged by public opinion to adopt a 'responsible' attitude in any serious controversy, being aware that if they succeed in defeating the Government of the day it will be they themselves who will have to deal with the situation. They are thus cautious not to indulge in criticism which they may have to face themselves, or to make promises which one day they may themselves be obliged either to repudiate or to execute. Only those who have observed and analysed the frequent failure of parliamentary institutions in other countries can estimate how great an influence for good has been introduced, perhaps unwittingly, by the responsibility clause of the Act of Settlement.

THE OPPOSITION OBLIGED TO BE RESPONSIBLE

A third element of chance that determined the development of British constitutional practice was the fortuitous circumstance that the Hanoverian George I was profoundly bored by English politics and could not understand or speak the English language. Charles II would always himself preside at meetings of the Cabinet, to the frequent amusement but occasional embarrassment of his Ministers. George I attempted at first to follow this precedent, but the language difficulty proved an insuperable barrier. For a few weeks he endeavoured to converse with his Ministers in Latin, but soon discovered that the Latin as pronounced at Göttingen was a totally different language from that taught at Eton, Westminster or Harrow. His Ministers were probably better Latin scholars than he was himself, but their pronunciation of that mighty language was wholly incomprehensible to the continental ear. So George I, in relief and boredom, ceased to preside over Cabinet meetings and

Left: *The Proclamation of the Accession of Queen Anne in 1701. Queen Anne still lay claim to the Crown of France, though Calais, the last English foothold in France, was relinquished by Queen Mary in 1558*

Engraving of the House of Commons about 1840, during Lord Melbourne's administration. The remains of the royal Palace of Westminster founded by Edward the Confessor, which had been badly damaged by fire in 1512, were destroyed, except for Westminster Hall, by another fire in 1834. The present buildings were erected on the site 1840-67

left that task to the senior Minister, who gradually came to be known as 'Prime Minister', or 'First Minister'. The haphazard ways in which British constitutional practice evolved is well illustrated by the development of the office of Prime Minister, now the dynamic centre of the realm. Originally the term was used as one almost of reproach, as when men would sneeringly refer to 'Marquis Pombal, Prime Minister to the King of Portugal'. Gradually it assumed a more reputable significance and is today a supreme title of honour and the target of many a young man's noblest ambition. Even to this day, however, the office of Prime Minister is unknown to British law. It is mentioned only three times in an Act of Parliament, notably in the Chequers Act of 1917. Disraeli, who relished odd designations, signed the Treaty of Berlin as 'Prime Minister of England'. And King

288

George I as a Roman emperor, a bust by Rysbrack. During his reign (1714-27), as a result of the operation of the Act of Settlement of 1701, the principle of responsible government was firmly established

Edward VII, in granting social precedence to his Prime Ministers, (having but recently observed Mr Balfour seated at a dinner party below the undergraduate son of a peer) assigned to the 'Prime Minister' by name, place and precedence immediately after those of the Archbishop of York.

In spite of the assumption by the Cabinet and House of Commons of almost all the prerogatives formerly held by the Sovereign, there remain certain 'discretionary powers' vested in the Crown. It is not generally

realised that these acts of 'delegated legislation' are still in frequent use and that they should be carefully scrutinised by all good Whigs in order to make sure that the Government in command of the House of Commons is not using these powers in order to by-pass Parliament.

Walter Bagehot, in his brilliant *English Constitution* of 1867, has given a list of acts that the Queen could perform without the consent of Parliament, under the heading of 'Royal Prerogative'. This delegated legislation, when set down in print, is sufficient to make the blood of any good Liberal run cold. Bagehot writes:

> The Queen could disband the army (by law she cannot engage more than a certain number of men, but she is not obliged to engage any men); she could dismiss all the officers, from the General Commander-in-chief downwards; she could dismiss all the sailors too; she could sell off all our ships of war, and all our naval stores; she could make peace by the sacrifice of Cornwall and begin a war for the conquest of Britanny. She could make every citizen in the United Kingdom, male or female, a peer; she could make every parish in the United Kingdom a university; she could dismiss most of the Civil Servants; she could pardon all offenders. In a word, the Queen could, by prerogative, upset all the action of civil government, could disgrace the nation by a bad war or peace, and could, by disbanding our forces, whether land or sea, leave us defenceless against foreign nations.

There is no legal safeguard against such extreme action on the part of the sovereign, other than the conventional theory that the sovereign can act only on the 'advice' of a responsible Minister. If the Queen really decided to sell the British Navy to the USSR she could only complete the transaction if her orders were counter-signed by the First Lord of the Admiralty. He, in his turn, would be questioned on the subject in the House of Commons, and would certainly be defeated in the resultant division. Under the doctrine of cabinet responsibility, the Prime Minister would be unable to evade the difficulty by saying that the First Lord had acted on his own and in a moment of personal aberration. He and the whole Cabinet would be forced to resign and, unless the Leader of the Opposition could form a Government commanding a substantial majority in the House of Commons, a General Election would follow.

Left: *Cartoon in Bell's 'Weekly Newsletter' on the Reform Act of 1832, which swept away rotten boroughs. The upper group includes Lord John Russell (3) and Lord Grey (4), the Prime Minister; the lower, Wellington (2)*

Stated in such fantastic terms, the Royal Prerogative appears a survival from the Middle Ages. Yet in fact it is employed for certain administrative and executive purposes to this day. In the eighteenth century, when there was still a danger that the sovereign might use the Prerogative as a device for extending his executive and legislative powers, the practice of making laws by Order in Council, by Proclamation or by Sign Manual, was regarded with deep suspicion. For instance, when in 1766 Lord Chatham found it expedient, at a time when Parliament was in recess, to lay by Royal Proclamation an embargo upon all grain ships in British ports, he found it necessary when Parliament reassembled to induce them to pass a Bill of Indemnity, justifying and confirming what at that date appeared an almost unconstitutional act. ' It was, ' he explained, ' but a forty days tyranny. '

THE USE OF
THE ROYAL
PREROGATIVE

Since then, we have become more reckless in the use of the Prerogative to by-pass parliamentary legislation. Thus in 1873 it was by Sign Manual that Queen Victoria abolished the old practice of officers purchasing their commissions in the army, since the Government foresaw that this necessary measure would not pass the House of Lords, who denounced it as an invasion of the hallowed rights of property. A far more serious use of delegated legislation was the Defence of the Realm Act of 1914, under which the King in Council was authorised to issue regulations, having all the force of law, affecting, not merely the armed forces, but the immemorial rights of private citizens. Among the innovations thus introduced under the Royal Prerogative was the right of the Government to arrest and imprison individual citizens without trial. The old power of ' purveyance ' or requisition was also revived, and the executive was authorised to seize buildings and properties required for the convenience of the State. This use of the Prerogative aroused a certain amount of public indignation and in 1920, in the case of *the Attorney-General versus Keyser's Hotel*, the House of Lords reaffirmed the provision of Magna Carta, by deciding in favour of the hotel against the Government. Under the Emergency Powers Act of 1920, the King in Council was empowered to proclaim if need arose ' a state of emergency ' and during the continuance of the emergency the Government could issue Royal Proclamations without the consent, or even the knowledge, of Parliament.

Right: *The House of Commons during Sir Robert Walpole's administration, 1721-42, from a painting by Hogarth and Sir James Thornhill. Sir Robert* (left, foreground) *was the first ' Prime Minister ' in the modern sense*

The Lobby of the House of Commons in 1886 (caricatures from Vanity Fair). *At this time Gladstone, having come to terms with Parnell, whose Home Rule party held the balance of power in the House, introduced his Home Rule Bill. MPs in the central group (left to right) Mr Chamberlain (with monocle), Mr Parnell, Mr Gladstone, Lord Randolph Churchill, Lord Hartington*

Were it not for the doctrine of responsibility, this might lead to the establishment of despotism: the public are protected against any permanent denial of their rights by the safeguard of rendering the Government ultimately responsible for all royal acts and all delegated legislation. Again, under the Foreign Jurisdiction Act, wide powers are accorded to the King in Council, and several important legislative acts have been issued without the consent of Parliament. The safeguard in such cases is that any instance of abuse would immediately be raised in either House and the Government held responsible for this exercise of the Prerogative and its consequences. In fact, in such instances of delegated legislation, the expression 'the Crown' signifies, not the monarch personally, but the Government of the day, which is responsible for all acts imposed under the device of Prerogative. Orders in Council, Signs Manual and Warrants are of great convenience to the executive, in enabling rapid legislation to be enforced and in avoiding the delays and complications of a formal Parliamentary Bill. Those who wish to preserve our ancient liberties, must be vigilant in seeing that the processes of indirect or delegated legislation are never abused by the Government, or the civil departments, in power.

In constitutional theory, moreover, it is the sovereign alone who can declare war, or make peace, or cede territory. In practice of course the issues of peace and war rest with Parliament as representing, or being deemed to represent, the will of the nation. Yet it is still not absolutely established that the treaty-making power, and the cession of territory, do not remain part of the Royal Prerogative. In 1904, when Mr Balfour, Conservative Prime Minister, announced the conclusion of the Anglo-French agreement, he promised to bring in a Bill ratifying that instrument and subjecting the slight cession of territory thereby entailed to the approval of the House of Commons. King Edward VII strongly objected to this interpretation of constitutional practice and contended that the cession of territory was a Royal Prerogative and could be effected by the sovereign directly, without the consent of Parliament. Mr Balfour insisted that Parliament must be informed, consulted and given an opportunity to accept or to reject the proposal. The King was obliged to give way.

The original Whig interpretation of the rights of kingship was given a more radical significance in the nineteenth century. Queen Victoria's protracted withdrawal from public life undoubtedly diminished the part that the monarch was expected to play in politics; she was continually asserting that she would 'never consent' to a given act of legislation, but in the end she invariably surrendered to the 'advice' of her Ministers. Mr Gladstone felt strongly on the subject. 'It would,' he wrote, 'be an evil and perilous day for the monarchy were any prospective possessor of the Crown to assume or claim for himself a preponderating, or even independent, power in any one department of State.' It may have been his tactless insistence on this radical doctrine, that explains Queen Victoria's passionate hostility to the great Prime Minister, an antipathy which has always seemed to me strange.

If, therefore, the exercise of the Royal Prerogative, although frequently resorted to for purposes of convenience, is a privilege accorded no longer to the sovereign, but used exclusively by Ministers and their departments, would it be correct to say that parliamentary kingship implies that the monarch retains no political function whatsoever? This would be an incorrect assumption. It may be true that under present constitutional practice the sovereign can only act on ministerial 'advice'

THE SOVEREIGN'S
POLITICAL
FUNCTION

and therefore on ministerial responsibility, but what happens when the Prime Minister resigns and is therefore in no position to tender that advice? An episode occurred in 1852 which illustrates the nicety of this point. Lord Derby had already delivered his seals of office to the Queen and went on to recommend that Lord Lansdowne should be chosen as his successor. 'I interrupted Lord Derby,' recorded the Prince Consort, 'saying that constitutionally it did not rest with him to give advice and to become responsible for it, and that nobody, therefore, could properly throw the responsibility of the Queen's choice of a new Minister upon him.' It was therefore Lord Aberdeen, unfortunately perhaps, who was sent for, and not Lord Lansdowne.

THE SOVEREIGN'S
DISCRETION

This episode illustrates the fact that there may occur occasions when the sovereign alone can decide who is to become Prime Minister, since by constitutional doctrine no Minister is after his resignation entitled to tender 'advice', or able to become responsible for it thereafter. Obviously, when the party in power is defeated at a General Election, the sovereign is obliged by custom and usage to send for the leader of the Opposition. Yet the situation is not always as clear-cut as that. It is always possible for the Crown to refuse a dissolution to an outgoing Prime Minister, on the ground that the leader of the Opposition can form a government without exposing the country to the expense and confusion of a General Election. Thus in 1925, Lord Byng, when Governor General of Canada, refused to grant Mr Mackenzie King a dissolution on the ground that the leader of the Opposition would be able to form and to maintain a government without having recourse to a General Election. Similar action was taken by Sir Andrew Duncan, then Governor General of the Union of South Africa, when he refused to grant General Hertzog a dissolution in 1939. In each of these two cases much criticism was aroused, on the ground that the Prime Minister, while still constitutionally Prime Minister, had 'advised' a given course of action and his advice had been rejected. Fortunately so difficult an issue has not presented itself in Great Britain, although it has been suggested, quite incorrectly, that King George V refused to grant Mr Asquith a dissolution, when 'advised' to do so, in 1910.

What generally happens is that a Prime Minister, conscious that he no longer commands the necessary majority in the House of Commons, 'advises' the sovereign to grant him a dissolution, that a General Election is then held, and that the leader of the party which wins the Election is then automatically 'sent for' by the sovereign and invited

Disraeli's last Cabinet, about 1876. Disraeli stands in front of the fireplace

to form a government. Occasions may occur however when a Prime Minister, still possessing a majority in the House of Commons, retires owing to ill health and when the sovereign alone can decide who is to be his successor. According to constitutional purists, such as the Prince Consort, a retiring Prime Minister is not in a position to 'advise' the sovereign whom to designate as his successor, since, being thereafter in retirement or dead, he will be unable to assume responsibility for the consequences of his 'advice'. In practice, however, the sovereign probably consults the retiring Prime Minister in cases of difficulty, in the same way that she consults her elder statesmen and Privy Councillors. Yet the situation is often more complicated. Thus on the sudden illness and retirement of Mr Bonar Law in 1923, King George had to exercise his discretionary power in sending for Stanley Baldwin rather than Lord Curzon. He once again made use of his Prerogative when persuading Ramsay MacDonald to head a National Government in 1931. Similarly in 1956 it was the Queen alone who was in the position to decide whether to appoint Mr Macmillan as her Prime Minister or Mr R. A. Butler. She possessed, of course, the right unofficially to consult the leading statesmen as to who would be most likely to command party support and the acquiescence of the House of Commons. But the responsibility for the ultimate and conclusive decision rested with the Queen alone.

THE SOVEREIGN AND FOREIGN AFFAIRS

The theory is sometimes advanced that the sovereign, since treaty making is in theory part of the Royal Prerogative, occupies a special position in regard to Foreign Affairs and possibly also Dominion Affairs. King Edward VII certainly regarded himself as justified in visiting foreign sovereigns and conducting conversations with them and their Ministers, without being accompanied by any Minister of the Crown. It must be said, in justice to the King, that this was due, not to any desire on his part to assume functions to which he might not be constitutionally entitled, but to the disinclination of Sir Edward Grey, who was then Foreign Secretary, to travel abroad. Yet King Edward's independent action in Foreign Affairs was sharply criticised in the House of Commons as being unconstitutional. In his usual lapidary manner, Sir William Anson defines the position admirably. He writes:

> The Sovereign does not, constitutionally, take independent action in Foreign Affairs. Everything which passes between him and foreign princes or ministers should be known to his own ministers, who are responsible to the people for policy, and to the law for acts done.

King Edward VII was scrupulous in informing his Ministers of what had passed between him and foreign princes at Cronberg, Ischl, Cartagena, Reval or Gaeta. But the Cabinet would have felt more at ease and the House of Commons less critical had a Minister of the Crown been present at such interviews.

A further difficulty might arise if the Queen's Prime Minister in Canada were to tender her 'advice' in complete contradiction to that furnished her by her Prime Minister in the Commonwealth of Australia. Such a collision of constitutional obligations might well have arisen at the time that South Africa embarked on the policy of apartheid and decided to leave the Commonwealth. A collision was avoided by the ingenuity of the several civil servants and private secretaries concerned. But it might possibly arise again.

A more serious problem is presented by the question whether the sovereign is invariably obliged to follow the 'advice' of the Prime Minister in power. Nobody but the sovereign can dismiss or appoint

a Prime Minister; nobody but she can summon, prorogue, or dissolve Parliament. No Bill, however great may be the majority supporting it, can become law without the royal assent. The extreme parliamentary doctrine holds that the sovereign is constitutionally bound to give her assent to any Bill passed by both houses, even one providing for her own abdication or death. If she were to refuse her obedience to the 'advice' of her Prime Minister, the Government would resign and the action of the sovereign would, as William IV realised to his cost, be dragged into the political arena at a General Election. Yet it is possible to conceive circumstances in which it would be the duty of the sovereign to refuse assent to a Bill unless and until the 'advice' of her Prime Minister were confirmed at a General Election by the mandate of the nation.

Supposing, for instance, that an unscrupulous Prime Minister, possessing an overwhelming majority in the House of Commons, were to pass a Bill prolonging the life of the existing Parliament for fifty years. The Sovereign at her Coronation solemnly swore an oath on the Bible to govern according to the 'laws and customs' of the realm. The establishment of a personal dictatorship which would be implied by the prolongation for fifty years of a Parliament which by then might have lost the support of the nation, would certainly be a violation of our constitutional law and customs. Is the sovereign to violate the coronation oath in order to satisfy the extreme believers in the doctrine of the absolute supremacy of Parliament? I do not think so. I should feel that in' such circumstances the sovereign had become the sole guardian of the Constitution, and was obliged in duty to submit the issue to the decision of the electorate.

It would generally be agreed that, although under the system of parliamentary kingship, the functions and privileges of the Crown have been reduced to those of being permitted ' to advise, to encourage and to warn', the influence of the Crown, especially in a long reign, is not to be estimated by its actual powers. Sir William Anson writes:

> It is impossible to be constantly consulted and concerned for years together in matters of great moment without acquiring experience, if not wisdom. Ministers come and go, and the policy of one group of Ministers may not be the policy of the next, but all Ministers in turn must explain their policy to the Executive Sovereign, must effect it through his instrumentality, must leave upon his mind such a recollection of its methods and its results as may be used to form and influence the action of their successors.

The survival of kingship depends upon the wish of the people to have a hereditary sovereign as head of the State rather than an elected President. It must be admitted also that the popularity of the monarchy is based on sentiment rather than on reason, on feelings rather than on thought. Yet, in the mass of the electorate, these feelings are even today deep and strong, and cannot possibly be disregarded by even the most demagogic politician.

On what sentiments is the wide popularity of the British monarchy founded?

The Queen, in the first place, is the symbol of continuity and tradition. Most people above the age of forty prefer the familiar to the unfamiliar and become devoted to symbols which they have known since childhood. Temperamentally they prefer recognition to surprise, the expected to the unexpected, the settled to the dynamic; from their school-days they have been taught to respect the ancient monarchy and to identify loyalty to the Crown with patriotism and love of country. The younger generation who, if they be of any value at all, react against the older tradition, may deride the monarchy and contend that it is expensive and out of date. They do not accept the fact that the Exchequer makes more than a million pounds annually out of the Crown lands which, had they not been handed over to the nation, would go to swell the private income of the Queen. They do not realise to what an extent foreign republicans, such as those of Germany, envy us our monarchical constitution as giving continuity, dignity and glamour to the realm. Yet to the mass of the nation it is the venerability and continuity of our monarchy that gives it so strong and wide a sentimental appeal.

The monarchy again is the symbol of unity and integration. The sovereign is, or should be, above class distinctions or party animosities. Every British subject and every citizen of a Dominion should feel that the Queen belongs to himself, whatever be his origin or occupation. The great regal ceremonies, such as a Coronation or a Jubilee, even as the occasions of mourning or rejoicing in the royal family, arouse a remarkable degree of uniform sentiment, rendering the whole people united in celebration or condolence. There is, of course, much exaggeration in the adulation voiced by some of the newspapers, even as there are waspish spurts of malice from republican quarters. But it is no exaggeration to contend that the nation as a whole does in fact regard the monarchy as symbolic of national unity. On occasions of national relief or triumph the crowds will flock spontaneously to Buckingham Palace and will wait for hours for the Queen to appear on the balcony. One need only have witnessed these memorable scenes to be convinced that the emotion shown by the crowd is a perfectly sincere emotion, or to reflect that a similar wave of public feeling would not be aroused were Mr and Mrs Johnson of the TUC to appear with their children on the gilded balcony and wave to the plaudits of the multitude. Such emotion may seem an unworthy and transient factor. But it assuredly exists and is operative in democratic decisions. The grief that was almost universally felt and expressed when King Edward VIII renounced his throne was a wholly spontaneous emotion: many millions of subjects felt that continuity had been interrupted.

A Queen and a royal family possess in addition a metaphysical attraction or what Max Weber has called a ' grace ' or ' charisma '. There is an element of curiosity in this attraction, based on the fact that most intelligent people are naturally inquisitive and are fascinated by the unusual. It seems wonderful to them that there should exist a family who lead lives akin to their own and yet widely different. There is also the natural tendency to admire and to seek to emulate someone set far higher than oneself. ' There is something, ' writes G. M. Young, ' in human nature which is gratified by liking people of exalted rank. The object elevates the sentiment, and the sentiment once evoked will not be content without an object. ' This sense of admiration, of almost

AWE OF
THE SOVEREIGN
ENHANCED BY
PAGEANTRY

The Mace, the symbol of royal authority, which said to represent the King in Parliament

awe, is enhanced by pageantry. Queen Victoria did much to diminish the popularity of monarchy when she remained secluded after her widowhood and refused obstinately to appear in public. The period during which republicanism, between 1870 and 1871, became a serious political factor in Great Britain was the period during which Queen Victoria was hardly ever witnessed by her subjects. Edward VII on his accession restored pageantry to the British monarchy and his somewhat perplexing popularity was largely based on the fact that again and again did he give the crowds occasion to enjoy the spectacle of splendid processions, with sleek horses and the chink and glitter of scarlet and gold. There exists in human nature a liking for the dramatic and a love of display. Pageantry ministers to these inclinations.

The sovereign thereby acquires an aura of grandeur and, as Professor Black has remarked, ' it nullifies in the ordinary subject his feeling of smallness '. It gives to royalty a glamour which as individuals they may not possess. The masses, not being really interested in abstract political theories, prefer to personify authority and to be more impressed by individuals seeming to perform interesting actions, than by institutions, organisations, and groups who perform what may appear to be uninteresting actions. Any good journalist, any advertising agent, is aware that the attention of the public is more readily aroused by personalities than it is by objects. It is the intense and yet glamorous personification of royalty that gives it a grace far deeper and wider than any President could acquire.

The sovereign, being accepted by her peoples as an example and symbol of the State, and being by her title head of the Church and defender of the faith, must, if she is to maintain the mystery so essential to the survival of monarchy, adopt and practise the highest moral code. In days of modern publicity it would not be possible for any monarch to retain among his subjects that sense of awe unless he were to practise the highest personal rectitude. The sovereign and the royal family are expected in their private lives to be patterns of perfect domesticity. The British public would today not tolerate self-indulgence such as that of George IV and flatter themselves that the sovereign and her family are stained-glass saints, shining as examples, and offering themselves as scapegoats for all the squalid sins of their people. It would be a shock to the British people if their scapegoat let them down.

This brings me in conclusion to one of the most difficult problems that assail parliamentary kingship in the present age. I refer to the question of publicity. Too much publicity will stain the mystery, even the dignity, of the Crown. Too little publicity will be regarded as undemocratic and will render the gulf that yawns between the sovereign and the ordinary subject an unfortunate barrier rather than a necessity of segregation. The real personality of monarchs is seldom revealed to their peoples until many years after their deaths. Few British subjects are aware that Queen Elizabeth II is a woman of exceptionally strong character and high intelligence. They realise that she and her husband are hard-working and possess a Coburg sense of duty. But they have little idea of what they are really like. I am grateful to destiny that I have not been chosen as public relations officer to Buckingham Palace, which is in truth a nightmare task. All we can hope is that the Queen will seize every opportunity to share the interests of the common people, their sorrows and their laughter, and realise that she remains Bretwalda of the English and must seek to represent, to symbolise, to enhance, to elevate and to integrate the finest elements in the national character. Such was the example set by her father and her grandfather. Let us hope that their example will be continued.

FIFTEEN

Regalia

THOSE WHO ATTENDED THE CORONATION of Queen Elizabeth II on 2 June 1953, or who watched it on television and the cinema, were above all else impressed by a sense of history. This century has witnessed the disappearance of five Emperors, eight Kings, and fifteen minor dynasties. The British monarchy, being sufficiently elastic to stand the strains and stresses of successive upheavals, has survived them all. It remains the most ancient institution in the country. Our Law Courts are eight hundred years old: our Parliament seven hundred years old; but our monarchy, as a political institution, is eleven hundred years old. Queen Elizabeth traces her descent from Egbert who was proclaimed Bretwalda in AD 829. Apart from the eleven years interlude of Cromwell's Republic, the descendants of Egbert have reigned in England ever since.

The Coronation service, in its main outlines, is the same as that instituted by St Dunstan for the crowning of King Edgar at Bath in 973. 'We are able,' writes Professor Schramm, 'to glean from the Coronation rite traces of the Teutonic, Christian and Norman-French heritages that have gone to make England what she is.' We can also trace vestiges of the several types of kingship that have been described in this volume.

The prehistoric element of magic is represented by the 'Stone of Destiny' which was brought by Kenneth MacAlpine to Scone, and on which the kings of Scotland were invariably crowned. In 1296 the Stone of Destiny was stolen from Scone by King Edward I and brought to Westminster where it is now inserted beneath the Coronation chair. All English kings, even Oliver Cromwell when installed as Lord Protector, have seated themselves at their coronation above this magic stone. On Christmas day, 1951, some enterprising Scottish undergraduates concealed themselves at night in Westminster Abbey, extracted the stone from under the chair, and took it back to Scotland. The episode was settled by negotiation and the stone brought back to London, where it awaits the coronation of King Charles III. It is not yet known whether the gesture of kidnapping and its few weeks concealment in Scotland has materially diminished the stone's palaeolithic magic. It has hitherto proved a perfectly efficient talisman, no less effective than the even more ancient coronation stone preserved at Kingston-on-Thames.

The element of magic is also reflected in the extraordinary ritual of the Coronation service. The Queen is acclaimed with all the pomp of a great temporal sovereign; she is at the same time dedicated, almost as a sacrificial victim, to the service of her God and her peoples. There she sits clad in a tunic of cloth of gold, solitary and humble, modest and majestic, lonely and yet encompassed by the dignitaries of State and Church, aloof and detached, an Iphigenia dedicated to the welfare of her realm.

The king-priest element is also suggested by the service. The Queen is dressed in sacerdotal robes, in cope and stole; she moves slowly backwards and forwards across the theatre to the sound of anthems and the shouts of welcoming acolytes; she holds a Bible in her hand. The Church proclaims her its servant and she kneels humbly to the ministrations of the Church. The ritual is predominantly ecclesiastical; deliberately the monarch becomes a hierophant.

The king-warrior element is symbolised by the great swords that are delivered to her and carried naked before her in the processions. Menacing and splendid the swords flash as they move down the aisle, and among them is 'Curtana,' the sword of Mercy, with its point stubbed and snapped.

The old Teutonic system of election is symbolised by the Recognition with which the service begins. The Queen is presented to the congregation and is acclaimed, not as was the old custom by the knights clashing their swords upon their shields, but by the boys of Westminster

School shouting, '*Vivat Regina Elizabetha! Vivat! Vivat! Vivat!*', in sturdy unison. The helmet with which the tribal leaders were crowned in Teutonic days has been replaced by a crown of velvet, fur, gold and jewels.

The anointing, which is regarded by the Church as the supreme ceremony of the Coronation, implies that, even as Zadok the priest and Nathan the prophet anointed Solomon, so also are the monarchs of England anointed by the heads of the Church. From the ampulla the Dean of Westminster pours a few drops of oil into the spoon which he hands to the Archbishop. The Archbishop then anoints the Queen upon her head, her hands and her breast. From then on the Queen becomes 'the Lord's anointed': her person is holy.

The Coronation ends with the purely feudal rite of homage. The dukes, the earls, the barons kneel before her, promising to become her 'Liege man of Life and Limb and of earthly worship'. Another feudal practice, which survived as late as the coronation of George IV, was the entry into Westminster Hall of 'the King's champion' who chal-

The entry of the King's Champion into Westminster Hall at the coronation of James II in 1687

'*The Blessing of Queen Victoria*' by Sir George Hayter. The high officers of State stand in attendance

lenges any man who may dispute the Sovereign's right to succession. This is a relic of the old system of ordeal by battle. The right to act as King's champion is hereditary in the Dymoke family as Lords of the Manor of Scrivelsby. The champion is no longer obliged to back his charger into Westminster Hall and to fling down his gauntlet clanging upon the pavement. In full armour, with red and white plumes tossing from

his casque, he would challenge to mortal combat 'any person who would gainsay our rightful lord to be right heir to the imperial crown of the realm'. In the nineteenth century public opinion became shocked by such charades. *The Times* newspaper denounced the whole pageant as 'compounded of the worst dregs of popery and feudalism'. The direct descendants of the Dymoke family died out in 1875, but King

Edward VII granted to a collateral branch, in the person of Mr H. S. Dymoke, the hereditary right to carry the standard of England in the procession.

A further feudal survival was that whereby the Lord of the Manor of Worksop was supposed, by hereditary right, to present the sovereign with a new pair of gloves; this has been superseded by the right possessed by the Lord of the Manor - at present the Duke of Newcastle, - to support the sovereign's right arm, 'as occasion may require'.

The status of Queen Elizabeth II as simultaneously Queen of the United Kingdom and of the several Dominions has led to many alterations in the wording of the Coronation Oath. These changes will be mentioned later in connection with the important constitutional significance of the Oath and its relation to the Dominions. It is now time to consider the historical development and the successive rites of the Coronation ceremony in greater detail.

WESTMINSTER
ABBEY
The Church of Edward the Confessor at Westminster, as designed and remodelled by Henry III in 1245, was deliberately intended to become the site of future coronations. The architect, Henry of Reyns, placed the choir to the west of the central crossing, thus providing, between the choir and the High Altar, a space for the 'scaffold' or 'theatre' in which the service would be held. Behind the altar was the chapel of Edward the Confessor, containing his tomb and the tombs of some of his successors. In this was erected 'the Traverse', namely a cubicle or robing room hung with brocade curtains, into which the monarch could retire during the service for easement or re-robing.

The theatre in Westminster Abbey has been the site of coronations for nine hundred years, and twenty-eight coronations of English kings have been celebrated in that small square.

The present ritual, based on that provided by St Dunstan for King Edgar, is a fusion between the ancient Teutonic ceremony and the 'hallowing' or anointing of Christian tradition. At the outset of the fourteenth century the old service was remodelled and the text embodied in the *Liber Regalis* still preserved in the Abbey library.

The ancient regalia of the British Crown were desecrated and dispersed at the time of the Civil War. It is said that the regicide, Henry Marten, having seized and destroyed the religious images in the Queen's Chapel at Somerset House, descended upon Westminster and, with the authority of Parliament, took over the royal regalia. Marten had a personal grudge against King Charles who had publicly denounced him

'*Emblem of England's Distraction*' *1658. Cromwell attended by Fame, tramples on Error and Faction: a cartoon by William Fairthorne*

as 'an ugly rascal' and a 'whore-master', which indeed he was. Having obtained the keys of the Treasury at Westminster, he 'forced open a great iron chest and took out the crowns, the robes, the sword and the sceptre belonging anciently to King Edward the Confessor and used by all our kings at their Inaugurations'. Having removed the regalia, he persuaded his friend, the poet George Wither, to put them on. 'Wither,' writes Antony Wood in his *Athenae Oxonienses*, 'being crowned and royally arrayed, had first marched about the room with a stately mien and afterwards, with a thousand apish and ridiculous actions, exposed these sacred ornaments to contempt and laughter'. The crowns and sceptres were then taken to the Tower and broken up. The jewels were sold, only the more remarkable among them, such as the balas ruby, known since the days of Horace Walpole as 'the Black Prince's Ruby', were preserved. The regalia now used at the Coronation were made for Charles II in 1661 at the cost of £ 21,978 9s 11d.

Cromwell in June 1657, conscious of the monarchical sentiments of the people and being anxious to revive emotions of continuity, had himself for the second time installed as Lord Protector. The Coronation chair was moved from the Abbey to Westminster Hall; Cromwell was invested with a robe of purple and ermine, and a gold sword and sceptre were placed in his hands. At his funeral, a crown was laid beside his coffin. Such was the symbolic significance attached to regalia even under the Commonwealth: 'Let the rich ore,' wrote Waller,

> Let the rich ore be forthwith melted down
> And the state fixed by making him a crown;
> With ermine clad and purple, let him hold
> A royal sceptre made of Spanish gold...

But Cromwell was obdurate. 'I cannot,' he said, 'undertake this government with the title of King.'

PAGAN RITUALS   The pre-historic magic rites, which figured prominently in the coronation ceremonies of the Irish kings, were not adopted in the English *ordo*. In Ireland, the 'border line between kings and gods appears to have been obliterated'. On his accession the new Irish king was expected to break in wild horses; to ride between two blocks of stone which would only admit a passage for a legitimate sovereign; and to induce a sacred palaeolithic stone to roar aloud in recognition. Such pagan rituals were omitted from the European *ordines*. Step by step the Christian clergy gained control over the ritual; it was Bishop Hincmar of Rheims who in the ninth century established the Frankish *ordo* which became a model for other coronation services. Under this system it was the bishop who anointed the king and eventually presented to him the secular insignia as well. In 919 the German Henry I refused to be anointed by the bishops, contending that the Church had no concern with temporal

The coronation of a king of Croatia in the tenth or eleventh century: a bas-relief in the Baptistry of St John, Split Cathedral, formerly the Temple of Jupiter in Diocletian's palace

affairs. Yet in 936 Otto I had himself solemnly crowned and anointed in Charlemagne's church at Aachen and in 961 a complete *ordo* was composed at Mainz, accepted by the Pope of Rome, and established as the continental rite.

In England, according to Professor Schramm, the Coronation service remained a 'specifically English rite'. In 785 Offa had caused his son Ecgferth to be anointed and acclaimed as the legitimate heir to the throne. Yet, as I have said, the detailed English order dates from

973 when the order of Edgar was accepted and became established. To the anointing and crowning by the Church was added a contractual element as symbolised by the homage and the oath. The king was thus not anointed and crowned only, but entered into a contract with the nobles and with the people. The ceremony of the oath was later imitated at some continental coronations. As late as 1825 King Charles X of France took the oath at his coronation in Rheims cathedral in words modelled on the *mandatum regis* of King Edgar of England.

WILLIAM THE
CONQUEROR'S
CORONATION

William the Conqueror, being anxious to stress his legitimate rights of succession, claimed to have been recognised as King of England (*hereditaria delegatione et sacramentis Anglorum*), by 'the testament of Edward the Confessor and by the sacraments of the English'. On Christmas Day, 1066, William was anointed and crowned in Westminster Abbey by the Archbishop of York. Being anxious to emphasise the ritual of election or 'recognition' he had packed the Abbey with his nobles, leaving the Norman knights to keep guard outside. The nobles shouted so loud that the guards outside the building imagined that a riot had broken out and began laying about them to right and left. A general panic followed, the nobles rushed out of the Abbey and the King and the Archbishop were left alone in the theatre, staring at each other in front of the altar. Calm was at length reimposed and the service continued.

The Church contended that, since it was the Archbishop who anointed and crowned the King, the secular power was subordinate to the ecclesiastical. At Easter 1070 William I permitted the papal legate to place the crown upon his head at a formal and solemn service. But when Pope Gregory VII claimed that this implied that the King was a vassal of the Papacy, William replied in undiplomatic language, 'I never intended, and do not now intend, to pledge my troth' (*Fidelitatem facere nolui nec volo*).

The relation between the English Crown and the Papacy remained uncertain until the Reformation. King John, it is true, did homage to the papal legate and surrendered his kingdom as a vassal of the Papacy. But this was repudiated by the nobles of the Royal Council as being a violation of his coronation oath. Minor modifications were also introduced in the course of centuries. In the old days the king was, before

Right: HM Queen Elizabeth II on her return to Buckingham Palace from Westminster Abbey after her coronation on 2 June 1953, photographed by Cecil Beaton. The 'Black Prince's Ruby' can be seen in the Imperial State Crown

taking the oath, expected to grovel in front of the altar, laying himself flat on the carpet with his arms outstretched in the form of a cross: this humiliation did not survive the Middle Ages. The details and wording of the service were also adjusted to accord with the religious prejudices of the sovereign. Elizabeth I refused to accept Communion and retired to her robing room while mass was being celebrated. James II was unwilling to accept a purely Protestant rite and a compromise *ordo* was drafted by Dr Compton, Bishop of London. William IV for reasons of economy abolished the banquet in Westminster Hall and the entry of the Dymoke champion. In the old days before the anointing the monarch was stripped to the waist and lay for a few minutes 'groveling afore the high aulter'. In 1838, on considering the impending coronation of Queen Victoria, *The Times* suggested that the ceremony of anointing was 'more recommended by antiquity than delicacy, and will probably be omitted altogether'. It was not omitted, but Victoria was anointed, not on the breast, but on the head and hands only. Further modifications were introduced in the present century in the wording of the oath to render it more relevant to the altered status of the Dominions. King George V refused to sign the Protestant Declaration which, in its original form, contained passages offensive to Roman Catholic sentiment. He merely swore that he was a faithful Protestant, as indeed he was. The constitutional aspects of the Coronation service are, however, even more important than the historical aspects.

It might have been expected that, with the Reformation, the coronation service would have been abandoned, as it had been abandoned in Aragon and Castile. Yet, owing to the English love of tradition, to the desire of the Bishops of the Reformed Church to acquire ecclesiastical prestige, and to the resolve of the nobles to reaffirm their rights under Magna Carta by the Coronation Oath, it persisted almost unchanged. Even to this day the Coronation service is run by the Church and the Lords: the Commons are herded together in an upper gallery, wearing their best suits and seated on small velvet chairs: they play no part whatsoever in the ceremony, less of a part than the choir boys of St Paul's Cathedral or the senior boys of Westminster School.

THE SURVIVAL OF THE CORONATION SERVICE

In spite of the amiable fiction that hereditary peers still serve as the most important officers of State, the Coronation service does significantly define the relation between the sovereign and the Church, the sovereign and the people, and the sovereign and law.

The ecclesiastical aspect is concentrated in the ceremony of the anointing. As has already been recounted, the French contended that the holy chrism or oil had been brought to the baptism of King Clovis at Tours in 508 by a milk-white dove direct from heaven. In order not to be outmatched by the French, we contended that our own oil and our own *lekythion* or ampulla had been given to Thomas Becket by the Virgin herself and was thus also possessed of magic qualities. Although it was for long suspected that the whole legend of the *sainte ampoule* had been invented by the canons of Rheims cathedral, this miraculous chrism was believed to give special divinity to the kings of France and was used at all French coronations. It was seized by the republicans in 1793 and smashed with a hammer in the centre of the Place Nationale at Rheims. Some portions of it were, however, picked up by the sentinels on duty and to these portions vestiges of the holy oil still adhered. Eventually they were returned to Rheims and placed in a reliquary. Our own ampulla is a vase or receptacle in the semblance of an eagle accompanied by a spoon, the handle of which is the most ancient of our existing or surviving regalia.

THE CEREMONY
OF THE
ANOINTING

The Vatican were opposed to the idea that a king could be anointed with holy oil, or chrism, similar to that used at the consecration of bishops. They feared that such a ceremony might tempt secular sovereigns to claim the right of interference in ecclesiastical affairs. An attempt was therefore made to have kings anointed, not with sacred chrism, but with the olive oil provided for catachumens. The French refused to agree to this, asserting their claim to the heavenly origin of the *sainte ampoule*. We countered by inventing the story of our ampulla and Thomas Becket. The Pope resolutely refused to admit that the ceremony of the anointing conferred upon secular kings any sacerdotal or magic sanctity. The kings, in order to buttress their claim to divine right, were thus forced to invent the legend of the royal touch for cases of scrofula. Cranmer regarded the legends of the *sainte ampoule* and the Becket ampulla as savouring of a superstition. In his allocution to Edward VI at the time of his coronation he stated that the anointing 'was nothing but a ceremony. If it be wanting, the King is yet a perfect monarch notwithstanding, and God's anointed, as well as if he was inoiled'. Even to this day the late Archbishop of Canterbury, Dr Fisher, has publicly asserted that he regards the anointing as the central and most significant ritual in the whole Coronation ceremony. The Archbishop, after all, is the only person who can anoint.

The coronation of Charles VI (1385–1422) at Rheims, from 'Chronique de Charles VII'
in the Bibliothèque Nationale. The Archbishop of Rheims is anointing the king on his breast.
Five bishops stand on the king's left, six peers on his right, and three Princes of the Blood face him

A further interesting survival is the ceremony of 'recognition' with which our modern coronation service opens. It concerns the question whether succession should be governed by primogeniture or by selection. In Anglo-Saxon times a monarch was selected by the Witan from among the members of the 'cuninge' or royal family. The *consensus* of the magnates was followed by the 'recognition' or *collaudatio* of the assembled people. The growth of feudalism, in which succession was invariably hereditary and not elective, diminished the prestige of the selective principle. In England the succession has been governed by primogeniture since the thirteenth century. Yet it should be noted that the proclamation of the accession is signed by Privy Councillors, the Lord Mayor and Aldermen, and by 'other gentlemen of quality'. These signatories are descendants of the Great Council which was the legal successor of the Witan. This is a vestigial remnant of the old elective principle. In times of usurpation, when primogeniture cannot be claimed as the basis of succession, the elective principle gains in importance. Thus Henry VII, who could claim but frail hereditary rights, was dubbed as 'elected, chosen and required by all estates of the land'. Thus, when the Westminster boys shout '*Vivat Regina Elizabetha! Vivat! Vivat! Vivat!*', they are echoing a cry that acclaimed Henry Tudor on Bosworth Field.

It is by the ceremony of the Oath that the monarch pledges himself to rule by law. In the *ordo* of St Dunstan the oath was styled the *mandatum regis* but in 973, when Edgar was crowned, it became the *promissio regis*. Under this solemn oath to God and his people the monarch publicly recognises that he is bound by the law of the land. It constitutes a contract between the monarch and his peoples, and two English kings (Edward II and Richard II) lost their thrones on the ground that they had violated their Coronation Oath. This contract is, as Professor Schramm remarks, 'the barometer of the history of the monarchy'. In fact by taking an oath 'to govern the peoples of this United Kingdom of Great Britain and Ireland and the Dominions thereto belonging, according to the Statutes in Parliament agreed on and the respective Laws and Customs of the same', our kings have pledged themselves to govern as constitutional monarchs. The implications of that grave undertaking have been considered in the previous chapter.

THE RITE OF RECOGNITION

Such was the solemn and exacting ceremony undergone by Queen Elizabeth II on 2 June 1953. It began with the rite of Recognition. The Archbishop advanced to the corners of the theatre, east, north, west and south, addressing each of the four corners of the Abbey with the words:

Sirs, I here present unto you Queen Elizabeth your undoubted Queen. Wherefore, all ye who are come this day to do your homage and service, are ye willing to do the same?

At which the trumpets sound and the boys of Westminster School shout four times, 'God Save Queen Elizabeth!'.

The regalia are then carried into the Abbey and laid on the altar.

The Archbishop then advances towards the Queen and asks her whether she is now ready to take the oath. She indicates assent. The Archbishop administers the oath in words that differed from that administered to her father and which will also have to be changed at the Coronation of Charles III. 'Will you,' the Archbishop begins in a ringing voice,

> Will you solemnly promise and swear to govern the peoples of the United Kingdom and Northern Ireland, Canada, Australia, New Zealand and the Union of South Africa, Pakistan and Ceylon, and of your Possessions and other territories to any of them belonging and pertaining, according to their respective laws and customs?

To which the Queen replies, 'I solemnly promise so to do'.

She is then asked, 'Will you, to the uttermost of your power, cause Law and Justice, in Mercy, to be executed in all your judgements?' To which the Queen replies, 'I will'.

The Queen is then asked whether she will maintain 'in the United Kingdom the Protestant Reformed religion established by the Law. And will you maintain and preserve inviolably the settlement of the Church of England and the doctrine, worship, discipline and government thereof, as by the law established in England? And will you preserve unto the Bishops and Clergy of the Church of England and to the Churches there committed to their charge all such rights and privileges as by law shall appertain to them or any of them?' This assuredly is asking a lot on behalf of the established Church and might, if disestablishment became a political issue, face the monarch with serious constitutional problems.

Having assented to these demands, the Queen advances to the altar, lays her right hand on the Bible and says, 'The things that I have herebefore promised, I will perform and keep. So help me God.' She then kisses the book, signs the oath and returns to her chair. Henry VIII when asked to swear an oath to protect the 'lawful' rights of the Church, added in his own handwriting the words, 'not prejudiciall to hys jurysdyction and dignitie royall'. It may be that Charles III will be advised to accept some further redrafting.

Communion follows and then comes the supreme ceremony of the anointing. The Queen is seated in King Edward's chair and the choir

THE
CORONATION
OATH

The coronation oath of Henry VIII, altered in his own hand at a later date, when he declared himself Head of the Church in England. It reads (the King's emendations are in Roman type): ' The King shall swere that he shall kepe and maytene the lawfull *right and the libertees of old tyme graunted by the rightuous Cristen kinges of England* to the holy Chirche nott preiudyciall to hys jurysdyction and dignitie ryall... *And that he shall graunte to holde lawes and approved customes of the realme and* lawfull and nott preiudiciall to hys crowne or imperiall juris (diction) '

sing the hymn *Veni Creator Spiritus*. Four Knights of the Garter hold above the Queen a canopy of cloth of gold. The Dean of Westminster takes the ampulla and the spoon from the altar and gives them to the Archbishop who then anoints the Queen on forehead, hands and breast, with the words, 'And as Solomon was anointed King by Zadok the priest and Nathan the prophet, so be you anointed, blessed and consecrated Queen over the peoples whom the Lord your God has given you to rule and govern'.

Thereafter the Queen, seated in King Edward's chair, is arrayed by the Mistress of the Robes and the Lord Great Chamberlain in the *Colobium Sindonis* and the *Supertunica*. The Lord Chamberlain presents her with the spurs, which are then returned to the altar. The sword in the scabbard is then presented to the Queen and thereafter laid on the altar. The senior Earl redeems it at the price of one hundred shillings and it is thereafter unsheathed and carried flaming before the Queen. The armils are then fixed to the Queen's wrist, the Archbishop saying, 'Receive the bracelets of sincerity and wisdom, symbols and pledges of that bond which unites you with your peoples'. The Queen is then invested with the Stole Royal, the Robe Royal, and the orb. The ring is placed on the fourth finger of her right hand and she is handed the sceptre with the cross and the rod with the dove, the former being the 'ensign of kingly power and justice', and the latter the 'rod of equity and mercy'.

Then comes the coronation. The Queen, seated above the Stone of Destiny, is crowned with King Edward's Crown, made by the jeweller Vyner in 1661 and a supposed replica of the ancient crown which was melted down by Cromwell. The Archbishop then utters the injunction that has been repeated at every Coronation since that of William the Conqueror: 'Stand firm and hold fast from henceforth the Seat and State of Royal and imperial Dignity which is this day delivered unto you, in the name and by the authority of Almighty God and by the hands of us the Bishops and servants of God, though unworthy'. At the same time the peers and the peeresses put on their coronets; the choir and the schoolboys shout, 'God Save the Queen'. The trumpets sound and at a signal conveyed from the Abbey towers the guns at the Tower of London round the bend of the great grey river thunder a salute.

The homage follows. The first to perform the act of homage is the Archbishop of Canterbury on behalf of the Church. The Duke of Edinburgh then kneels before the Queen and recites the formula:

THE
CORONATION

'I Philip Duke of Edinburgh become your liege man of life and limb and of earthly worship.'

He then rises, touches the crown on the Queen's head, and kisses her left cheek. He is followed by the royal dukes of Gloucester and Kent and thereafter the peers of the realm do homage in the person of the senior representative in each category. The senior duke, earl, viscount and baron kneels before the Queen, places his hands between the Queen's hands and kisses her right hand. The choir sings anthems during this ceremony and when it is concluded, the drums beat, the trumpets sound, and the people (or more accurately the choir boys) shout, 'God Save Queen Elizabeth! Long live Queen Elizabeth! May the Queen live for ever!'.

The Queen then exchanges the heavy crown of King Edward for the Imperial crown, made for Queen Victoria in 1838 by Toundell and Bridge. It contains a section of the Cullinan diamond and bears in its front the great ruby which, according to Horace Walpole, was worn in his helmet by Henry V at the battle of Agincourt.

After the Communion, the Queen then retires to the Traverse, and exchanges the Robe Royal for the Robe of purple velvet. Carrying the orb in her left hand and the jewelled sceptre in her right and followed by her maids of honour, the Queen then slowly leaves the Abbey for her golden coach.

In the days of ancient Egypt the regalia were worshipped as a sacred object in themselves. The newly crowned king would worship his own diadem, hailing it in high-pitched recitative as 'Oh Red Crown! Oh Great one! Oh magician! Oh fiery snake!'. No such ceremony follows the British service. The crown is sent back to the Tower of London where it and its scintillating companions sparkle in the jewel room to the delight of many million tourists. In Egypt also there was a mystery play of the Coronation performed through the provinces of Upper and Lower Egypt by a touring company. In this play, the script of which has been preserved for two thousand years, the 'Keeper of the Great Feather' places the crown of Upper and Lower Egypt, 'the eye of Horus', on the head of the actor who impersonates the Pharaoh. The audience bow low in an ecstasy of subservience and are given small baked loaves for their trouble. In England and the Commonwealth, as

Left: *An illustration from the 'Liber Regalis,' probably the Order of Service used by the sovereigns themselves from Henry IV to Elizabeth I, and thought to have been written for Anne of Bohemia, Richard II's Queen*

well as abroad, the place of this mystery play was taken by a very excellent film of the ceremony. But no buns, so far as I am aware, were distributed to the audience. In New Zealand and the more loyal sectors of the Commonwealth many of those attending the cinema wept with loyalty.

It was in truth a moving ceremony. Few of those present felt that it was little more than an anachronism or that the prominence temporally accorded to ecclesiastical dignitaries and the nobility bore any relation to the possession of actual power. Was it in fact no more than a magnificent charade, symbolising with splendour the memories of a mighty imperial past? Or was it more accurately a pageant of British history repeating symbolically the stages of development from palaeolithic to democratic kingship? Certainly it was rich in symbolism. The Queen was acclaimed as the old Teutonic chieftain had been acclaimed. She was anointed with the holy oil, the *olium sanctificatum*. She was crowned seated above the Stone of Destiny and in the chair in which so many of her predecessors had been enthroned. The lords of the land, both spiritual and temporal, knelt down in homage before her. And she swore a solemn oath to preserve the laws and customs of her realm, even as King John seven-hundred-and-thirty-six years before, had with hatred in his heart signed the Magna Carta in the water meadow beside the Thames.

That, from the constitutional point of view, is the central act of the whole ritual. The Queen is the Lord's anointed, but she swears to Almighty God to obey the House of Commons. The nobles who are grouped in velvet and ermine around her well know that she recognises where the true power lies.

The golden coach, in the drizzling rain of that June afternoon, rocked its slow way through the packed streets of London. The Queen in her crown and holding her sceptre acknowledged the plaudits of the multitude. That royal progress added further symbols to the ceremony. The symbol of national and imperial unity; the symbol of national pride.

List of Books

AILLOUD, HENRI. *Suétone*, 1931.

ALDERSON, A. L. *The Structure of the Ottoman Empire.*

ALLEN, BERNARD M. *Augustus Caesar.* Macmillan, 1937.

ALLEN, J. W. *English Political Thought* 1603-1660. Methuen, 1938.

ANSON, SIR WILLIAM. *The Law and Custom of the Constitution.*

ARISTOTLE. *Politics.* Loeb Edition.

ARNOLD, SIR THOMAS. *The Caliphate.* Clarendon Press, 1924.

ARNOLD, W. T. *Studies of Roman Imperialism.* Manchester University Press, 1906.

ARRIAN, *Anabasis Alexandri*, Loeb Edition.

BARKER, SIR ERNEST. *The Political Thought of Plato and Aristotle.* Methuen, 1906.

BAUDIER, M. *The History of the Serrail.* English translation, 1655.

BAYNES, NORMAN. *The Byzantine Empire.* Oxford University Press, 1945.

BELL, GERTRUDE. *Amurath to Amurath*, Heinemann, 1911.

BELLOC, HILAIRE. *Monarchy. A Study of Louis XIV.* Cassell, 1936.

BENEDICT, RUTH. *The Chrysanthemum and the Sword.* Secker, 1947.

BENGSSON, FRANS. *Charles XII.*

BESNIER, MAURICE. *Histoire Ancienne. Vol. IV.* Presses Universitaires, 1937.

BLACK, PERCY. *The Mystique of Modern Monarchy.* Watts and Co, 1953.

BOLINGBROKE. *The Idea of a Patriot King.* Oxford, 1826.

BOURGEOIS, EMILE. *Le Grand Siècle.* Paris, 1896.

BRAKELOND, JOCELIN DE. *Chronicle.* The King's Classics, 1903.

BRENTANO, FUNCK. *La Cour du Roi Soleil.* Grasset, 1937.

BROCHER, HENRI. *Le Rang et l'Étiquette sous l'Ancien Régime.* 1934.

BRYCE, JAMES. *The Holy Roman Empire.* 1904 edition.

Cambridge Ancient History. Vols. X and XI. Cambridge University Press, 1936.

CARCOPINO, JEROME. *Cicero. The Secrets of his Correspondence.* Routledge and Kegan Paul, two vols. 1951.

CHURCHILL, WINSTON. *History of the English Speaking Peoples.* Dodd Mead, 1956.

CICERO. *Letters.* Loeb Edition. Six vols. Heinemann, 1925.

CICERO. *Philippics.* Loeb Edition, Heinemann, 1926.

CLAUDEL, PAUL. *Sous le Signe du Dragon.* Le Choix, 1948.

COLLIS, MAURICE. *The Great Within.* Faber, 1941.

CONSTANTINE VIII PORPHYROGENITUS. *Le Livre des Cérémonies.* Translated by Albert Vogt. Société Edition, 1935.

CUTOLO, A. *Viaggio nel Medioevo Italiano.* Bompiani, 1956.

DANGEAU, MARQUIS DE. *Journal.* Paris 1854. 19 vols.

DANTE. *De Monarchia.* Oxford, 1916.

DAVIS, H. W. C. *Mediaeval Europe.* Williams and Norgate, 1911. *Charlemagne.* Putnam's, 1899. *England under the Normans and Angevins.* Methuen, 1905.

DEMOSTHENES. *The Philippics.* Loeb Edition.

DIEHL, CHARLES. *Theodora.* Eugène Rey publisher, Paris, 1911.

DIO's *Roman History.* Loeb Edition, Heinemann, 1917, nine vols.

DROYSEN, JOHANN. *Alexandre le Grand.* 1935.

DUTAILLIS, CH. PETIT. *La Monarchie Féodale.* Paris, 1933.

DUVIQUET, GEORGES. *Héliogabale.* Mercure de France, 1953.

Encyclopaedia Britannica, 1944 edition.

FEILING, KEITH. *A History of England.* Macmillan, 1948.

FERRERO, GUGLIELMO. *Grandezza e Decadenza di Roma.* Treves, Milan, five vols. 1902.

FIGGIS, J. N. *The Divine Right of Kings.* Cambridge University Press, 1896.

FISHER, H. A. L. *Bonapartism.* 1908. *Napoleon,* 1904.

FOWLER, W. WARDE. *Julius Caesar.* Putnam's, 1925.

FOX, RALPH. *Genghis Khan.* John Lane, 1936.

FRANKFURT, HENRI. *Kingship and the Gods.* Chicago Press, 1948.

FRAZER, SIR J. G., O.M. *The Golden Bough.* Macmillan, nine vols. 1890-1951. *Lectures on the Early History of Kingship,* Macmillan, 1905.

FREEMAN, EDWARD A. *William the Conqueror.* Macmillan, 1888. *Norman Conquest.*

FUSTEL DE COULANGES. *Histoire des Institutions Politiques de l'Ancienne France.* Hachette, 1888.

GANSHOF, PROF. F. *Qu'est ce que la Féodalité?* Lebègue, Brussels, 1947.

GAUTIER, LEON. *La Chevalerie*, Delagrave.

GUEDALLA, PHILIP. *The Second Empire.* 1922.

HAMMOND, MASON. *The Augustan Principate.* Harvard Press, 1933.

HASLIP, JOAN. *The Sultan.* Cassell, 1958.

HAY, J. STUART. *The Amazing Emperor Heliogabalus.* Macmillan, 1911.

HOCART, A. M. *Kingship.* Oxford University Press, 1927.

JAMES I. *Basilikon Doron.* 2 vols. ed. by J. Craigie. Blackwood, 1950.

JONES, W. STUART. *The Roman Empire.* Putnam and Sons. New York. 1905.

LA BRUYÈRE, *Caractères*, 1908 edition.

LAMB, HAROLD. *Tamerlaine*, Thornton Butterworth, 1929.

LASKI, HAROLD. *The Foundations of Sovereignty*, Allen and Unwin, 1921. *Parliamentary Government in England.*

LATOUCHE, ROBERT. *Le film de l'histoire médiévale.* Arthaud, 1959.

LAVISSE, ERNEST. *Histoire de France.* Hachette, 1911.

LENOTRE, G. *Versailles au temps des rois.* Paris, 1935.

LIUDPRAND VON CREMONA. *Werke.* Becker edition, Hahnsche Buchhandlung, 1915.

LOCATELLI, FRANÇOIS. *Voyage de France*, 1905 edition.

LOUIS XIV, *Memoires*, 1927 edition.

MACHIAVELLI, NICOLO. *Il Principe e Discorsi.* Feltrinelli, 1960.

MAINTENON, MARQUISE DE. *Souvenirs.* Edited by Hanotaux.

MARAÑON, GREGORIO. *Tiberius.* Hollis and Carter, 1956.

MARCUS AURELIUS ANTONINUS. *Meditations.* Heinemann, 1924.

MARGOLIOUTH, D. S. *Mohammed.* Putnam's, 1905.

MARKHAM, SIR CLEMENTS. *The Incas of Peru.* Smith Elder, 1910.

MARSH, FRANK BURR. *A history of the Roman World.* Methuen, 1953. *Founding of the Roman Empire.* Oxford University Press, 1923.

MAURRAS, CHARLES. *Louis XIV.* Flammarion, 1937.

McKECHNIE, W. S. *Magna Carta.* Maclehose, 1905.

MILTON, JOHN. *Tenure of Kings.* Columbia edition, Vol. V.

MITFORD, A. B. (Lord Redesdale). *Tales of Old Japan.* Macmillan, 1871.

MOHL, RUTH. *Studies in Spenser, Milton and the Theory of Monarchy.* Columbia University, 1949.

MONGREDIEN, GEORGES. *Vie Privée de Louis XIV.* Hachette, 1938.

MORET, ALEXANDRE. *Rois et Dieux d'Egypte.* Colin, 1922.

Mum and the Sothsegger. Edited by Day and Steele, 1936.

NEAVE, LADY. *Romance of the Bosphorus.* Hutchinson, 1949.

NITOBE, INAZO. *Japan.* Ernest Benn, 1951.

ORLEANS, ELIZABETH CHARLOTTE DUCHESS OF, *Letters.* edited by Helmolt.

PETIT-DUTAILLIS. *La Monarchie Féodale.* 1933.

PETRIE, SIR CHARLES. *Monarchy*. Eyre and Spottiswoode, 1933. *The Modern British Monarchy*. Eyre and Spottiswoode, 1961.

PLATO. *The Republic* and *Laws*. Loeb edition.

PLUTARCH. *Lives*. Loeb edition, eleven Vols. 1928.

PRICE, WILLARD. *The Son of Heaven*. Heinemann, 1945.

PROCOPIUS. *Secret History*, Loeb edition Vol. VI, 1935. *History of the Wars*. Loeb edition. *Buildings*. Loeb edition.

REYNOLDS, BEATRICE. *Proponents of Limited Monarchy*. Columbia, 1931.

ROSNER, DR KARL. *Der König*.

RUSSELL, CHARLES. *Charlemagne*. Thornton Butterworth, 1931.

SAINT-SIMON, duc de. *Mémoires*. Pléiade edition.

SANDERS, HENRY A. (Editor). *Roman Historical Sources*, Macmillan, 1904.

SCHRAMM, P.E. *A History of the English Coronation*. Clarendon Press, 1937.

SEIGNOBOS, CHARLES. *The Feudal Régime*. Henry Holt, New York, 1902.

SÉVIGNÉ, MARQUISE DE. *Letters*. Pléiade edition.

STUBBS, BISHOP. *Select Charters*. 9th edition. Oxford, 1929. *Seventeen Lectures*. Oxford, 1887.

SUETONIUS. *Lives of the twelve Caesars*.

TACITUS. *Histories*. Two vols, Loeb edition. *Annals*. Four vols. Loeb edition. *Germania*. Loeb Edition.

TANNER, L. R. *The History of the Coronation*. Pitkin, 1952.

TARN, W. W. On *Alexander the Great*. Cambridge Ancient History, Vol. VI.

THOMPSON, FAITH. *Magna Carta*. Minnesota Press, 1948.

TREVELYAN, GEORGE. *English Social History*, Longmans, 1944. *History of England*. Longmans, 1926.

TWINING, LORD. *A History of the Crown Jewels of Europe*. Batsford, 1960.

VAILLANT, GEORGE. *The Aztecs of Mexico*. Penguin edition.

VISCONTI, ABBÉ PRIMI. *Memoires sur Le Cour de Louis XIV*. Lemoine, 1908.

VOLTAIRE. *Siècle de Louis XIV*. 1852 edition. *Charles XII*.

WADDELL, HELEN. *The Wandering Scholars*. Constable, 1927.

WALES, H. G. *The Mountain of God*. Bernard Quaritch, 1953.

WARREN, W. L. *King John*. Eyre and Spottiswoode, 1961.

WEBER, MAX. *Wirtschaft und Gesellschaft*. 1947.

WHITALL, SIR WILLIAM. *Frederick the Great on Kingcraft*, Longmans, 1901.

WILCHEN, ULRICH. *Alexander the Great*. Chatto and Windus, 1932.

WOLLASTON, ARTHUR. *The Sword of Islam*. John Murray, 1905.

WOODRUFF, DOUGLAS. *Charlemagne*. Peter Davies, 1934.

WRIGHT, F. A. *The Works of Liudprand of Cremona*. Routledge, 1930.

WYCLIFF. *Tractatus de Officio Regis*, London, 1887.

YOUNG, G. M. *The Government of Britain*, 1941. *The Origin of the West Saxon Kingdom*, 1934.

Index

331

REPRODUCTIONS PRINTING AND BINDING EXECUTED
BY THE ISTITUTO ITALIANO D'ARTI GRAFICHE OF
BERGAMO (ITALY) AUGUST 1962